# State-building and State Formation in the Western Pacific

T0347562

This book provides a rigorous and cross-disciplinary analysis of this Melanesian nation at a critical juncture in its post-colonial and post-conflict history, with contributions from leading scholars of Solomon Islands. The notion of 'transition' as used to describe the recent drawdown of the decade-long Regional Assistance Mission to Solomon Islands (RAMSI) provides a departure point for considering other transformations – social, political and economic – under way in the archipelagic nation. Organised around a central tension between change and continuity, two of the book's key themes are the contested narratives of changing state–society relations and the changing social relations around land and natural resources engendered by ongoing processes of globalisation and urbanisation. Drawing heuristically on RAMSI's genesis in the 'state-building moment' that dominated international relations during the first decade of this century, this book also examines the critical distinction between 'state-building' and 'state formation' in the Solomon Islands context. It engages with global scholarly and policy debates on issues such as peacebuilding, state-building, legal pluralism, hybrid governance, globalisation, urbanisation and the governance of natural resources. These themes resonate well beyond Solomon Islands and Melanesia, and this book will be of interest to a wide range of students, scholars and development practitioners. This book was previously published as a special issue of *The Journal of Pacific History*.

**Matthew G. Allen** is a Fellow at The Australian National University. A human geographer who has worked extensively across post-colonial Melanesia, he is the author of *Greed and Grievance: Ex-militants' perspectives on the Conflict in Solomon Islands* (2013).

**Sinclair Dinnen** is a Senior Fellow at The Australian National University and a sociolegal scholar with longstanding experience as a researcher and policy adviser in the Melanesia region.

# State-building and State Formation in the Western Pacific

Solomon Islands in transition?

*Edited by*
**Matthew G. Allen and Sinclair Dinnen**

LONDON AND NEW YORK

First published 2017 by Routledge

2 Park Square, Milton Park, Abingdon, Oxfordshire OX14 4RN
711 Third Avenue, New York, NY 10017

*Routledge is an imprint of the Taylor & Francis Group, an informa business*

First issued in paperback 2018

*British Library Cataloguing in Publication Data*
A catalogue record for this book is available from the British Library

ISBN 13: 978-1-138-20684-7 (hbk)
ISBN 13: 978-0-367-02837-4 (pbk)

Typeset in BaskervilleMT
by diacriTech, Chennai

**Publisher's Note**
The publisher accepts responsibility for any inconsistencies that may have arisen
during the conversion of this book from journal articles to book chapters, namely
the possible inclusion of journal terminology.

**Disclaimer**
Every effort has been made to contact copyright holders for their permission to
reprint material in this book. The publishers would be grateful to hear from any
copyright holder who is not here acknowledged and will undertake to rectify any
errors or omissions in future editions of this book.

# Contents

# Citation Information

The chapters in this book were originally published in *The Journal of Pacific History*, volume 50, issue 4 (December 2015). When citing this material, please use the original page numbering for each article, as follows:

**Chapter 1**
*Solomon Islands in Transition?*
Matthew G. Allen and Sinclair Dinnen
*The Journal of Pacific History*, volume 50, issue 4 (December 2015) pp. 381–397

**Chapter 2**
*The Teleology and Romance of State-building in Solomon Islands*
Jon Fraenkel
*The Journal of Pacific History*, volume 50, issue 4 (December 2015) pp. 398–418

**Chapter 3**
*Honiara: Arrival City and Pacific Hybrid Living Space*
Clive Moore
*The Journal of Pacific History*, volume 50, issue 4 (December 2015) pp. 419–436

**Chapter 4**
*From* Taovia *to Trustee: Urbanisation, Land Disputes and Social Differentiation in Kakabona*
Rebecca Monson
*The Journal of Pacific History*, volume 50, issue 4 (December 2015) pp. 437–449

**Chapter 5**
*Customary Authority and State Withdrawal in Solomon Islands: Resilience or Tenacity?*
Debra McDougall
*The Journal of Pacific History*, volume 50, issue 4 (December 2015) pp. 450–472

**Chapter 6**
*Big Money in the Rural: Wealth and Dispossession in Western Solomons Political Economy*
Edvard Hviding
*The Journal of Pacific History*, volume 50, issue 4 (December 2015) pp. 473–485

# CITATION INFORMATION

**Chapter 7**

*Maasina Rule beyond Recognition*
David Akin
*The Journal of Pacific History*, volume 50, issue 4 (December 2015) pp. 486–503

**Chapter 8**

*Urban Land in Honiara: Strategies and Rights to the City*
Joseph Foukona
*The Journal of Pacific History*, volume 50, issue 4 (December 2015) pp. 504–518

For any permission-related enquiries please visit:
http://www.tandfonline.com/page/help/permissions

# Notes on Contributors

**David Akin** is a Lecturer in Anthropology at the University of Michigan, USA, and author of *Colonialism, Maasina Rule, and the Origins of Malaitan Kastom* (2013). He is also the managing editor of the journal, *Comparative Studies in Society and History*.

**Matthew G. Allen** is a Fellow at The Australian National University. A human geographer who has worked extensively across post-colonial Melanesia, he is the author of *Greed and Grievance: Ex-militants' perspectives on the Conflict in Solomon Islands* (2013).

**Sinclair Dinnen** is a Senior Fellow at The Australian National University and a sociolegal scholar with longstanding experience as a researcher and policy adviser in the Melanesia region.

**Joseph Foukona** is a doctoral student at the School of Culture, History and Language, College of Asia and the Pacific, Australian National University. His research examines land legislation and reform in the Pacific.

**Jon Fraenkel** is a Professor in Comparative Politics at the School of History, Philosophy, Political Science and International Relations, Victory University of Wellington, New Zealand. He is the author of *The Manipulation of Custom: from Uprising to Intervention in the Solomon Islands* (2004) and the Pacific Islands correspondent for *The Economist*.

**Edvard Hviding** is a Professor in the Department of Social Anthropology, University of Bergen, Norway. His work explores the Melanesian South Pacific and he is the founding director of the Bergen Pacific Studies Research Group.

**Debra McDougall** is a Senior Lecturer in Anthropology and Sociology, School of Social Sciences, Faculty of Arts, University of Western Australia. Her book, *Engaging with Strangers: Love and Violence in the Rural Solomon Islands*, was published in 2016.

**Rebecca Monson** is a Lecturer at the ANU College of Law, Australian National University. Her current research focuses on housing, land and property rights, natural resource management, and disaster and emergency management.

**Clive Moore** is an Emeritus Professor in the School of Historical and Philosophical Inquiry, University of Queensland. His research examines the history of Australia, Queensland, Pacific Islands, New Guinea, Papua New Guinea and Solomon Islands.

# Solomon Islands in Transition?

## MATTHEW G. ALLEN AND SINCLAIR DINNEN

## ABSTRACT

The notion of 'transition' as used to describe the recent drawdown of the decade-long Regional Assistance Mission to Solomon Islands (RAMSI) provides an obvious departure point for considering what other transformations – social, political and economic – are under way in the archipelagic nation. Yet the contributions to this special issue collectively reject the teleological language of transition and transformation deployed by many development actors in favour of a more nuanced and historically informed understanding of the central dialect between change and continuity, with change in Solomon Islands occurring slowly and in distinctly non-linear ways. This dialectic is traced and interrogated in various ways by the contributors to this issue. One broad theme concerns the contested narratives of changing state–society relations and, in particular, those between the central government and the rural localities where most Solomon Islanders continue to reside. Another is the changing social relations around land and natural resources engendered by ongoing processes of globalisation and persistent patterns of demographic change, migration and urbanisation. These and other processes of historical change, including state formation and capital accumulation, are also shaped by the enduring realities of scale and distance integral to Solomon Islands archipelagic geography. In this essay we explore these themes of change and continuity in Solomon Islands, positioning the individual contributions within this larger trajectory of slow-paced and distinctly non-linear change. Drawing heuristically on RAMSI's genesis in the state-building moment that dominated international relations during the first decade of this century, we also examine the distinction between 'state-building' and 'state formation' in the Solomon Islands context and, in doing so, contrast the tropes of state failure, weakness and fragility against narratives of resilience, tenacity, innovation and experimentation.

*Acknowledgements*: The authors thank the anonymous readers and reviewers of this paper for their insightful comments and suggestions and wish to acknowledge the excellent support provided by the editors of this journal. Matthew Allen acknowledges support provided under Australian Research Council fellowship DE140101206.

This volume had its genesis in a two-day workshop convened at the Australian National University in November 2013. The workshop was titled 'Solomon Islands in transition' (*without* a question mark). Its purpose was to take the occasion of the so-called 'transition' of the then ten-year-old Regional Assistance Mission to Solomon Islands (RAMSI) as an opportunity to consider and debate other types of transitions that had been taking place in Solomon Islands over recent decades. The discourse of RAMSI transition was narrow, technical and managerialist. It addressed the shift from one modality of external assistance to another, namely, from a multilateral peace- and state-building intervention to a more regular bilateral aid engagement. As convenors of the workshop, we were concerned to widen the frame and to shift the focus to Solomon Islands itself. In the workshop blurb, we wrote that the discourse of RAMSI transition 'should not obscure the other significant transitions underway in Solomon Islands … the many transformations occurring within Solomon Islands' societies'.

Now we stand corrected. While forgiving the rhetorical licence afforded to a workshop description, participants were quick to challenge our transition framing. By lunchtime on the first day, a salient tension had emerged between change and continuity, a dialectic that deepened over the ensuing proceedings and has ultimately necessitated the addition of a question mark to the title of the present volume. RAMSI transition may have served us well as a point of departure, a moment around which to gather and debate. But collectively the contributions presented here reject the lexicon of transition and transformation. Instead they chronicle slow-paced and distinctly non-linear processes of change that have been in train in Solomon Islands for many decades. Foremost among these are the changing relationships between state and society, widely perceived, from the vantage point of the rural majority, as a gradual retreat of the central government from their everyday lives. Alongside this perceived retreat has occurred an expansion of clientelist institutions and a proliferation of alternative, non-state structures and configurations of local-level governance. Another of the grinding processes documented here is the changing social relations around land and natural resources engendered by the ongoing encounter with globalisation. Several of the contributions also remind us of the Solomons' enduring demographic conditions: high rates of population growth, a very young and mobile population, and the steady growth of peri-urban and urban areas, especially the capital Honiara.

Contouring these processes of change are what we might term immutable geographies. Tobias Haque, whose workshop paper has been published elsewhere, reminds us that the realities of scale and distance – which are compounded by Solomon Islands' archipelagic geography – have long confounded the conventional models of economic growth and development.[1] They have also presented challenges to those seeking to govern, to the projection of the functional authority of the state to a

---

[1] Tobias Haque, 'Economic transition in Solomon Islands', State, Society and Governance in Melanesia Program, Discussion Paper 10 (2013).

widely dispersed rural population.[2] Several of the contributions here show us how the Solomons' immutable geographies have shaped, and continue to shape, state formation and capital accumulation in profound ways, just as they have done in other geographically challenging contexts both in Oceania and further afield.[3]

Returning to our central dialectic of change and continuity, the decade-long RAMSI intervention brought about far less change than its architects, proponents and early implementers had envisaged. Jon Fraenkel's paper in this volume demonstrates that RAMSI marked a distinctive period in the history of Solomon Islands but not a transformative one. Indeed, he questions whether the intervention should even be characterised as a state-building project, an issue that we take up below. Yet the broader point, upon which few would disagree, is that following the rapid restoration of law and order and financial stability, political and economic trends during the remainder of RAMSI's tenure were characterised by much more continuity than change. The notoriously unsustainable logging industry expanded, constituency development funds grew, the state continued its physical retreat from rural areas, voting behaviour during elections arguably became more parochial than ever before, and parliamentary politics continued to be characterised by instability and money politics and, in the case of the riots that followed the national election of April 2006, violence. All of this is a far cry from the massively ambitious and hubristic aspiration, pronounced by Australian Prime Minister Howard and Foreign Minister Downer in early 2003, to 'radically re-engineer' and 'completely redesign the place' (quoted in Fraenkel this volume).

It has now become abundantly clear that RAMSI failed to realise these lofty state- and nation-building ambitions. Fraenkel argues that from its outset the mission differed from other multilateral state-building interventions, such as those in Iraq and Kosovo, in that it did not assume executive authority or attempt constitutional change. While these are important contrasts to draw, RAMSI nevertheless represented a stark departure from Australia's hitherto hands-off policy towards its Pacific Islands neighbours, which led some observers to cite it as the exemplar of Australia's 'new interventionism'.[4] Moreover the shift in policy was in large part informed by contemporaneous developments at the global scale. The imperatives of the war on terror had brought about what Mark Duffield described as a securitisation of

---

[2]Graham Teskey, 'State-building and development: getting beyond capacity', in Rupert Jones-Parry (ed.), *Commonwealth Good Governance 2011/12: democracy, development and public administration* (London 2012), 44–48.

3 For Oceania, see Geoffrey Betram and Ray Watters, 'The MIRAB economy in South Pacific microstates', *Asia Pacific Viewpoint*, 26:1 (1985), 497–512. For mainland Southeast Asia, see James C. Scott, *The Art of Not Being Governed: an anarchist history of upland Southeast Asia* (New Haven 2009), 1–39. For the Horn of Africa, see Jeffrey Herbst, *States and Power in Africa: comparative lessons in authority and control* (Princeton 2000), 12–31.

[4] Greg Fry and Tarcisius Tara Kabutaulaka, 'Political legitimacy and state-building intervention in the Pacific', in Greg Fry and Tarcisius Tata Kabutaulaka (eds), *Intervention and State-Building in the Pacific* (Manchester 2008), 1–36.

development.[5] Weak and failing states came to be seen not as benign objects of humanitarian and development assistance but as potent security threats to the West. This is precisely the framing that was applied in the Australian Strategic Policy Institute (ASPI) report 'Our failing neighbour', released just prior to the deployment of RAMSI in July 2003, as well as that used by Australia's political leaders to explain the deployment to their domestic audience.[6] While RAMSI may have differed in its design and legal basis from other multilateral – mainly United Nations – state-building operations,[7] it no doubt was conceived and executed during state-building's apotheosis, and as we have argued elsewhere, it exhibited all the hallmarks of a classic 'liberal peace' intervention.[8]

Before moving on to expand on the key themes of the volume, we wish to note how RAMSI, specifically its genesis in the state-building moment, provides two further heuristic tensions that assist us in ordering our themes. First, we can foreground a distinction between 'state-building' as a linear, predictable and technical project and 'state formation' as a messy, organic and highly contingent historical process that plays out in multiple institutional spaces. Several of the contributions chronicle the latter, adding significantly to our understanding of how state formation is unfolding in Solomon Islands. Second, we can contrast the tropes of state failure, weakness and fragility against more positive narratives of resilience (or, as Debra McDougall prefers in her paper, 'tenacity'), innovation and experimentation.

## CHANGE AND CONTINUITY

The first presentation at the workshop, by Tarcisius Tara Kabutaulaka, critiqued the very notion that Solomon Islands was, or had been, experiencing transitional or transformative change. His paper reminded us that trajectories of change and development are shaped by specific social and cultural contexts that defy the teleological tropes of modernisation and demographic transition. Subsequent presentations reinforced and

---

[5] Mark Duffield, *Global Governance and the New Wars: the merging of development and security* (London 2001), 22–43.

[6] Elsina Wainwright on behalf of the Australian Strategic Policy Institute, 'Our failing neighbour: Australia and the future of Solomon Islands', June 2003, https://www.aspi.org.au/publications/our-failing-neighbour-australia-and-the-future-of-solomon-islands/solomons.pdf (accessed 16 Sep. 2015). See also Alexander Downer, 'Security in an unstable world', Archive 1995 to 2012: Australian Ministers for Foreign Affairs, 26 June 2003, http://www.foreignminister.gov.au/speeches/2003/030626_unstableworld.html (accessed 16 Sep. 2015).

[7] Michael Fullilove on behalf of the Lowy Institute for International Policy, 'The testament of Solomons: RAMSI and international state-building', March 2006, http://www.lowyinstitute.org/files/pubfiles/Fullilove%2C_The_testament_web_version.pdf (accessed 16 Sep. 2015).

[8] Matthew Allen and Sinclair Dinnen, 'The North down under: antinomies of conflict and intervention in Solomon Islands', *Conflict, Security & Development*, 10:3 (2010), 299–327; also see Michael J. Mazaar, 'The rise and fall of the failed-state paradigm: requiem for a decade of distraction', *Foreign Affairs*, 93:1 (2014), 113–21.

affirmed the view that the most important changes taking place in Solomon Islands have, in fact, been in train for many decades and are, therefore, more representative of continuity than rapid transformational change. Three of these slow-paced processes of change are highlighted in the contributions to this volume, though others were raised and discussed at the workshop.[9] Here we focus on changing relations between the political centre and rural communities, changing social relations engendered by globalisation and resource capitalism, and demographic change, mobility and urbanisation.

*State–Society Relations*

Several of the papers presented at the workshop addressed the theme of changing relations between central government and the rural communities in which most Solomon Islanders continue to reside. Some of these papers, or the research on which they are based, have been published elsewhere.[10] In terms of the present volume, the papers by Akin, McDougall, Hviding and Monson address, in various ways, the changing relationships between state and society and, especially, between the centre and rural communities. This is a contested narrative. Widespread community perceptions of a gradual withdrawal of the postcolonial state in its service delivery guise must be set against the steady expansion of Member of Parliament (MP) constituency development funds that has occurred since their introduction in 1993.[11] These funds, the disbursement of which is highly discretionary, now exceed central government grants to the provinces by a factor of six.[12] For Craig and Porter, who presented at the workshop, the expansion and contemporary primacy of constituency funds is best interpreted as a reordering of political power that brings into question the narrative of a state in retreat. Rather than retreating,

[9] See Matthew Allen and Sinclair Dinnen, 'Solomon Islands in transition: workshop report', State, Society and Governance in Melanesia Program, Working Paper 2 (2013).

[10] David Craig and Doug Porter, 'Political settlement in Solomon Islands: a political economic basis for stability after RAMSI?', State, Society and Governance in Melanesia Program, Working Paper 1 (2013); Matthew Allen, Sinclair Dinnen, Daniel Evans and Rebecca Monson, 'Justice delivered locally: systems, challenges, and innovations in Solomon Islands', World Bank research report, Aug. 2013, http://www-wds.worldbank.org/external/default/WDSContentServer/WDSP/IB/2013/09/27/000356161_20130927130401/Rendered/PDF/812990WP0DL0Se0Box0379833B00PUBLIC0.pdf (accessed 16 Sep. 2015); Debra McDougall, 'Sub-national governance in post-RAMSI Solomon Islands', State, Society and Governance in Melanesia Program, Working Paper 3 (2014).

[11] On perceptions of the withdrawal of the state, see Allen et al., 'Justice delivered locally', 9–12; McDougall, 'Sub-national governance', 4–5. On constituency development funds, see Jon Fraenkel, 'The atrophied state: a supply-side perspective on politician "slush funds" in western Melanesia', in Ron Duncan (ed.) *The Political Economy of Economic Reform in the Pacific* (Mandaluyong City 2011), 303–26.

[12] David Craig and Doug Porter, 'Political settlement, transitions, and lasting peace in Solomon Islands? Some institutional perspectives', unpublished paper (2013), 23.

the exercise of state power in rural areas is taking on a different form, they would contend.

Indeed, even if the state is interpreted primarily in terms of its service delivery and developmental functions, the narrative of its steady, lineal retreat from rural areas during the postcolonial period demands nuance and inflection. Some services, for example education in the form of government-run schools, expanded quite significantly after independence in 1978, albeit unevenly and to an insufficient extent to meet the demand from an ever-growing population.[13] Government health and education services do reach into many rural communities in contemporary Solomon Islands – perhaps more so as a consequence of the RAMSI intervention – and recent improvements in basic health and education outcomes have occurred. Yet other areas of government service delivery have unambiguously retreated from rural areas over the past several decades. As noted in McDougall's paper in this volume, formal governance and justice services are largely absent or moribund in rural communities, and the perception is widespread that the state has withdrawn its support to local customary authorities in such places.[14]

To be sure, the postcolonial history of government-sponsored local-level governance and justice services is one of decline. British colonial authorities established 'Native councils' and 'Native courts' as cornerstones of a system of indirect rule that was eventually implemented around the time of World War II.[15] These fora enabled 'traditional leaders' ('chiefs' or 'elders') to assume a formal role in dispute resolution. At independence, Native councils and Native courts became area councils and local courts, respectively. Area councils consisted of elected members, whose functions included raising basic taxes and licence fees as well as formulating policies relating to local issues such as land use and tourism. 'Council messengers' and later 'area constables' were empowered by the Local Government Act to assist in the enforcement of by-laws and local court decisions. They also acted as critical intermediaries among traditional leaders, local council areas and the wider state justice system, linking different levels and forms of authority. Designated offences were referred upwards to the police and state court hierarchy.

This system of local-level government was dismantled when area councils were officially suspended – effectively abolished – in 1998 as a consequence of both domestically and internationally driven structural adjustment programs.[16] Some

---

[13] David Oakeshott and Matthew Allen, 'Schooling as a "stepping-stone to national consciousness" in Solomon Islands: the last twenty years', State, Society and Governance in Melanesia Program, Discussion Paper 8 (2015).

[14] Also see Allen et al., 'Justice delivered locally', 9–12, 43–57; McDougall, 'Sub-national governance', 4–5.

[15] Judith A. Bennett, *Wealth of the Solomons: a history of a Pacific archipelago, 1800–1978* (Honolulu 1987), 280–82; David W. Akin, *Colonialism, Maasina Rule, and the Origins of Malaitan Kastom* (Honolulu 2013), 50–60.

[16] A detailed account of the demise of area councils is provided in Allen et al., 'Justice delivered locally', 10. An alternative explanation for their demise is the introduction of constituency development funds for national members of parliament in 1993; see Ian Scales 'The flourishing of local

328 councillors, and a significant number of administrators and officials, were set aside and, with them, the raft of bylaws that had been administered at this level. While local courts still exist in many areas, they are, for the most part, moribund and, where they do operate, only hear customary land disputes rather than the more extensive repertoire of local disputation managed previously.[17]

Another important dimension of the relations between central government and the citizens of Solomon Islands concerns trans-local political and social movements, some of which have found expression at the scale of the island, as was the case with Maasina Rule, which is the subject of David Akin's paper in this volume. His carefully argued reinterpretation of the movement as fundamentally political in nature – a comprehensive account of which can be found in his recently published book on the subject[18] – exhorts us to rethink the many other movements that have occurred in different parts of the archipelago at different times, and which have tended to be portrayed in terms of their millenarian as opposed to political orientation.[19]

While Maasina Rule primarily operated at the scale of 'Malaita', noting that its influence also extended to neighbouring islands, other movements have mobilised at sub-island scales, as is the case with the Christian Fellowship Church that is discussed in the papers by Hviding and McDougall, or at regional scales, as was the case with Western Breakaway movement that encompassed all of present-day Western and Choiseul provinces. The latter movement emerged in the lead-up to independence in the context of debates about the sharing of power between different tiers of government. Despite calls from several 'federalist' islands and regions for greater devolution, including Guadalcanal and Western, a unitary system was introduced that included provincial governments with their own assemblies, executives and premiers. The relationship between these two tiers of government has remained unclear, with considerable uncertainty about the division of responsibilities, as well as perennial problems of underfunding for provincial administrations.[20] In concert, the elimination of local government through the abolition of area councils, the weakness of the provincial government system and the rise of constituency funds largely

---

level governance after the coup in Solomon Islands: lessons for reform of the state', paper presented at the Development Research Symposium on Governance in Pacific States: Reassessing Roles and Remedies, University of the South Pacific, Suva, 30 Sep. 2003, 9.

[17] Daniel Evans, Michael Goddard and Don Paterson 'The hybrid courts of Melanesia: a comparative analysis of village courts of Papua New Guinea, island courts of Vanuatu and local courts of Solomon Islands', World Bank, Justice and Development Working Paper 13 (2011), 11.

[18] Akin, *Colonialism, Maasina Rule, and the Origins of Malaitan Kastom.*

[19] This dichotomisation of politics and religion is particularly problematic in Melanesia, where ritual is profoundly pragmatic, world oriented and politically entwined. See Bronwen Douglas 'From invisible Christians to gothic theatre: the romance of the millennial in Melanesian anthropology', *Current Anthropology*, 42:5 (2001), 615–50.

[20] John Cox and Joanne Morrison, 'Solomon Islands provincial governance information paper', unpublished AusAID report (Canberra 2004).

explain the parlous condition of local-level governance and justice services in Solomon Islands today.

### The Social Relations of Land and Natural Resources

Several of the papers herein provide case studies of what Edvard Hviding has described elsewhere as 'entanglements between the local and the global'[21] and 'compressed globalisation'.[22] Historically, these entanglements have taken many shapes. Yet over recent decades it has been the encounter between transnational resource capitalism – predominantly taking the form of Malaysian logging companies – and local social and political economic contexts that has been most productive of (mostly negative) change. A recent multi-sited ethnographic study of local-level disputation and access to justice in rural Solomon Islands, titled 'Justice delivered locally', found that the presence or otherwise of natural resource development, especially logging, was the most significant determinant of social cohesion in rural localities.[23] While the political economy of logging has been well documented at the national scale, however, only a handful of detailed studies of its local social impacts has been conducted.[24]

Hviding's paper in this volume provides a welcome expansion to the latter literature. Drawing upon David Harvey's concept of 'accumulation by dispossession', he describes the political economic impacts of several decades of commercial logging on customary lands in the New Georgia group of islands. His central concern is with how these impacts have played out differentially across New Georgia's two dominant church communities, Seventh-day Adventist (SDA) and Christian Fellowship Church (CFC). Two different processes of accumulation by dispossession are identified, each informed by changing forms of chiefly authority, but with the same outcome in both cases, namely a reduction of collective agency over customary land and the

---

[21] Edvard Hviding, 'Knowing and managing biodiversity in the Pacific Islands: challenges of environmentalism in Marovo Lagoon', *International Social Science Journal*, 58:187 (2006), 69.

[22] Edvard Hviding, 'Contested rainforests, NGOs, and projects of desire in Solomon Islands', *International Social Science Journal*, 55:178 (2003), 542.

[23] Allen et al., 'Justice delivered locally', xi.

[24] The most authoritative account of the logging industry in Solomon Islands is Judith A. Bennett, *Pacific Forest: a history of resource control and contest in Solomon Islands, c. 1800–1997* (Knapwell, UK, and Leiden 2000). For a more recent review of the literature on the political economy of logging at the national scale, see Matthew Allen, 'The political economy of logging in Solomon Islands', in Duncan, *The Political Economy of Economic Reform*, 278–301. For studies of its local impacts, see Karen Lummis, 'Local level impacts of commercial forestry operations and forest conservation initiatives on customary land in the Solomon Islands', MPhil thesis, Australian National University (Canberra 2010); Ian Scales, 'The social forest: landowners, development conflict and the state in Solomon Islands', PhD thesis, Australian National University (Canberra 2003); Morgan Wairiu and Gordon Nanau, 'Logging and conflict in Birao Ward of Guadalcanal, Solomon Islands', Islands Knowledge Institute, Working Paper 1 (n.d.).

concomitant concentration of its control in the hands of a few. In the case of SDA communities, a disintegrative process has occurred whereby many landholding groups have effectively become 'chiefless' – as chiefs have chosen to use their logging royalties to reside in town – allowing power to shift to men who are adroit at dealing with companies but uninterested in the broader leadership of the collective. In the CFC case, by contrast, a highly centralised, hierarchical and religiously sanctioned authority structure has seen power over land and resources concentrated in hands of a single leader. Hviding's analysis arrives at an ironic and sobering conclusion. It is the very collective agency over land, grounded in kinship relations, that has long provided Melanesians with a 'safety net against material dispossession', which is being 'appropriated and accumulated by a few to the ultimate detriment of the dispossessed majority'.

A pertinent link exists here to the retreat of the state discussed above. Late in the colonial period, as the administration was attempting to establish a perpetual 'forest estate', Solomon Islanders were becoming increasingly aware of the possibility that they could sell their timber rights directly to the loggers without having to turn their land over to the government.[25] The desire for 'direct dealing' became a popular cause on the eve of independence and was seized upon by then chief minister Peter Kenilorea, who introduced the necessary amendments to the Forest and Timber Act. This resulted in a shift from government-owned to customary land, a sharp expansion in both geographical scope and production levels, and an increase in the use of corrupt practices by the foreign companies that started entering the country.[26] Moreover, since the abolition of area councils, provincial governments now conduct the timber rights hearings that are required under the forestry regulations and were previously the responsibility of the councils. Anecdotal evidence suggests that this has seen an increase in logging-related corruption at the provincial level and the manipulation of the timber rights acquisition process in favour of logging companies and their local collaborators.

Rebecca Monson's paper deals with processes closely analogous to those described by Hviding, but in relation to land disputes in Kakabona, the peri-urban area immediately west of and contiguous with Honiara. The processes of social differentiation that she describes have been occurring, to greater or lesser degrees, wherever customary land has been registered for the purposes of sale, lease or commercial development. Indeed, they can be discerned wherever customary groups have been, through some sort of legal process, defined as land- or resource-owning groups for the purposes of receiving economic benefits associated with land or extractive resource industries, such as logging and mining. In the case of Kakabona, Monson describes how the legal act of registration has concentrated control over land and the wealth that flows from it in the hands of those, invariably local 'big men', listed as 'duly authorised representatives' – or trustees – of the 'landowning group', of whom up to five can be named on each registered title. Through this process, Monson

---

[25] Bennett, *Pacific Forest*, 182–85.

[26] Ian Frazer, 'The struggle for control of Solomon Island forests', *Contemporary Pacific*, 9:1 (1997), 45–48.

demonstrates, the mutual constitution of 'big man' and 'trustee' works to entrench the authority of a relatively small group of male leaders over land. Read against Hviding's paper, Monson describes a third pathway to collective dispossession, which, like the two described by Hviding, involves an interplay of 'traditional authority' and power over land. Set against Hviding's contrasting processes of centralisation and disintegration, that described by Monson could perhaps be characterised as one of consolidation whereby traditional leaders, in this case big men, have consolidated their power and authority by virtue of their trusteeship over land that was previously held under customary tenure.

In the case of Kakabona, some trustees have abused their authority over land by transacting it without consulting other members of their landholding groups and without sharing the proceeds of such transactions, a story that will resonate with readers who are familiar with the political economy of land and extractive resource industries in Melanesia. Monson reminds us that these land transactions were a significant source of the intragroup and intergenerational conflicts that played an important part in the genesis of the social and political unrest of 1998–2003 (known locally as the 'Ethnic Tension' or simply the 'Tension').[27] Elsewhere, Monson extends these arguments to draw attention to the centrality of struggles over land to processes of state formation.[28] Her work also shows that disputes over land and natural resources are fundamentally gendered, and through their entanglements with the state legal system, the gender inequalities that attend land disputation in the *kastom*[29] realm are reproduced in formal state institutions.

### Demographic Change, Migration and Urbanisation

The most recent census, conducted in 2009, enumerated 515,870 people living in Solomon Islands, but owing to an 'undercount', the National Statistical Office estimates the actual population at the time of the census as 552,000.[30] Taking account of this adjustment, the average annual population growth rate over the inter-census period 1999–2009 was 3%, compared with previous inter-census growth rates of

---

[27] Also see Tarcisius Tara Kabutaulaka, 'Beyond ethnicity: the political economy of the Guadalcanal crisis in Solomon Islands', State, Society and Governance in Melanesia Program, Working Paper 1 (2001); Matthew Allen 'Land, migration and conflict on Guadalcanal, Solomon Islands', *Australian Geographer*, 43:2 (2012), 163–80.

[28] Rebecca Monson, '*Hu nao save tok?* Women, men and land: negotiating property and authority in Solomon Islands', PhD thesis, Australian National University (Canberra 2012).

[29] While local usage of *kastom* often approximates the English word 'custom', the term should not be interpreted as referring to a timeless and unchanging pre-European way of life. It has specific historical, political and place-based meanings and is often invoked in ways that emphasise change and adaptation as well as continuity with the past.

[30] Solomon Islands Government, *Report on 2009 Population & Housing Census*, vol. 2: *National Report* (Honiara n.d.), xxvi.

2.8% (1986–99), 3.5% (1976–86) and 3.4% (1970–76).[31] A population growth rate of 3% is high by global standards. Moreover, the age structure of the population is very young, even in comparison with other developing countries, with around 41% of the population under the age of 15, and 60% under the age of 25, in the 2009 census.[32] These demographic trends take on additional significance against the backdrop of extremely constrained employment opportunities in the country's small formal economy.

Around 82% of the population resides in rural areas. This is changing, however, because the urban population is growing more quickly than the rural population (4.7% as opposed to 1.8% during the last inter-census period). Honiara is easily the largest urban centre, accounting for around 78% of the total urban population.[33] The 2009 census records the population of Honiara as 64,609, which increases to 80,082 when the 'urban population' of Guadalcanal – presumably referring to Honiara's peri-urban fringes – is included.[34] As Moore notes in this volume, Honiara's population has increased fivefold since independence in 1978.

We can infer several trends from this demographic data that point to both change and continuity but mostly the latter. While the overall population growth rate is declining gradually, it is still relatively high, and the age structure of the population is still very young. Urban centres are growing more rapidly than rural areas, but the vast majority of the population still resides in rural areas. Moreover, internal migration and circulation continue to be important phenomena. In the 2009 census, 36% of people were enumerated in a ward other than that in which they had been born, while 11% were enumerated in a different ward to that in which they had lived five years earlier.[35] As has been the case with previous censuses, Malaita is the most important 'source' of migrants for all provinces in Solomon Islands, with urban Honiara and Guadalcanal being the main destinations. Considerable census-based, observational and anecdotal evidence suggests that the nature of Malaitan mobility has changed over time, with a trend toward permanent settlement as opposed to circulation, though both circulation and migration remain important.

With a collective focus on Honiara and its peri-urban surrounds, the papers in this volume by Moore, Monson and Foukona illustrate how the processes of internal migration and urbanisation have been playing out on the ground. In his history of Honiara, Clive Moore engages with an influential book by Doug Saunders to ask whether Honiara fits the 'arrival city' model.[36] Saunders's framework highlights the role of urbanisation in creating the economies of scale and population concentrations required for service delivery and economic development. It also points to the importance of informal networks, markets and institutions in underpinning migrants'

---

[31] Ibid.; Matthew Allen, *Greed and Grievance: ex-militants' perspectives on the conflict in Solomon Islands* (Honolulu 2013), 37.

[32] Solomon Islands Government, *Report on 2009 Population & Housing Census*, 22.

[33] Ibid., xxi.

[34] Ibid.

[35] Ibid., 195.

[36] Doug Saunders, *Arrival City: the final migration and our next world* (Sydney 2010).

transition into the urban world. Moore finds that Honiara shares some of the characteristics of the arrival city – for example the circulation of people, money and ideas between rural and urban areas and the salience of social networks in the urban context – but that its small scale unsettles any comparison with classic arrival cities, such as the mega-metropolises of Manila and Mexico City. He concludes that while the continued growth of Honiara may still see it come to have more in common with other developing world cities, its distinguishing and enduring characteristic since its foundation in the 1940s has been its comparatively small size. This smallness has enabled the continuation of what Moore describes as 'pre-urban' social and economic forms and their adaptation into a 'hybrid living space'.

Joseph Foukona also engages with a particular conceptual framework of urbanisation, Henri Lefebvre's notion of 'right to the city',[37] to examine the strategies that people employ to gain access to land and services in Honiara's ever more densely populated urban space. Foukona demonstrates how exclusion from urban land and housing markets has occurred through a combination of supply and demand, the manipulation of the urban property market through corrupt dealings, and the mismanagement of the government's temporary occupation licence scheme. This has resulted in a rapid expansion of informal settlements such that these now number 30, six of which have encroached onto areas of customary land beyond the town boundary. Foukona argues that the politics of access to urban land have been framed by identity narratives. Guadalcanal landowners invoke indigeneity to underwrite their claims to alienated land in and around Honiara. Migrant-settlers, in contrast, link their identity narratives to the legitimacy of the state, which underpins their rights to reside within the Honiara town boundary. Identity narratives are also salient in Honiara's informal settlements, each of which is based on provincial/island or sub-provincial/language affiliations. Foukona concludes that, collectively, these dynamics point to multilayered tensions between inclusion and exclusion and that, when assessed in terms of Lefebvre's framework, Honiara is, above all, a space of exclusion.

Monson's paper, discussed above, is also, ultimately, a tale of urbanisation. The processes of land disputation and social differentiation that she analyses have occurred in the context of post-World War II migration to north Guadalcanal and the growth of Kakabona as a peri-urban extension of Honiara. In Kakabona, as in parts of the Guadalcanal plains to the east of Honiara, migrants, especially from Malaita, acquired access to land through marriage into the local matrilineal landholding groups and through both *kastom* and market-based transactions, increasingly the latter. For Monson, Kakabona's 'dangerous' land disputes – which, for its residents, give rise to profoundly ontological questions of identity and belonging – are rooted in the broader process of urbanisation. She concludes that urbanisation in this case has deepened social fragmentation and inequality, particularly along gender and intergenerational lines, rendering Kakabona a site of instability and insecurity.

---

[37] Henri Lefebvre, *Writings on Cities* (Oxford 1996 [1968]).

## STATE-BUILDING AND STATE FORMATION

Somewhat ironically, RAMSI's almost exclusive focus on the agencies of central government in Honiara has enabled a continuation of the 'governance without government' that has arguably prevailed in most of Solomons rural communities over the past several decades and that intensified markedly during the Tension period. Several of the contributions to this volume shed light on the plethora of innovative informal governance arrangements and projects that are occurring in these spaces of 'statelessness'.[38] Globally, scholarly and policy interest in such spaces is growing, as is their significance as sites of innovation and transformation, which is giving rise to analytical concepts such as 'twilight institutions',[39] 'mediated states'[40] and 'hybrid political orders'.[41] This scholarship is redirecting attention away from 'state-building' as a linear, predictable and technical project and towards 'state formation' as a messy, organic and highly contingent process that plays out in multiple institutional spaces.

Questions of scale and agency are paramount here. The 'Justice delivered locally' project, which carried out ethnographic research in five provinces of Solomon Islands, found that informal governance arrangements are being implemented, discussed and planned at different scales: the village and sub-village, the trans-local sub-island/province, and the island/province.[42] At the village or sub-village level, local experimentation is evident across a range of informal governance arrangements, including 'village committees', 'village councils', 'village associations' or 'advocacy committees'. It also occurs through the elaboration of informal community 'rules', 'laws', 'by-laws' and 'ordinances'. While having no recognised status under national law, these are, in large part, a response to the absence of effective state regulation at local levels. By emulating the form and, in some cases, the substance of national law, local leaders also anticipate an enhanced prospect of external support to enforce them.

These developments are illustrated in Debra McDougall's paper, a historically grounded village-level case study of the interplay of what she describes as customary authority and state withdrawal. With an empirical focus on the work of village chiefs and a chiefs committee at Pienuna on Ranongga in Western Province, McDougall describes how Ranonggan chiefs have long been engaged in codifying customary

---

[38] Maria H. Brons, *Society, Security, Sovereignty, and the State in Somalia: from statelessness to statelessness?* (Utrecht 2001), particularly ch. 8.

[39] Christian Lund, 'Twilight institutions: public authority and local politics in Africa', *Development and Change*, 37:4 (2006), 685–705.

[40] Ken Menkhaus, 'The rise of a mediated state in northern Kenya: the Wajir story and its implications for state-building', *Afrika Focus*, 21:2 (2008), 23–38.

[41] Volker Boege, Anne Brown, Kevin Clements and Anna Nolan, 'On hybrid political orders and emerging states: state formation in the context of "fragility"', in Martina Fischer and Beatrix Schmelzle (eds), *Building Peace in the Absence of States: challenging the discourse on state failure*, Berghof Handbook Dialogue 8 (Berlin 2009), 15–35.

[42] Allen et al., 'Justice delivered locally', 69–78.

rules and formalising dispute resolution processes, efforts that intensified following the abolition of area councils and the de-funding of local courts in the late 1990s. These projects have had the dual purpose of attempting to integrate local content into the apparatus of government law and seeking recognition from external actors, including the withdrawing state and international conservation NGOs. While McDougall's primary conceptual concern is to critique the characterisation of institutions of customary authority as 'resilient' (see below), her paper sheds light on some of the village-level dynamics of state formation that are taking place, in various ways, throughout the archipelago.

McDougall's paper also touches upon some of the informal governance arrangements that have emerged at the trans-local and island/province scales. The most remarkable example of the former is the CFC, also discussed by Hviding in this volume. Elsewhere, Hviding has written about the CFC as 're-placing the state', a form of state formation from below.[43] 'Re-placing' in this context has a dual meaning because, as Hviding demonstrates, the CFC operates in critical ways with and within the state, as well as occupying the governance space created by its absence. In this manner the CFC represents a way of reconfiguring authority and repositioning the state in a manner that aligns more closely with local social forms and priorities.

In terms of the scale of the island/province, McDougall's paper refers to the distinctive 'tripod' governance structure of Isabel, which combines chiefs, the Anglican church and the provincial government;[44] and to Choiseul's Lauru Land Conference of Tribal Communities, founded by Reverend Leslie Boseto, an influential member of the Uniting Church and national-level politician. David Akin's paper in this volume reminds us that these island-wide social and political institutions have an impressive and very successful antecedent in the form of Maasina Rule. His paper explores the question of why so much misinformation about the movement has been published by historians, anthropologists and others over the past 65 years. In doing so, Akin shows us that contra the 'virtually undisputed' claim that Maasina Rule was supressed by colonial authorities and largely failed as a political movement, it was, in fact, remarkably successful in achieving most of its main political objectives. Foremost among these was for Malaitans to have a greater say in their own affairs, which they effectively achieved in 1952, when an agreement with the government established a popularly selected Malaita Council and a Malaitan president elected by the council.

## FAILURE AND RESILIENCE

The dialectic of failure and resilience speaks to some of the most durable tropes in outsiders' depictions of the western Pacific. On the one hand, the region is seen as being

---

[43] Edvard Hviding, 'Re-placing the state in the western Solomon Islands: the political rise of the Christian Fellowship Church', in Edvard Hviding and Knut M. Rio (eds) *Made in Oceania: social movements, cultural heritage and the state in the Pacific* (Wantage, UK 2011), 51–89.

[44] Graham Baines, 'Beneath the state: chiefs of Santa Isabel, Solomon Islands, coping and adapting', State, Society and Governance in Melanesia Program, Working Paper 2 (2014).

rife with failures and frailties that encompass the spheres of governance, development, security and the environment. In the 1990s these depictions coalesced in a 'new doomsdayism' that selectively deployed data from Melanesia, especially PNG, to portray the entire Pacific Islands as a region in crisis.[45] And while this crisis was said to be Pacific-wide, its western edge was seen as especially troublesome. Indeed, it had become the core of a so-called 'arc of instability', the metaphorical geometry of which betrayed the increasingly securitised view of the region from Australia.[46] More recently, these framings of Melanesia, and Solomon Islands in particular, found a natural home in the discourse of 'state-failure', epitomised by the ASPI paper mentioned earlier.

Set against, and largely in opposition to, these discourses of failure and weakness are longstanding depictions of the western Pacific that highlight the strength and resilience of its many societies. As discussed by McDougall in this volume, 'resilience' has become a buzzword across a range of fields and is the core theoretical concern of the growing body of research on social-ecological systems (which includes a number of recent studies conducted in Solomon Islands).[47] In the case of Solomon Islands, McDougall observes that the term has found its way into descriptions of a range of subjects under the broad rubric of social and political systems. Indeed, the dialectic of failure and resilience finds expression in the contrast between a weak state and strong society, which, as McDougall astutely points out, figures in the discourse of those who make the case for 'neo-liberal state-building' as well as those who have critiqued such projects.

The key contribution of McDougall's paper lies in her empirically and historically grounded critique of the resilience discourse as it has been applied to depictions of Indigenous sociality in Solomon Islands. She argues that, far from being self-sustaining systems that have held their shape against outside forces – as the term 'resilience' implies – customary institutions in Pienna and elsewhere in the Solomons have been profoundly shaped by their intensive engagement with the apparatus of state. For these reasons, she prefers the term 'tenacious' to 'resilient', as it emphasises the 'efforts of actors to transform their local communities by gaining recognition and resources from the state and other trans-local actors'. David Akin's work on Maasina Rule, both in this volume and elsewhere, complements McDougall's arguments by demonstrating the eagerness with which Malaitans have engaged with and adopted new forms of social and political organisation. McDougall's arguments

---

[45] Greg Fry, 'Framing the Islands: knowledge and power in changing Australian images of "the South Pacific"', *Contemporary Pacific*, 9:2 (1997), 305–44.

[46] Robert Ayson, 'The "arc of instability" and Australia's strategic policy', *Australian Journal of International Affairs*, 61:2 (2007), 215–31.

[47] These studies include Anette Reenberg, Torben Birch-Thomsen, Ole Mertz, Bjarne Fog and Sofus Christiansen, 'Adaptation of human coping strategies in a small island society in the SW Pacific – 50 years of change in the coupled human-environment system on Bellona, Solomon Islands', *Human Ecology*, 36:6 (2008), 807–19; Ioan Fazey, Nathalie Pettorelli, Jasper Kenter, Daniel Wagatora and Daniel Schuett, 'Maladaptive trajectories of change in Makira, Solomon Islands', *Global Environmental Change*, 21:4 (2011), 1275–89.

also resonate with Monson's and Hviding's accounts of how contemporary forms of power and authority over land are being actively shaped by the ongoing encounters with urbanisation and globalisation, respectively.

IMMUTABLE GEOGRAPHIES?

As one would expect in a volume on Solomon Islands, questions of political and economic geography loom large across all the contributions. As John Gillis reminds us, islands are good to think with.[48] The pioneering work of Epeli Hau'ofa and the more recent florescence in thinking and writing about islands has done much to reform the way we think about islands; they are no longer perceived as essentially remote, static, backward, small and isolated.[49] One of the defining characteristics of islands, or of the condition of 'islandness' as it has been elucidated in the island studies literature, is the contradiction between openness and closure, and the corollary dialectic of fixity and movement, eloquently captured in Joel Bonnemaison's metaphor of '*l'arbre et la pirogue*' – the 'tree and canoe'.[50]

This maps onto capitalism's own dialectic of fixity and movement and of its contradictory logic of de- and re-territorialisation.[51] Just as globalisation breaks down some territorial boundaries, such as those associated with the traditional nation-state, it creates new ones: new enclaves, new frontiers, new spaces for production, exploitation, dispossession and accumulation. To invoke again Hviding's term, in the western Pacific these processes have been experienced as 'compressed globalisation': seen on a macro-historical timescale, the recent and rapid entanglement of Melanesia's 'communities' with an array of globalised projects, not least of which is capitalism. With the much-anticipated collapse of the logging industry – for several decades now a woeful tale of mismanagement, corruption and unsustainability – discussion is intensifying regarding what a mining future might look like for Solomon Islands, and indeed whether mining will replace logging in the latest sequence of accumulation by dispossession and de- and re-territorialisation.[52]

---

[48] John Gillis, *Islands of the Mind: how the human imagination created the Atlantic world* (New York 2004), 1–4.

[49] Epeli Hau'ofa, 'Our sea of islands', in Eric Waddell, Vijay Naidu and Epeli Hau'ofa (eds), *A New Oceania: rediscovering our sea of islands* (Suva 1993), 2–16, reprinted in *Contemporary Pacific*, 6:1 (1994), 148–61. On island studies, see Godfrey Baldacchino, 'The coming of age of island studies', *Tijdschrift voor Economische en Sociale Geografie*, 95:3 (2004), 272–83.

[50] Joël Bonnemaison, *The Tree and the Canoe: history and ethnography of Tanna* (Honolulu 1994).

[51] Neil Brenner, 'Beyond state-centrism? Space, territoriality, and geographical scale in globalization studies', *Theory and Society*, 28:1 (1999), 39–78.

[52] See for example Phillip Tagini, 'What should sustainable mining look like in Solomon Islands?', in Clive Moore (ed.), *Looking beyond RAMSI: Solomon Islanders' perspectives on their future* (Honiara 2013), 17–26; Graham Baines, 'Solomon Islands is unprepared to manage a minerals-based economy', State, Society and Governance in Melanesia Program, Discussion Paper 6 (Canberra 2015); Doug Porter and Matthew Allen, 'The political economy of the transition from logging to mining in Solomon Islands' (under review).

Yet before we turn to these, and other, anticipated economic shifts in more depth, we must first acknowledge a large body of research that demonstrates that geography does matter when it comes to economic development. The 2009 World Development Report titled 'Reshaping economic geography' argued, based on the evidence of two centuries of economic development, that distance from global markets is a critical determinant of economic growth.[53] Analysis by the World Bank shows that Pacific Island countries are uniquely challenged by the combination of small population sizes and distance from global markets and centres of production.[54] Moreover, Solomon Islands is especially challenged owing to the dispersal of its population at low densities over many islands. Tobias Haque, who presented at the workshop, argues that the experience of other small islands states shows that higher living standards can be achieved but not through the standard policy nostrums that emphasise the creation of regulatory environments conducive to investment and productivity gains. He suggests that lasting improvements in living standards in Solomon Islands will come about only through 'deeper economic integration with larger economies, including through sharing service delivery and regulatory responsibilities and working to remove constraints to cross-border movements of people, capital, goods and services'.[55]

These observations further highlight the tension between change and continuity. While Solomon Islands experienced relatively spectacular economic growth rates during RAMSI's tenure, they were based on unprecedented rates of logging and a boom in Honiara's service economy brought about by a combination of increased public sector expenditure (much of it funded by aid) and the post-conflict influx of expatriate development workers. In this manner, the economic reforms implemented by RAMSI have done little to effect structural change and diversification in the economy or to establish a foundation for broad-based growth.[56]

As we contemplate the Solomons' economic prospects, we are reminded of the tight imbrication of society and economy and, in particular, of the socially disintegrative impacts of certain types of economic development, as illustrated in this volume by Monson and Hviding. A 2010 World Bank study pointed to large-scale mining and urbanisation as the most likely 'sources of growth' for Solomons in the coming decades.[57] It also cautioned, and we concur, that the costs and benefits of these will have to be carefully managed, with the assistance of the international community, if the gains made during the RAMSI period are to be sustained and perhaps, eventually, translated into transformational change.

---

[53] World Bank, 'Reshaping economic geography', 2009, 73–95, http://www-wds.worldbank.org/external/default/WDSContentServer/WDSP/IB/2008/12/03/000333038_20081203234958/Rendered/PDF/437380REVISED01BLIC1097808213760720.pdf (accessed 18 Sep. 2015).

[54] Cited in Haque, 'Economic transition in Solomon Islands', 11–12.

[55] Ibid., 1.

[56] Ibid., 4.

[57] World Bank, 'Solomon Islands growth prospects: constraints and policy priorities', Oct. 2010, 9–12, http://www-wds.worldbank.org/external/default/WDSContentServer/WDSP/IB/2010/11/09/000333037_20101109234611/Rendered/PDF/577950ESW0P1111urcesofGrowthSummary.pdf (accessed 18 Sep. 2015).

# The Teleology and Romance of State-building in Solomon Islands

## JON FRAENKEL

ABSTRACT

The 2003–13 Regional Assistance Mission to Solomon Islands (RAMSI) is widely depicted as an ambitious 'state-building' project in the mould of contemporary interventions in Bosnia, Iraq, East Timor and Kosovo. Yet no new constitution was put in place in Solomon Islands, and, in practice, the core Australian policing components of the mission were largely substituted for their local counterparts. Unlike most state-building missions, RAMSI did not assume executive authority, and the critical relationship with the Indigenous government soon deteriorated, particularly after the election-related riots of April 2006. The teleological framing of RAMSI as a 'state-building' operation largely draws on heroic claims about future intentions made during the early phase of the mission, whereas, after the crises of 2006–07, RAMSI officials were engaged mostly in playing down expectations, narrowing the mission's objectives and preparing an exit strategy.

> We only begin to understand this momentous historical process – the formation of national states – when it begins to lose its universal significance. Perhaps, unknowing, we are writing obituaries for the state.
>
> Charles Tilly[1]

The Australian-led Regional Assistance Mission to Solomon Islands (RAMSI) has regularly been seen as a 'comprehensive' or 'integrated state-building operation', both by its architects and by its critics.[2] Within Australia, the 2003–13 mission was often

---

[1] Charles Tilly, 'Western state-making and theories of political transformation', in Charles Tilly (ed.), *The Formation of National States in Western Europe* (Princeton 1975), 638.

[2] Regional Assistance Mission to Solomon Islands, 'Annual performance report 2005/2006', July 2006; Elsina Wainwright 'How is RAMSI faring? Progress, challenges, and lessons learned' Australian Strategic Policy Institute, Strategic Insights 14 (2005), 2. Most scholarly accounts of RAMSI centrally figure the state-building framing. To mention only those that include the term in their

extolled as possessing a 'unique kind of authority in the world of state-building' and as providing a 'model for future deployments'.[3] On the ground in Solomon Islands, the early RAMSI special coordinators frequently described their task as 'state-building' or 'nation-making', terms that were often used interchangeably. The mission's first special coordinator, Nick Warner (2003–04), told a press conference in February 2004: 'Nation building is what we really came here to do, laying down the foundations of law and order, a foundation to begin the process to rebuild the nation'.[4] That delayed timing became more compressed for Warner's successor, James Batley (2004–06), who said in 2005 that 'at its core, RAMSI is a state-building exercise', a task he deemed necessary because 'prior to RAMSI's arrival in mid-2003, the Solomon Islands state had ceased to function in a minimally acceptable way'.[5]

Two distinct perspectives help to explain why RAMSI has been so widely viewed in this light.

titles: Francis Fukuyama, 'State-building in Solomon Islands', *Pacific Economic Bulletin*, 23:3 (2008), 1–17; Sinclair Dinnen, 'Dilemmas of intervention and the building of state and nation', in Sinclair Dinnen and Stewart Firth (eds), *Politics and State Building in Solomon Islands* (Canberra 2008), 1–38; Greg Fry and Tarcisius Tara Kabutaulaka (eds), *Intervention and State-Building in the Pacific: the legitimacy of 'cooperative intervention'* (Manchester, UK 2008); John Braithwaite, Sinclair Dinnen, Matthew Allen, Valerie Braithwaite and Hilary Charlesworth, *Pillars and Shadows: statebuilding as peacebuilding in Solomon Islands* (Canberra 2010); Sinclair Dinnen, 'State-building in a post-colonial society: the case of Solomon Islands', *Chicago Journal of International Law*, 9:1 (2008), 511–78; Sinclair Dinnen, 'A comment on state-building in Solomon Islands', *Journal of Pacific History*, 42:2 (2007), 255–63; Shahar Hameiri, 'The future of RAMSI: Australian state building abroad and its discontents', *Asia View*, 17 (2007), 2–3; Shahar Hameiri 'State building or crisis management? A critical analysis of the social and political implications of the Regional Assistance Mission to Solomon Islands', *Third World Quarterly*, 30:1 (2009), 35–42; Shahar Hameiri, 'Mitigating the risk to primitive accumulation: state-building and the logging boom in Solomon Islands', *Journal of Contemporary Asia*, 42:3 (2012), 405–26; Shahar Hameiri, 'Capacity and its fallacies: international state building as state transformation', *Millennium*, 38:1 (2009), 55–81; Julien Barbara, 'Antipodean statebuilding: the Regional Assistance Mission to Solomon Islands and Australian intervention in the South Pacific', *Journal of Intervention and Statebuilding*, 2:2 (2008), 123–49; David Hegarty, Ron May, Anthony Regan, Sinclair Dinnen, Hank Nelson and Ron Duncan, 'Rebuilding state and nation in Solomon Islands: policy options for the regional assistance mission', State, Society and Governance in Melanesia Program, Discussion Paper 2 (2004).

[3] Michael Fullilove on behalf of the Lowy Institute for International Policy, 'The testament of Solomons: RAMSI and international state-building', March 2006, 14–15, http://www.lowyinstitute. org/files/pubfiles/Fullilove%2C_The_testament_web_version.pdf (accessed 16 Sep. 2015); see also Michael Fullilove, 'Strategy sound so far: now to finish shaping a nation', *Australian*, 10 Mar. 2006; James Watson, 'A model Pacific solution? A study of the deployment of the Regional Assistance Mission to Solomon Islands', Land Warfare Studies Centre, Working Paper 126 (2005), 37.

[4] Warner, Nick, 'RAMSI's Objectives for 2004', press conference, Lelei Resort, Guadalcanal, 16 Feb. 2004.

[5] James Batley, 'The role of RAMSI in Solomon Islands: rebuilding the state, supporting peace', paper presented at the Peace, Justice and Reconciliation Conference, Brisbane, 31 Mar. 2005.

## 1. The Failed State Diagnosis

In July 2003, Prime Minister John Howard of Australia described the objective of RAMSI as being to rescue a 'failed state' that might otherwise jeopardise Australian security interests.[6] Several weeks earlier, Foreign Minister Alexander Downer had launched a pamphlet prepared by the Australian Strategic Policy Institute (ASPI) titled 'Our failing neighbour: Australia and the future of Solomon Islands', which identified Solomon Islands as a 'petri dish in which transnational and non-state security threats can develop and flourish' and which set out a framework for a ten-year reconstruction plan.[7] In retrospect, these interpretations of a security threat posed by the Solomons conflict were widely rejected[8] but occasionally defended as politically convenient warnings aimed at persuading a reluctant Australian public to back a costly and protracted regional intervention. After it became clear that Solomon Islands and Papua New Guinean politicians resented the 'failed state' label, many Australian and New Zealand diplomats switched to use of the terms 'fragile' or 'weak' states rather than 'failed' states, as did the aid agency AusAID. Nonetheless it was the failed state diagnosis that informed the Australian Coalition government's claim in mid-2003 that remedial action would entail a long-run state rebuilding or construction program, without any explicit exit timetable. Prime Minister Howard and Foreign Minister Downer thought that it would be necessary to radically 're-engineer' and 'completely redesign the place'.[9]

## 2. The Unfinished Colonial State-building Hypothesis

A second, more sophisticated and better historically grounded strand in the state-building framing of RAMSI was to suggest that states across western Melanesia 'were entirely external creations overlaid on top of indigenous social orders' and that threadbare colonial administrations had left only a 'light footprint'. As a result, the state remained 'incomplete' at independence in 1978. From this perspective, the 'failed state' diagnosis was badly wrong:

[6] John Howard, 'Address to the Sydney Institute, Intercontinental Hotel, Sydney', PM Transcripts, http://pmtranscripts.dpmc.gov.au/release/transcript-20769 (accessed 21 Sep. 2015).

[7] Elsina Wainwright on behalf of the Australian Strategic Policy Institute, 'Our failing neighbour: Australia and the future of Solomon Islands', June 2003, https://www.aspi.org.au/publications/our-failing-neighbour-australia-and-the-future-of-solomon-islands/solomons.pdf (accessed 16 Sep. 2015), 41 and 47.

[8] Terence Wesley Smith, 'There goes the neighbourhood: the politics of failed states and regional intervention in the Pacific', in Jenny Bryant-Tokalau and Ian Frazer (eds), *Redefining the Pacific? Regionalism past, present and future* (London 2006), 121–26; Jon Fraenkel, 'Myths of Pacific terrorism', in John Henderson and Greg Watson, *Securing a Peaceful Pacific* (Christchurch 2005), 120–26; Tarcisius Tara Kabutaulaka, '"Failed state" and the War on Terror: intervention in Solomon Islands', East–West Center, Asia-Pacific Issues 72 (2004).

[9] Quoted in Braithwaite and Charlesworth, *Pillars and Shadows*, 51.

> The labelling of states as 'failed' or 'failing' has little analytical value and is ultimately more about legitimating intervention than explaining failure. Moreover, the notion that a state has 'failed' implies that at some earlier point it was 'successful' … [This] has never been the case in Solomon Islands. On the contrary, the problem with post-colonial states in Melanesia, including Solomon Islands, is not so much that they are prone to falling apart but rather that they have yet to be properly built.[10]

Similarly, the influential ASPI pamphlet 'Our failing neighbour' argued that 'the crisis in Solomon Islands is less about the collapse of a coherent functioning state, and more about the unravelling of the apparatus of colonial rule'.[11] For Elsina Wainwright, the pamphlet's author, it was the weak engagement of the British colonial authorities that explained why 'the institutions of statehood never firmly took root', and the key question was 'whether Solomon Islands was ever a properly functioning state'.[12] Like the 'failed state' diagnosis, the incomplete colonial state-building hypothesis pointed in the direction of a long-run state construction mission, but it offered a closer fit with the perceived difficulties RAMSI was to encounter on the ground.

This paper does not revisit debates about whether or not the weakness of the state was the critical catalyst for the 1998–2003 conflict. Those issues have been considered elsewhere.[13] Instead, the focus of attention here is on the RAMSI years and how these are best interpreted. The paper argues that much of the literature on state-building in Solomon Islands exaggerates the degree of external control and downplays the significance of local forces working in different directions. The state-building framing contested the sovereignty of the host state (whether owing to state-failure or the absence of a 'proper state'), but most Solomon Islanders saw RAMSI primarily as a mission to restore law and order. As studies of ostensibly state-building operations in other parts of the globe have found, even weak or troubled states can sustain internal political dynamics

---

[10] Sinclair Dinnen, 'The Solomon Islands intervention and the instabilities of the post-colonial state', *Global Change, Peace & Security*, 20:3 (2008), 352. See also Sinclair Dinnen, 'Lending a fist? Australia's new interventionism in the southwest Pacific', State, Society and Governance in Melanesia Program, Discussion Paper 5 (2004), 6; Dinnen, 'Dilemmas of intervention', 3. See also Organisation for Economic Co-operation and Development, 'DAC peer review: Australia', 2005, 45, http://www.oecd.org/dac/peer-reviews/34429866.pdf (accessed 25 Sep. 2015). This line of analysis is echoed in Barbara, 'Antipodean statebuilding', 130–31; Benjamin Reilly, 'State functioning and state failure in the South Pacific', *Australian Journal of International Affairs*, 58:4 (2004), 488.

[11] Wainwright, 'Our failing neighbour', 27.

[12] Elsina Wainwright, 'Responding to state failure – the case of Australia and Solomon Islands', *Australian Journal of International* Affairs, 57:3 (2003), 487–88.

[13] Jon Fraenkel, *The Manipulation of Custom: from uprising to intervention in the Solomon Islands* (Canberra 2004), 9–12, 181–86.

that work contrary to overseas-orchestrated institutional designs.[14] The first part of the paper looks at the initial framing of RAMSI under the Pacific Islands Forum's Biketawa Declaration and the extent to which this shaped the mission's architecture. The second part considers the objectives set out by RAMSI and what these meant in practice.[15] The third part examines how local politics shaped the mission, setting limits that ultimately frustrated the more ambitious objectives. In conclusion, we consider what lessons the RAMSI story offers for the broader state-building literature.

## THE CONTEXT AND LEGAL FRAMING OF RAMSI

RAMSI commenced in July 2003 in the wake of five years of low-intensity civil warfare but at a time when a reconfiguration of domestic conflict eased the path to a foreign intervention mission, at least on the law-and-order front. The initial phase of the conflict, over late 1998 to 2000, entailed the emergence first of the Isatabu Freedom Movement (IFM) on Guadalcanal and then, in response, the Malaita Eagle Force (MEF). The IFM drove around 25,000 Malaitan settlers from their homes in rural Guadalcanal during 1998–99, many of whom fled to the capital, Honiara (also located on the island of Guadalcanal), or else returned to the neighbouring island of Malaita.[16] The MEF initially emerged out of pressures by disgruntled Malaitans in Honiara on the government of Bartholomew Ulufa'alu to provide compensation for properties lost during the troubles on Guadalcanal.

In June 2000, a 'joint operation' between the MEF and the Royal Solomon Islands Police Force's paramilitary arm, the Police Field Force, overthrew the Ulufa'alu government, precipitating clashes between the MEF and the IFM, mostly centred on Honiara's outskirts. Four months later, an Australian-brokered peace agreement signed in Townsville ended the MEF/IFM fighting around Honiara, but this failed to deliver a robust peace. Critically, one faction of the Guadalcanal militias signed up to the Townsville Peace Agreement while the other did not. A phase of intra-factional fighting commenced, which was particularly acute among militants from

---

[14] Nicolas Lemay-Hébert, 'Coerced transitions in Timor Leste and Kosovo: managing competing objectives of institution-building and local empowerment', *Democratization*, 19:3 (2012), 465–85; Simon Chesterman, Michael Ignatieff and Ramesh Thakur, 'The future of state-building', in Simon Chesterman, Michael Ignatieff and Ramesh Thakur (eds), *Making States Work: state failure and the crisis of governance* (Tokyo 2005), 359–87.

[15] This section of the report draws on the findings in Jon Fraenkel, Joni Madraiwiwi and Henry Okole on behalf of the Solomon Islands Government and the Pacific Islands Forum, 'The RAMSI decade: a review of the Regional Assistance Mission to Solomon Islands, 2003–2013', 14 July 2013, http://pidp.eastwestcenter.org/pireport/2014/July/Independent%20RAMSI%20Review%20Report%20Final.pdf (accessed 25 Sep. 2015).

[16] The figure of 35,000 is regularly given, but this includes those displaced also from within Honiara and probably underestimates the latter since the heaviest urban displacement occurred in 2000 after the census had been completed. For an analysis, see Fraenkel, *The Manipulation of Custom*, 56.

Guadalcanal's Weather Coast. This second phase of the conflict entailed a greater focus on criminal activity, including widespread extortion and the use of state finances to bankroll the militia groups, helping to explain why so many of the political elite were willing to endorse foreign intervention in mid-2003. Per capita GDP shrank by around one-quarter over 2000–02, and most rural industries were closed down, including the Gold Ridge mine and the palm oil plantations on northern Guadalcanal. In total, around 200 people were killed as a result of the 1999–2003 fighting.

When RAMSI arrived on 24 July 2003, its authorisation had been established under the Pacific Islands Forum's Biketawa Declaration (2000), which specified a need for the consent of the nation concerned.[17] The key legal provision, the Facilitation of International Assistance Act, gave the 'visiting contingent' (as RAMSI was legally called) extensive powers, particularly as regards policing, carriage of weapons, tax exemption and immunity from prosecution, but it depended on a 'notice' from the governor-general affirming that 'the Government has requested assistance', and it gave the Solomon Islands parliament an annual right of review of that notice, together with the possibility of terminating the mission within three months.[18]

This framing differentiated RAMSI from other so-called state-building missions, such as those in Kosovo, East Timor, Iraq or Bosnia, where foreign authorities acquired considerably greater powers. The enabling legislation for the United Nations Interim Administration Mission in Kosovo (UNMIK), for example, entitled the mission to 'provide an interim administration for Kosovo' and perform 'basic civilian administrative functions'.[19] Regulations specified that 'all legislative and executive authority with respect to Kosovo, including the administration of the judiciary, is vested in UNMIK and is exercised by the Special Representative of the Secretary-General'.[20] Both Iraq (UN Security Council Resolution 687) and Kosovo (UN Security Council Resolution 1244) 'uniquely impose[d] a mandatory international regime

---

[17] 'Forum Leaders recognised the need in time of crisis or in response to members' request for assistance, for action to be taken on the basis of all members of the Forum being part of the Pacific Islands extended family'. Pacific Islands Forum, '"Biketawa" declaration', Oct. 2000, sec. 2, http://www.forumsec.org/resources/uploads/attachments/documents/Biketawa%20Declaration,%2028%20October%2020002.pdf (accessed 25 Sep. 2015). The use of the word 'or' leaves open the possibility of a regional intervention without an invitation by the member state concerned, though in practice unsolicited intervention would be unlikely to gain Pacific Islands Forum approval.

[18] Facilitation of International Assistance Act 2003 (Solomon Islands), secs 3.1, 23.

[19] United Nations, Security Council, UN Doc. S/RES/1244(1999), 'On the deployment of international civil and security presences in Kosovo', 10 June 1999, undocs.org/S/RES/1244(1999) (accessed 25 Sep. 2015).

[20] United Nations, UNMIK regulation no. 1999/1, 'On the authority of the interim administration in Kosovo', 25 July 1999, sec. 1.1, http://www.unmikonline.org/regulations/1999/re99_01.pdf (accessed 25 Sep. 2015). An almost identical provision was set out for East Timor but adds: 'In exercising these functions the Transitional Administrator shall consult and cooperate closely with representatives of the East Timorese people'. United Nations, UNTAET regulation no. 1999/1, 'On the authority of the transitional administration in East Timor', 27 Nov. 1999, sec. 1.1, http://www.un.org/en/peacekeeping/missions/past/etimor/untaetR/etreg1.htm (accessed 25 Sep. 2015).

on a sovereign state'.[21] Nor was there to be any gradual expansion in the degree of control exerted by RAMSI, analogous to Bosnia after the Dayton Peace Accord of 1995, where 'the international powers of administration, under the Office of the High Representative, [were] vastly increased, reducing the Bosnian institutions established by Dayton to administrative shells'.[22]

All conflict-triggered foreign interventions might, at least in theory, be seen as 'state-building' missions in the minimal sense that they aim to resolve or subdue challenges to domestic government authority and to restore a state's monopoly on the use of armed force, but the term 'state-building' has more usually been confined to those broader intervention missions that go beyond peace-keeping and entail a significant civilian deployment. Like foreign interventions in Bosnia, Iraq, Kosovo and East Timor, RAMSI was such an integrated mission, characterised by a 'merging of development and security' objectives,[23] but it lacked the tools of enforcement available elsewhere.[24] Just as RAMSI's commencement relied on the consent of the host nation, so too did the suite of reforms it intended to implement. Although that limitation was soon to be sorely tested, the uneasy relationship with the Indigenous government critically shaped RAMSI's activities.

Before examining how RAMSI interacted with the local political environment, let us consider the range of objectives set out in RAMSI's enabling legislation and examine what the mission entailed in practice.

## RAMSI's Objectives and the Impact on the State

In the July 2003 'Framework for strengthened assistance to Solomon Islands', the objectives of the mission were set out as being not only to restore law and order but also to 'promote longer-term economic recovery and revive business confidence' and 'rebuild the essential machinery of government to support stability and the delivery of services', including 'focused efforts to deal with corruption', 'downsizing the civil service, cleansing the payroll and stopping extortion'.[25] In the wake of protracted

---

[21] Thomas Franck, 'Lessons of Kosovo', *American Journal of International Law*, 93:4 (1999), 858; Richard Caplan, *The International Governance of War-Torn Territories: rule and reconstruction* (Oxford 2005).

[22] David Chandler, 'From Dayton to Europe', *International Peacekeeping*, 12:3 (2005), 336; see also Gerald Knaus and Felix Martin, 'Travails of the European Raj', *Journal of Democracy*, 14:3 (2003), 60–74.

[23] Mark Duffield, *Global Governance and the New Wars: the merging of development and security* (London 2001).

[24] Similarly, Shahar Hameiri's depiction of RAMSI as a 'form of emergency rule' neglects that emergency rule everywhere entails unfettered control over government. Hameiri, 'State building or crisis management?', 35.

[25] Australian Government, 'Framework for strengthened assistance to Solomon Islands: proposed scope and requirements', 24 July 2003, as reproduced in Foreign Relations Committee, 'Inquiry into the Facilitation of International Assistance Notice 2003 and RAMSI intervention', Nov. 2009, 22–24, http://www.parliament.gov.sb/files/committees/foreignrelations/FRC%20Final%20Report.pdf (accessed 29 Oct. 2015).

behind-the-scenes negotiations distilling these objectives into programmatic form, 'law and justice', 'economic reform' (or 'development' or 'governance') and 'machinery of government' emerged as the three civilian 'pillars' of the mission (in language inherited from the Kosovo mission via East Timor).[26] RAMSI was envisaged as a three-phase process: an initial restoration of law and order, a subsequent stabilisation of government finances, and thirdly, a longer-term phase of state-building and 'capacity development'.[27]

Although it was the civilian programs that most contributed to RAMSI's reputation as a state-building mission, the number of RAMSI personnel initially involved in these was relatively small. In total, only 17 expatriate personnel were deployed as part of the mid-2003 civilian stabilisation team, though numbers subsequently climbed. On average, around 150 RAMSI expatriate civilian personnel worked in Solomon Islands during 2007–13. At first, easily the largest component of the mission was the military operation, the 'combined task force' (CTF), composed mostly of Australian Defence Force personnel but also soldiers from New Zealand, Papua New Guinea, Fiji and Tonga. The CTF deployment peaked at close to 2,000 personnel in mid-2003, but as the absence of any local resistance became clear, military numbers rapidly shrank. For the 2003–13 decade as a whole, the most sizable RAMSI deployment in both numerical and financial terms was the Participating Police Force (PPF), which was mainly composed of officers from the Australian Federal Police (AFP) but also included smaller numbers from New Zealand and the Pacific Islands. An oversight role was granted to a 'special coordinator', required to be 'a person nominated by the Government of Australia', who dealt with the local and international media profile of the mission and with lines of accountability back to Canberra, but the CTF and PPF commanders had control over daily military and policing operations.[28]

Unlike interventions in Kosovo and East Timor, where police forces were reconstituted under United Nations auspices, the PPF was kept organisationally separate from the Royal Solomon Islands Police (RSIP). A combined police force was deemed impossible, on the grounds that the RSIP had been too heavily compromised by its activities during the conflict years, not least owing to its complicity in the June 2000 coup.[29] Nevertheless the RAMSI Treaty provided that the head of the PPF was

[26] Susannah Gordon, 'Evaluating success of peacekeeping missions: lessons from East Timor and Solomon Islands', in Jacob Bercovitch and Karl DeRouen Jnr, *Unraveling Internal Conflicts in East Asia and the Pacific: incidences, consequences, and resolutions* (Lanham, MD 2011), 249.

[27] RAMSI, 'RAMSI medium term strategy 2007–2012', Jan. 2007, 3.

[28] 'Agreement between Solomon Islands, Australia, New Zealand, Fiji, Papua New Guinea, Samoa and Tonga concerning the operations and status of the police and armed forces and other personnel deployed to Solomon Islands to assist in the restoration of law and order and security' (otherwise known as, and hereinafter described as, the RAMSI Treaty), 24 July 2003, art. 4.1.

[29] The Police Field Force, which had collaborated with the MEF in overthrowing the elected government in June 2000, was disbanded.

to be sworn in as deputy commissioner of the RSIP,[30] and several Australian and New Zealand officers also assumed line positions in the RSIP. For the initial years, the PPF was largely focussed on executive policing. As 2005–07 PPF commander Will Jamieson acknowledged, the force initially 'pushed aside a somewhat dysfunctional SIPF [RSIP]' despite the risk of 'collateral damage'.[31] Stationed at the Guadalcanal Beach Resort outside the capital, Honiara, the PPF was mostly supplied externally from Australia, drawing on funds that did not pass through Solomon Islands government accounts. Like the deployment to East Timor, the PPF did entail a dramatic restructuring of Australia's overseas policing capabilities, but the key step in this respect was the formation of the AFP's International Deployment Group.[32] If any state was built by this particular innovation, it was the Australian state.

RAMSI did entail a major domestic police-training operation organised in considerable part through the Solomon Islands Police Academy. Around two-thirds of the RSIP had been retired, removed or replaced by the end of the 2003–13 decade, with a slightly larger number of new recruits. Even at the conclusion of this period, the PPF command preferred to look to generational change to restructure the RSIP.[33] A RAMSI-commissioned 2009 review of the PPF found that the 'two forces' model had encouraged a public contrast between 'the well-equipped, efficient, highly motivated and exceptionally visible PPF officers in their PPF vehicles' and the seemingly 'less efficient, less competent and less trustworthy' RSIP officers.[34] The six annual RAMSI People's Surveys reinforce this claim of a negative public perception of the RSIP.[35] The decision to continue AFP assistance beyond 2013, when other elements of the RAMSI package were discontinued, reflected an official awareness that success in rebuilding the Solomon Islands police force had been patchy.

Closely linked to the police programs, RAMSI facilitated a civilian deployment to the judiciary (both High Court and Magistrates Court), the Office of the Director of Public Prosecutions and the Office of the Public Solicitor. Extensive

---

[30] RAMSI Treaty, art. 5.2

[31] Will Jamieson, 'Rebuilding a police service – restoring law and order: an overview of the activities of the PPF in the Solomon Islands', paper presented at a State, Society and Governance in Melanesia Program seminar, Australian National University, 15 Nov. 2007.

[32] Chris Ellison (minister for justice and customs), 'Australia boosts regional law enforcement capacity', press release, 2 Feb. 2004; Gordon Peake and Kaysie Studdard Brown 'Policebuilding: the International Deployment Group in the Solomon Islands', *International Peacekeeping*, 12:4 (2005), 520–32.

[33] Regional Assistance Mission to Solomon Islands Participating Police Force, 'The status of the Royal Solomon Islands Police Force and its capability as of 30th June 2013', 2011–13 transition outcome report, 20.

[34] 'Independent review of the RAMSI Participating Police Force's (PPF's) capacity development of the Royal Solomon Islands Police Force (RSIPF): final report', 29 Sep. 2009, 31. See also Sinclair Dinnen and Matthew Allen, 'Paradoxes of postcolonial police-building: Solomon Islands', *Policing and Society*, 23:2 (2013), 222–42.

[35] Available from 'People's survey', RAMSI, http://www.ramsi.org/media/peoples-survey/ (accessed 29 Sep. 2015).

construction activities occurred later in the decade, entailing new or refurbished courts and accommodation in both Honiara and the provincial centres. The key early focus of these activities was on seeing through the Tension trials. From 2009, the number of external advisors and inline personnel in this sector was considerably scaled down.

Under the 'economic reform' pillar, the crucial deployment was to the Ministry of Finance, with expatriates assuming powerful positions such as accountant-general, undersecretary of finance and commissioner of inland revenue. Repayment of debt arrears helped to stabilise government finances. Concerted efforts directed towards tax and customs compliance led to substantial increases in government revenue. This was classic state-building, at least for that school of thought that sees state acquisition of tax revenue as central to the creation of robust accountability institutions,[36] but RAMSI's economists and accountants had much less control over government expenditure. For example, during 2006–07, RAMSI had only a single official deployed to the Ministry of Development Planning and Aid Coordination (MDPAC), which had responsibility for much of the capital account spending and at the time included supervision of controversial cash grants delivered to MPs in the form of Taiwanese-aid-funded rural constituency development funds.[37] In reaction to these and other domestic political influences over government expenditure, Australia, New Zealand and the multilateral organisations sought to ring-fence at least donor funds from being diverted for domestic political purposes.[38]

The third civilian component, 'rebuilding the essential machinery of government' (MOG) was, in the early days, often depicted by special coordinators as central to RAMSI's 'nation building' objectives.[39] It commenced later than the other programs and included assistance to key accountability institutions, such as the Auditor-General's Office, the Electoral Commission and the Parliamentary Support Services, as well as the offices of the ombudsman and the Leadership Code Commission.[40] Under the leadership of Speaker Sir Peter Kenilorea and

---

[36] Mick Moore, 'How does taxation affect the quality of governance?', Institute of Development Studies, Working Paper 280 (2007).

[37] See Peter Coventry, 'The hidden mechanics of Solomon Islands budget processes – understanding context to improve reforms', State, Society and Governance in Melanesia Program, Discussion Paper 3 (2009). Peter Coventry was the one RAMSI adviser deployed to the MDPAC for the three years ending 2008.

[38] David Craig and Doug Porter 'Political settlement in Solomon Islands: a political economic basis for stability after RAMSI?', State, Society and Governance in Melanesia Program, Working Paper 1 (2013).

[39] Office of the Special Coordinator, 'RAMSI military contingent 200 days detailed miscellaneous fact sheet', 2004.

[40] James Batley, speech announcing the commencement of the 'machinery of government' programs, 'Solomon Islands government – development partners high level meeting', Honiara, 17 Nov. 2004. These programs got underway in 2005.

Clerk Taesi Sanga, the Parliamentary Support Services were dramatically transformed, as was the Auditor General's Office under Floyd Augustine Fatai, but MOG eventually became a smorgasbord of loosely connected programs, for which both domestic and international enthusiasm steadily waned.[41] Some originally anticipated activities, such as assistance to the Office of the Prime Minister and Cabinet, were particularly politically sensitive and thus eventually scaled back, while 'provincial government strengthening' was never a major priority. Programs changed in reaction to shifting policy concerns in Canberra, and at times in response to Solomon Islands government priorities, as with the temporary Solomon Islands Government Housing Management Project.[42]

Placement of RAMSI expatriate personnel affected mainly three ministries – justice, police and finance – whereas the other 21 ministries remained largely untouched. Ministries covering agriculture, lands, rural development, commerce, mines, fisheries, infrastructure development, forestry and national reconciliation experienced either very little contact with RAMSI or no contact at all (though Australian bilateral assistance to the lands ministry continued for several years after the commencement of RAMSI). In all these ministries, Melanesian state processes remained predominant, even if constrained by restrictions on procurement and cash advances emanating from the Ministry of Finance.

In practice, RAMSI steered clear of assisting or encouraging any fundamental reshaping of the institutions of state, for example by rewriting the constitution or redesigning the electoral system, again dramatically differentiating RAMSI from missions to Bosnia, Kosovo or East Timor. The Solomon Islands government had committed itself to introducing a federal constitution at the Townsville Peace Agreement in 2000, and extensive consultations on decentralisation had taken place over 2002–03, but RAMSI 'adopted a position of quiet but effective opposition to the proposed constitutional reforms'.[43] On the ground, many RAMSI personnel were keen on electoral reform and saw the introduction of preferential voting or party strengthening

---

[41] For example, the 2010 annual RAMSI report warned of 'diminishing returns to investment' in this area. Sue Emmot, Manuhuia Barcham and Tarcisius Kabutaulaka, 'Annual performance report 2010: a report on the performance of the Regional Assistance Mission to the Solomon Islands', 21 Mar. 2011, ii. See also Prime Minister Sikua's comments that MOG had become 'problematic in many ways'. Derek Sikua in Solomon Islands Parliament, *Hansard*, 24 July 2008, 8th parliament, 8th meeting, 2.

[42] World Bank, 'Building post-crisis capacity: cases from the Solomon Islands – second phase of the Government Housing Management Project: government housing management and policy', 1 Oct. 2008, http://www-wds.worldbank.org/external/default/WDSContentServer/WDSP/IB/2012/05/16/000333037_20120516013354/Rendered/PDF/687280WP0P11400ng0case0Sols0Oct2008.pdf (accessed 29 Sep. 2015).

[43] See Katy Le Roy, 'Participatory constitution making: lessons from Fiji and Solomon Islands', PhD thesis, University of Melbourne (Melbourne 2013), 209–10. See also Braithwaite and Charlesworth, *Pillars and Shadows*, 78–79; Ashley Wickham cited in Gordon Leua Nanau, 'Intervention and nation-building in Solomon Islands: local responses', in Fry and Kabutaulaka, *Intervention and State-Building in the Pacific*, 156.

legislation as a sensible echo of nation-building strategies with which they were familiar from the Australian historical experience, but the key decision-makers in Canberra were wary of the cost implications of electoral system change and saw a new federal set-up as empowering another potentially expensive tier of government.[44]

The state was built in one critical respect during the RAMSI years (if state-building is conceived in raw numerical terms), but this was not at the behest of RAMSI. In the 2003 'Framework for strengthened assistance to Solomon Islands', one objective had been 'downsizing the public service', but in practice the public sector doubled in size over the RAMSI decade, from 8,466 civil servants in 2003 to 15,933 in 2013.[45] Public spending rose from 25 to 50% of GDP between 2003 and 2009.[46] In part, this reflected the economic recovery after 2003 and corrected a sizable contraction during 1998–2003. Even after the expansion, the civil service was no larger in per capita terms than that of its Pacific neighbours.[47]

Growth in state spending relied on the substantial pickup in government revenue during the RAMSI years. Over 2003–13, foreign aid composed around 38% of Solomon Islands GDP. Yet much of the aid associated with RAMSI had only a small direct impact on levels of civil service employment, as is often the case with foreign intervention missions. In the 2007–08 financial year, for example, only 10.5% of RAMSI's expenditure remained within the country.[48] Bilateral donor funding tends to have greater domestic impact, but the World Bank estimates that around 75–80% of total official aid to Solomon Islands is spent overseas.[49] Rental incomes paid by expatriate personnel, local hiring by RAMSI and its associated contractors, and the hotel, hospitality and catering trade all increased as a result of the mission's presence, generating incomes or expenditures that could be directly or indirectly taxed. Although notorious for tax evasion, the round log export industry – which boomed after 2003 – generated around 17% of government revenue on average during the RAMSI years. More rigorous enforcement of tax compliance lifted revenue acquired from the commercial and retail trade, including the increasingly Chinese-dominated small-scale retail sector. Recovery in the local economy

---

[44] Le Roy, 'Participatory constitution making', 212.

[45] K.G. Gannicott, 'The size and cost of the public service in Solomon Islands', Remuneration Review, Briefing Paper 1 (2003), 2.

[46] World Bank, 'Solomon Islands growth prospects: constraints and policy priorities', 1 Oct. 2010, 1, http://www-wds.worldbank.org/external/default/WDSContentServer/WDSP/IB/2010/11/09/ 000333037_20101109234611/Rendered/PDF/577950ESW0P1111urcesofGrowthSummary.pdf (accessed 18 Sep. 2015); Tobias Haque 'Economic transition in Solomon Islands', State, Society and Governance in Melanesia Program, In Brief 16 (2013).

[47] K.G. Gannicott, 'Public sector remuneration in Solomon Islands: some economic issues', Oct. 2013, 9, chart 2. (Publicly undisclosed consultancy report in possession of the author.) See also Le Roy, 'Participatory constitution making', 212.

[48] Peace Dividend Trust, 'The economic impact of peace and humanitarian operations in Solomon Islands', Sep. 2010, 15.

[49] World Bank, 'Solomon Islands sources of growth: summary of findings' 2010, 8.

clearly benefitted from RAMSI's restoration of the rule of law, but the associated upsizing of the state was never among the mission's initial objectives.


## THE UNEASY STANDOFF WITH THE INDIGENOUS STATE

RAMSI's absence of executive authority may have distinguished the mission from state-building operations in Iraq, East Timor and Kosovo, but on the ground Australia nevertheless had considerable financial clout. The Howard–Downer government wanted to use the strong domestic political support for RAMSI's core policing and military functions to leverage its 'good governance' and economic liberalisation reforms. At the inception of the mission, Prime Minister John Howard had insisted on an 'all or nothing' approach, most importantly entailing extensive controls over the Ministry of Finance.[50]

When RAMSI arrived in mid-2003, the government of Sir Allan Kemakeza was in office. Most governments in Solomon Islands are coalitions of loosely aligned factions and independents. Many fall to mid-term no-confidence challenges. Yet Kemakeza's government was the first since independence to survive a full parliamentary term. With a relatively extensive deployment in place, RAMSI's political influence was at its zenith. Prime Minister Kemakeza had staked his political reputation on the success of the mission. His administration was – as historian Clive Moore has expressed it – more 'subservient' than its successors.[51] During 2003–06, no-confidence votes were discouraged as destabilising, and key figures in the opposition were encouraged to cross the floor and join the government. Ironically, this phase included the dismembering of what remained of the loose reformist coalitions that had assumed office under prime ministers Francis Billy Hilly (1993–94) and Bartholomew Ulufa'alu (1997–2000).[52]

Despite strong public support for the mission, many in the political elite were ambivalent or opposed to RAMSI's economic reforms, to the strengthening of oversight institutions, to the open-ended time horizon of the mission and to the lack of any 'exit strategy'. A December 2004 'Report of the cabinet committee to review "Intervention Task Force report on RAMSI"' claimed that RAMSI's Ministry of Finance deployment had 'caused undesirable and unnecessary delays to the delivery of

---

[50] Fraenkel, *The Manipulation of Custom*, 165.

[51] Clive Moore, 'Uncharted Pacific waters: the Solomon Islands constitution and the government of Prime Minister Manasseh Sogavare, 2006–07', *History Compass*, 6:2 (2008), 494. See also Clive Moore 'External intervention: the Solomon Islands beyond RAMSI', in M. Anne Brown (ed.), *Security and Development in the Pacific Islands: social resilience in emerging states* (Boulder and London 2007), 177. In the wake of the 2006 election, Patrick Cole described Kemakeza as the unsurpassed local 'numbers man' best fitted to lead the country. Patrick Cole, pers. comm., Honiara Hotel, Apr. 2006.

[52] Jon Fraenkel, 'The impact of RAMSI on the 2006 elections in the Solomon Islands', *Political Science*, 58:2 (2006), 158.

goods and services' and objected to RAMSI personnel assuming inline positions. The report recommended that RAMSI should be 'confined to its original mandate of security and civic order and economic recovery' and that the Ministry of Finance deployment should be 'scale[d] down immediately' until a 'total withdrawal in mid 2005'.[53] One of the report authors, finance minister Francis Zama, complained that RAMSI was primarily accountable to Canberra rather than to the Solomon Islands government, while police minister Michael Maina was critical of the 'deepening gap' between the PPF and RSIP. Both were sacked by Kemakeza, and both were subsequently arrested on charges of corruption.[54]

Nevertheless resistance from the political and civil service elite continued. In 2006, RAMSI public affairs manager Mary-Louise O'Callaghan gave an insider account of the 'daily, endless and time-consuming struggle to push on with [our] reforms, with little or no support from all but a few of Solomon Islands' senior bureaucrats'. She described RAMSI's efforts to deal with corruption or placement of personnel in the finance ministry as attracting 'resentment, suspicion and active undermining from the country's political and bureaucratic élite'.[55] The debacle following the election of April 2006 had intensified these difficulties. Kemakeza's former deputy Snyder Rini was selected as the new prime minister, much to the consternation both of RAMSI and of the crowds gathered outside parliament awaiting the formation of the new government. Riots broke out, culminating in the burning down of Honiara's Chinatown district and including the torching of several RAMSI vehicles.[56] Eight days later, Snyder Rini resigned to avoid a no-confidence challenge on the floor of parliament.

In his place, Manasseh Sogavare, who had previously served as prime minister at the height of the conflict in 2000–01, was selected as the new head of government, again to the dismay of RAMSI. Sogavare's cabinet featured several vociferous opponents of the mission, including at least one politician formerly closely associated with the MEF, Charles Dausabea, who became minister of police and national security but was soon arrested for allegedly orchestrating the April riots. The deterioration of bilateral relations was further fuelled by Sogavare's termination of the attorney-general, solicitor-general, legal draftsman and director of public prosecutions in a bid to tighten his control over state power that Clive Moore has called a 'creeping coup'.[57] After he protested against the removal of the attorney-general, Australian

[53] Solomon Islands Cabinet Committee, 'Report of the cabinet committee to review "Intervention Task Force report on RAMSI"', Dec. 2004, 13, 16.

[54] Robert Iroga, 'Kemakeza fires two Solomon Islands ministers', *Solomon Star*, 4 Feb. 2005; Tarcisius Tara Kabutaulaka, 'Melanesia in review: issues and events, 2005: Solomon Islands', *Contemporary Pacific*, 18:2 (2006), 425–26. Maina was subsequently cleared of these charges.

[55] Mary-Louise O'Callaghan, 'RAMSI – the way ahead', in Sinclair Dinnen and Stewart Firth (eds), *Politics and State-Building in Solomon Islands* (Canberra 2007), 187.

[56] In April 2006, a leaked internal RAMSI email recounting the behind-the-scenes efforts of Australia's high commissioner, Patrick Cole, to avoid the election of Snyder Rini reinforced allegations of foreign political interference. 'Solomons advisor sacked over email', *Solomon Star*, 3 May 2006.

[57] Moore, 'Uncharted Pacific waters', 498–501.

High Commissioner Patrick Cole was declared persona non grata on 12 September 2006. Australian Federal Police stationed in Port Moresby tried in vain to stop Sogavare's intended replacement attorney-general, Fiji national Julian Moti, from entering Solomon Islands.[58] Moti evaded capture and flew into the country surreptitiously on a Papua New Guinea Defence Force carrier. In October, Australian police officers stationed in the Solomon Islands as part of RAMSI's PPF raided the prime minister's office, seeking evidence that Moti's entry had been illegal. Having ordered the raid despite serving as a line officer in the RSIP, police commissioner Shane Castles, another AFP officer, was declared an undesirable immigrant in December.[59]

In reaction to the September crisis, Australia's foreign minister, Alexander Downer, reiterated that RAMSI was a 'take it or leave it package' and that the Solomon Islands government preference to 'cherry pick' only selected parts of the mission would not be tolerated:

> RAMSI is an integrated package and we're not going to have RAMSI salami sliced or neutered in any way in delicate areas like improvement in the operation of public finances in the Solomon Islands ...
> We won't have RAMSI, in other words, sliced up so that some of the more effective areas of RAMSI dealing with the fight against financial corruption, the need for integrity within the legal system, that they must remain in place, otherwise the whole program will fail.[60]

Downer claimed that the reluctance of many in the Solomon Islands elite to accept the RAMSI reform package was motivated by corruption and self-interest, while Sogavare accused Australia of bankrolling his opponents.[61] The Sogavare government did not revoke the RAMSI-enabling legislation, perhaps mindful of broad popular support for the mission and the difficulty of assembling a parliamentary majority for such a course of action. In August 2007, however, the Solomon Islands prime minister did persuade parliament to agree to a future review of the Facilitation of

---

[58] For a fuller account of the 'Moti affair', see Hank Nelson, 'The Moti affair in Papua New Guinea', State, Society and Governance in Melanesia Program, Working Paper 1 (2007); Moore, 'Uncharted Pacific waters', 499–500. Julian Moti was 'wanted' in Australia on charges of having had sex with an underage girl in Vanuatu in 1997.

[59] When RAMSI arrived, a British police officer, Bill Morrell, had been chief of the RSIP, but Canberra preferred to have an Australian occupying the role.

[60] 'The Solomon Islands facing "very difficult situation"', *Insiders*, television program, ABC (Australia), 21 May 2006; 'RAMSI won't be "salami sliced" says Downer', *AM*, radio program, ABC Radio (Australia), 22 Sep. 2006.

[61] Hameiri, 'State building or crisis management', 37. In the wake of the expulsion of Patrick Cole, Downer said, 'I think some of the politicians there see RAMSI as standing between them and the honeypot'. 'Ambassador expelled from Solomons', *Age*, 12 Dec. 2006. In 2007, responding to allegations of Australian heavy-handedness in the region and intrusion on sovereignty, he said, 'Frankly, the cry of sovereignty is occasionally used as a smokescreen meant to distract attention from corrupt and illegal behaviour'. 'Downer blasts corrupt Pacific leaders', *Sydney Morning Herald*, 8 Aug. 2007.

International Intervention Act.[62] Yet by October, fissions had emerged in cabinet, and in December 2007 Sogavare was ousted in a no-confidence vote.

The end of 2007 proved a watershed for RAMSI, both because of the failure of the Howard–Downer reform strategy and because of changes in government in both Australia and Solomon Islands. This period also set the pattern for the second half of the RAMSI decade. The new government of Derek Sikua was considerably more sympathetic to RAMSI than its predecessor, but it included many of the same ministers. Sikua used reformist policies and declarations of support for RAMSI to leverage financial backing for government objectives, such as rural development.[63] Weaker government finances as a result of the global financial crisis also encouraged appeals to Australia and New Zealand for increased support, but New Zealand in particular was experiencing financial stress and cutting back its aid program. At this stage, RAMSI officials were reluctant to embrace new commitments. The later special coordinators Tim George (2006–09) and Graeme Wilson (2009–11) focused on a minimalist interpretation of RAMSI's responsibilities, emphasising the restricted 'mandate' of the mission.[64] Encouraged by the Pacific Islands Forum reports on the mission's progress, the main focus now was on RAMSI's 'exit strategy', though the mantra was that this was to be 'task bound' rather than 'time bound', implying that RAMSI would steadily achieve its objectives and then depart.[65]

In the wake of the 2006–07 crisis, state-building objectives no longer figured centrally in RAMSI official statements. Senior Solomon Islands civil servants – most still in place from the Sogavare years – left RAMSI personnel to follow through the mission's various proposed reforms but with little more than perfunctory local participation, as for example during negotiations around the 2009 'Partnership' agreement, setting out funding priorities for the 2009–13 Australian budgetary cycle.[66] Sikua served out the remainder of the parliamentary term ending 2010, but towards its end his governing coalition splintered. The 2010 polls brought into office another loosely aligned governing coalition headed by veteran Western Province politician Danny Philip, who insisted upon a five-year exit strategy and recommended that

---

[62] Solomon Islands Parliament, *Hansard*, 27 Aug. 2008, 8th parliament, 4th meeting, 1–48.

[63] Coalition for National Unity and Rural Advancement, 'Policy statement', Jan. 2008.

[64] An 11-page speech given in 2009 by special coordinator Graeme Wilson, for example, used the term 'mandate' 12 times, and the emphasis throughout was on RAMSI's restricted roles and responsibilities. See Graeme Wilson, 'The Solomon Islands government – RAMSI Partnership Framework: towards a secure and sustainable Solomon Islands', speech to the State, Society and Governance in Melanesia Program, Canberra, 17 Dec. 2009, http://www.ramsi.org/wp-content/uploads/2014/07/091217-State-Society-and-Governance-in-Mework-Towards-a-secure-and-sustainable-SI-Address-at-ANU-by-SC-Graeme-Wilson.pdf (accessed 20 Sep. 2015).

[65] Pacific Islands Forum Eminent Persons Group, 'Mission helpem fren: a review of the Regional Assistance Mission to Solomon Islands', May 2005, 6, http://pidp.eastwestcenter.org/pireport/special/Forum_RAMSI_review.pdf (accessed 30 Sep. 2015).

[66] As acknowledged by ex-RAMSI 'machinery of government' manager Julien Barbara. See Julien Barbara, 'From intervention to partnership – prospects for development partnership in Solomon Islands after the RAMSI', *Asia & the Pacific Policy Studies*, 1:2 (2014), 400.

'RAMSI should concentrate on rebuilding of the RSIP and implementation of the capability program including training, logistics, and police housing in Honiara, other urban centres and the rural areas'.[67] New allegations of Australian political interference echoed those of 2006. In early 2011, a garbled 'intel report' issued from within the Office of the Prime Minister accused Australia of fast-tracking convictions of government ministers and of luring defections to the opposition.[68] Those claims were subsequently dropped, but they nevertheless indicated just how ingrained hostility to RAMSI had become among key sections of the governing elite. In mid-2013, on the tenth anniversary of the mission, RAMSI was dismantled: the military component was ended, the civilian programs were transferred to bilateral control, and only a residual police-building program was continued under the mission's umbrella, initially entailing around 150 PPF officers but expected to draw down over the 2013–17 period.

CONCLUSION

Whether or not missions such as RAMSI are seen as 'state-building' operations may depend on the criteria adopted – interpretive or empirical. This paper has explored both possible approaches. From an interpretative perspective, RAMSI was plausibly a state-building operation because these *were* the stated intentions or aspirations of at least some of the early special coordinators, even if those goals went largely unfulfilled. The sheer inappropriateness of the initial rhetoric about 'failed states' and threatening 'petri dishes' opened the way for a variety of alternative perspectives about what RAMSI would do in Solomon Islands. Into this opening, some development-oriented practitioners on the ground heroically sought to interact with local champions in an effort to build the state.[69] Others critiqued RAMSI for not deepening such commitments.[70] Reformist politicians and expatriate business owners similarly wanted

[67] Coalition for Reform and Advancement, 'Policy statement', Oct. 2010, 26.

[68] Intel report, 28 Jan. 2011, copy in possession of the author. This report became the subject of a lawsuit against the prime minister. See *Wale v. Philip* [2011] SBHC 144 (Solomon Islands).

[69] Looking back at the early days of the mission, James Batley has said that the use of the expression 'state-building' was 'shorthand for saying that RAMSI's mandate covered core functions of government as opposed to its broader service delivery functions, such as health and education. So it was partly a way of resisting mission creep. It was also a way of saying RAMSI was not about nation-building (in particular the peace and reconciliation agenda, which we always said had to be taken forward by Solomon Islanders themselves)'. James Batley, pers. comm., 28 Oct. 2014.

[70] Hence the state-building orientation – it was argued – needed to be supplemented by a 'nation-making' focus, or it needed to become less 'Honiara-centric', and it needed to engage more effectively with local-level or informal institutions. See Sinclair Dinnen, 'Beyond state-centrism: external solution and the governance of security in Melanesia', in Fry and Kabutaulaka, *Intervention and State-building in the Pacific*, 102–18; Matthew Allen, Sinclair Dinnen, Daniel Evans and Rebecca Monson, 'Justice delivered locally: systems, challenges, and innovations in Solomon Islands', World Bank research report, Aug. 2013, http://www-wds.worldbank.org/external/default/WDSContentServer/WDSP/IB/2013/09/27/000356161_20130927130401/Rendered/PDF/812990WP0DL0Se0Box0379833B00PUBLIC0.pdf (accessed 16 Sep. 2015).

RAMSI to overhaul the state more extensively and take a firmer stand on the protection of private property and on anti-corruption, but most Solomon Islanders saw RAMSI primarily as a policing program. The official RAMSI strategy prioritised the restoration of the rule of law and the stabilisation of government finances but envisaged a subsequent protracted state-building project. The 2006–07 Sogavare crisis disrupted that longer-run strategy and encouraged a minimalist reshaping of the mission.

Just as the Howard–Downer strategy entailed a thinly veiled threat of withdrawal in the event of non-compliance, so too did Sogavare's stance imply a threat to revoke the RAMSI-enabling legislation. For very different reasons, neither the Australian nor the Solomon Islands government chose to go down those routes. After Sogavare had called Canberra's bluff by expulsion of senior Australian personnel, the insistence on far-reaching good governance and economic liberalisation reforms as the price for security assistance was politically unsustainable, even if the Rudd–Gillard government had been so inclined. The option of an Australian withdrawal raised reputational issues both because of the finance and effort previously invested and because of the risk of renewed violence.[71]

The empirical case for interpreting RAMSI as an integrated state-building exercise is still weaker. First, RAMSI did not acquire executive authority but relied on the continuing consent of the Solomon Islands government. Second, the core policing component of the mission was in practice largely delivered outside the RSIP, through a 'two forces' model, and the AFP's efforts to adjust to a later 'capacity building' phase were fraught and limited and largely oriented towards generational change. Third, RAMSI steered clear of radically restructuring the Solomon Islands state, believing that any change would be costly for Australia. Fourth, the vast majority of RAMSI expenditures did not pass through the Solomon Islands government budget. Although these entailed assistance in kind, they had limited impact on the long-run character of the Solomon Islands state. Finally, to the extent that the state was 'built' – or changed in significant and durable ways – this occurred largely under Indigenous auspices. Most of the ministries were little affected by the presence of RAMSI personnel, with the exceptions of justice, police and finance.

The analytical bases of contemporary state-building perspectives also merit scrutiny. The 'failed state' hypothesis was inherently contradictory: RAMSI was in the Solomon Islands at the behest of that same state, and ultimately it was the actions of the Indigenous state that set limits on the mission's activities. A similar blind spot exists in that perspective that centres on the unfinished colonial nation-making project, with its teleological emphasis on the absence of a 'properly functioning state'.[72] The idealised 'properly built' end point implied some continuum of state

[71] Dan Halvorson, 'Reputation and responsibility in Australia's 2003 intervention in the Solomon Islands', *Australian Journal of International Affairs*, 67:4 (2013), 439–55.
[72] As Charles Tilly pointed out in the wake of his research team's monumental study of the formation of Western European 'national states', phrases like 'state-building' and 'state formation' quickly 'took on teleological tones in the literature on political change. Contrary to our intentions,

capacity spanning from the deficient or dysfunctional to the robust, and a set of interventions along that known trajectory that could deliver a fully fledged state. But the Solomon Islands state had not stood frozen in a semi-constructed mould since independence in 1978. A new postcolonial elite had emerged, with strong links to foreign logging and, to a lesser degree, mining companies, and with access to powers of licencing and taxation.[73] Under Kemakeza, 20 ministries delivered rudimentary services at least to urban Honiara and some provincial capitals and provided employment for 15,000 Solomon Islanders, and Sogavare raised the number to 24 ministries. Ministers and permanent secretaries thus had considerable powers, as did the chairs of state-owned enterprises, such as the Solomon Islands Water Authority, Solomon Islands Electricity Authority and Solomon Airlines Ltd. The state may not have been 'properly built' on an Australian or European template, but it had firmly taken root on a Melanesian pattern also discernible in Papua New Guinea and Vanuatu.

The unfinished colonial state-building hypothesis relied on a romanticised image of European state-building. 'Nationalism, constructed around the symbols and ideals of shared community and identity, was a potent force in the development of many of these [European] states', Sinclair Dinnen has written, whereas in Melanesia 'little sense of shared political community' existed, and thus what eventuated in Solomon Islands was a 'state without a nation'.[74] That idea of a necessary congruence between state and nation is indeed familiar from the European experience, but the extent of intellectual emphasis on 'the nation' was often inversely related to national political homogeneity. In France the 18th-century Jacobin revolutionaries battled to transcend multiple dialects, localised legal arrangements and regionalist movements (for example, the Vendée) in the name of 'the nation'. Yet in the mid-19th century, Karl Marx could justly describe the French peasantry as possessing 'no national bond'.[75] A more homogeneous sense of French national identity did not emerge

students of state formation in Latin America, Africa, the Middle East, or Asia began taking the European experience as a model, and asking why their regions had failed to form proper states'. Charles Tilly, 'Why and how history matters', in Robert E. Goodin and Charles Tilly (eds), *The Oxford Handbook of Contextual Political Analysis* (Oxford 2006), 419; see also 'Charles Tilly interview: concepts and state formation', YouTube, https://www.youtube.com/watch?v=b51Dkbh8 XCA&index=4&list=PL73ABDF5D9781DF91 (accessed 30 Sep. 2015).

[73] Ian Frazer, 'Resource extraction and the postcolonial state in Solomon Islands', in Raymond Frederick Watters and T.G. McGee (eds), *Asia Pacific: new geographies of the Pacific Rim* (Wellington 1997), 318–34; Judith A. Bennett, *Pacific Forest: a history of resource control and contest in Solomon Islands, c. 1800–1997* (Knapwell, UK, and Leiden 2000).

[74] He concluded that 'despite the passing of 30 years, the underlying assumption as to the historical inevitability of the cementing of state and nation has yet to be fulfilled'. Dinnen, 'The Solomon Islands intervention', 344 and 347; see also Dinnen, 'Dilemmas of intervention', 56.

[75] Karl Marx and Frederick Engels, 'The Eighteenth Brumaire of Louise Bonaparte', in Karl Marx and Frederick Engels, *Selected Works* (London 1968), 171. For an assessment of the accomplishments of the French revolution, in this respect, see Peter McPhee, *The French Revolution, 1789–1799* (Oxford 2002), 187–88.

until the last quarter of the 19th century, centuries after the formation of a centralised absolutist state.[76] Those German philosophers, contemporaries of the French revolution, renowned for identifying an intimate connection between a common language and a legitimate state nonetheless recognised that the aspiration for national unification was 'utterly alien' to most Germans and thought this something that had to 'be instilled in them'.[77] Few modern historians see the 1870s unifications of both Germany and Italy as a direct response to a popularisation of nationalist sentiment.[78]

Although much aspired to by 19th-century European intellectuals, the idea that state-building and nation-making were inherently interconnected acquired international authority only later in the European state formation experience, particularly in Woodrow Wilson's 'right of nations to self-determination' (also a key theme of Bolshevik thought in Russia) and in article 22 of the League of Nations covenant's acknowledgement of 'certain communities' that have 'reached a stage of development where their existence as independent nations can be provisionally recognized'.[79] Modern ideas of state-building owe a considerable debt to the 1919 Treaty of Versailles's notions of trusteeship over 'mandated' territories. Ever since, the prevailing international system has nurtured, legitimised and protected even weak states, and in so doing brought into being a radically different global context for would-be nation-builders to that which spawned the 16th- and 17th-century European states.[80] As a result, emerging states outside Europe – including those of East Asia – have not followed in the footsteps of their European forebears. In this sense, the new postcolonial states that acquired independence in the 1960s and 1970s do indeed (as Tilly speculated) entail an obituary for the state in its classical European form.

With overseas assistance, the Solomon Islands state not only survived the Tension years of 1998–2003. It was also protected under the Biketawa provisions and expanded at least in raw numerical terms under RAMSI's auspices. RAMSI wanted to establish a police force, prisons, courts and oversight institutions that reflected 'an irreducible minimum of functions that a state should provide, and

---

[76] Eugene Weber, *From Peasants into Frenchmen: the modernization of rural France, 1870–1914* (Stanford 1976).

[77] Johann Gottlieb Fichte, cited in Erica Benner, 'Nationalism: intellectual origins', in John Breuilly (ed.), *The Oxford Handbook of the History of Nationalism* (Oxford 2013), 45.

[78] John Breuilly, 'Nationalism and national unification in nineteenth-century Europe', in Breuilly, *The Oxford Handbook of the History of Nationalism*, 149–74; John Breuilly, 'Reflections on nationalism', in Stuart Woolf (ed.), *Nationalism in Europe, 1815 to the Present: a reader* (London 1996), 137–54; William Carr, 'The unification of Germany', in John Breuilly (ed.), *The State of Germany* (New York 1992), 80–102.

[79] Quoted in Lisa Anderson, 'Antiquated before they can ossify: states that fail before they form', *Journal of International Affairs*, 58:1 (2004), 7.

[80] Robert H. Jackson and Carl G. Rosberg, 'Why Africa's weak states persist: the empirical and the juridical in statehood', in Atul Kohli (ed.), *The State and Development in the Third World* (Princeton 1986), 1–24; Jeffrey Herbst, *States and Power in Africa: comparative lessons in authority and control* (Princeton 2000); Karen Barkey and Sunita Parikh, 'Comparative perspectives on the state', *Annual Review of Sociology*, 17 (1991), 531.

some irreducible minimum standards that governments should observe'.[81] Although those standards seemed uncontroversial and even apolitical for those from relatively prosperous neighbouring countries,[82] in the very different Solomon Islands context, this was essentially a radical reform strategy that would be delivered from above, and from outside, and which entailed a showdown with the political elite, despite the absence of any groundswell of popular social mobilisation. Successive Solomon Islands governments wanted the security assistance and the increased foreign aid, but – as we have seen – many Indigenous politicians were less well-disposed towards a restructuring of the state. The type of state that most Solomon Islands politicians wanted to assemble was a radically decentralised one, focused on constituency-level control of expenditures by MPs and/or federal arrangements. A politically significant number also wanted a porous state that was amenable to manipulation for personal or communal advantage. Unable to assemble a majority to eject RAMSI, the middle position became to allow the mission to undertake its work relatively unfettered but with minimal buy-in. As a result, Solomon Islanders post-RAMSI encounter many of the same dilemmas that they faced before RAMSI, but at least – and fortunately – without the former ascendancy of the militant factions.

---

[81] Batley, 'The Role of RAMSI'.

[82] Although decisions about the configuration of intervention missions are ultimately deeply political, the much-criticised 'technocratic' tone of much official comment arises from the fact that civilian operations are managed mostly on the ground by public servants.

# Honiara: Arrival City and Pacific Hybrid Living Space

## CLIVE MOORE

### ABSTRACT

Honiara is a Pacific arrival city and hybrid living space that retains many village-like qualities. It shares similarities with Doug Saunders's 'arrival city' model: new arrivals are sustained by established networks that enable them eventually to integrate into urban life, along with considerable circulation through a constant flow from and to the provinces. Yet the relatively small size of Honiara and Solomon Islands, plus the resilience of aspects of village culture, bring into question theoretical models based on much larger, more anonymous developing world cities. Settlement and squatter areas are more dominant than fixed-tenure suburbs. *Wantokism*, *kastom* and linguistic diversity permeate this urban diversity and extend family networks. The conclusion argues that authorities must come to terms with new arrivals, squatters and settlements/urban villages and incorporate them into planning or face future urban turmoil.

Honiara is a name in the Ghari language for the area of land west of Point Cruz on Guadalcanal Island. *Naho-ni-ara* means 'facing the Ara', the place where the southeast winds meet the land. The main village sites were Matanikau (or Mataniko) to the east and Kakabona to the west of Point Cruz. Between the 1880s and the 1930s, with little compensation or permission, the Honiara area was divided into several coconut plantations. In June and July 1942 it was briefly a Japanese base, and from August 1942 to 1945 the area became a huge American military garrison, replete with hospitals, movie theatres and a complex road system leading out to major airfields (Figure 1). Some of the heaviest fighting on Guadalcanal in 1942 took place in what is now central Honiara, with the Matanikau River a 'no-man's land' for several months. At war's end, the military base passed to the British as the site for a new capital to replace the 1897–1942 protectorate headquarters on Tulagi in the Nggela (Florida) Islands, which had been destroyed. The possibilities were good: several airfields existed, the area abutted extensive plain land, and its lower rainfall meant less prevalence of

*Acknowledgements*: I am indebted to David Akin, Graham Baines, Murray Chapman, Terry Brown, Ben Burt, Daniel Evans, Christine Jourdan, Rodolfo Maggio and Paul Roughan for advice on this paper.

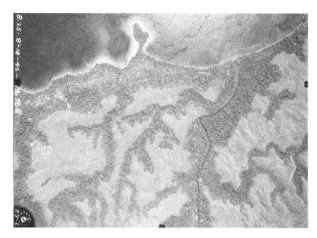

FIGURE 1: The American invasion of Guadalcanal began on 7 Aug. 1942. This 18 Aug. photograph is of the area that became central Honiara, taken at 10,700 feet (3,261 metres) on one of the daily B17 reconnaissance missions. Point Cruz is in the centre, and the Matanikau River divides the area. The site of Matanikau village can be seen in a clearing near the coast just west of the mouth of the river; it was burnt down on 19 Aug. by American marines.
Source: United States National Archives and Records Administration, United States Air Force, RP Bishop Guad 08181942-004B.

malaria. What was ignored was that Honiara had no natural port and only a narrow area of coastal flat land. In addition, the rivers in the area are capable of flash floods, and Guadalcanal Plains are also flood prone. This was very clear in April 2014, when heavy rain brought devastating floods to Honiara, made worse because the river systems and hills behind Honiara have been denuded of forests through gardening.

Initially just a government settlement and a small Chinatown – with a population of 3,000 in the 1950s, 79% male – Honiara slowly became a substantial city that families call home. It drew Solomon Islanders from across the nation, the majority from neighbouring Malaita Island. The largest urban area in Solomon Islands, with roughly 18% of the nation's 550,000 inhabitants,[1] Honiara suffers from significant social pressures. Many Solomon Islands issues during and since the 1998–2003 Tension years relate to Honiara.[2] Malaitan migration, one major issue behind the civil unrest, has

---

[1] The latest census suggests only 12%. See Solomon Islands Government, *Report on 2009 Population & Housing Census*, vol. 2: *National Report* (Honiara n.d.), 2. But a more recent survey estimates the greater Honiara population at more than 100,000. Ministry of Lands, Housing and Survey, 'Draft Honiara local planning scheme 2015', 18 Dec. 2014, 13, http://www.honiaracitycouncil.com/wp-content/uploads/2014/09/Honiara-Local-Planning-Scheme-2015-draft-v1.pdf (accessed 29 Oct. 2015).

[2] 'Tension' refers to the 1998–2003 period, when Honiara was caught in a civil war, anarchy and widespread breakdown of civil life. Clive Moore, *Happy Isles in Crisis: the historical causes for a failing state in Solomon Islands, 1998–2004* (Canberra 2004); Jon Fraenkel, *The Manipulation of Custom: from uprising to intervention in the Solomon Islands* (Wellington 2004); Clive Moore, 'The misappropriation of Malaitan labour: historical origins of the recent Solomon Islands crisis', *Journal of Pacific History*, 42:2 (2007), 211–32; Mary-Louise O'Callaghan (ed.), *Rebuilding a Nation: ten years of the Solomon Islands –*

been mostly to Honiara and Guadalcanal Plains. Understanding Honiara's history and social dynamics will be crucial to all future development in Solomon Islands. This paper describes Honiara as a hybrid living space, a combination of pre- and post-urban social and economic forms. I argue that, as in other developing- world cities,[3] authorities must come to terms with the arrival communities and incorporate their hybrid living patterns into their planning, or face future urban turmoil.

Contemporary Honiara's approximately 22 square kilometres are surrounded by customary lands over which the government has little jurisdiction. Expanding the city's boundaries thus seems unfeasible; a higher population density, division of the larger land blocks and more high-rise buildings seem likely solutions. A population movement to the new Doma urban area on Guadalcanal and expansion of provincial capitals might also slow Honiara's growth.[4] The census figures in Table 1 indicate that the population increased from 3,534 in 1959 to 64,609 in 2009. Official figures from the 1990s and 2000s are considered unreliable, however, and the 2015 Honiara City Council estimates suggest a population of 100,000 in the greater Honiara area.[5] The difference can be accounted for because the urban population considerably overflows the municipal boundaries onto surrounding Guadalcanal customary lands and into the now truncated Queen Elizabeth II National Park at the back of Honiara, mainly through use as garden lands. A comparison of Figures 2 and 4 shows the expansion of Honiara's boundaries. Honiara's population has been growing at 6.2% annually, nearly twice the national average. Many residents who fled Honiara in the late 1990s returned after 2003, when the Regional Assistance Mission to Solomon Islands (RAMSI) arrived and new arrivals came from the provinces. In the three years after 2003, the growth rate was 26%.[6]

\* \* \* \* \*

Honiara is in a rain shadow and is often hot and dusty, that is, when it is not wet and muddy. After all, it is on a tropical island eight degrees from the equator. Honiara balances on a series of undulating ridges and valleys. The middle classes and the rich usually live on hills with picturesque views out to volcanic Savo Island

---

*RAMSI partnership* (Honiara 2013); Clive Moore (ed.), *Looking beyond RAMSI: Solomon Islanders' perspectives on their future* (Honiara 2014).

[3] Gordon McGranahan, Diana Mitlin and David Satterthwaite, 'Land and services for the urban poor in rapidly urbanizing countries', in George Martine, Gordon McGranahan, Mark Montgomery and Rogelio Fernández-Castilla (eds), *The New Global Frontier: urbanization, poverty and environment in the 21st century* (London 2008), 77–97.

[4] *Solomon Star*, 6 Feb. 2014.

[5] The 1986 projection for Honiara's 2006 population was 73,855, with an annual increase of 4.8%. Considering the disturbances of 1998–2003, this projection was reasonably accurate. Ko Groenewegen, 'Demographic estimates and projections based on the 1986 census', Solomon Islands Census Office, Working Paper 2 (1988), 26.

[6] Satish Chand and Charles Yala, 'Informal land systems within urban settlements in Honiara and Port Moresby', in Australian Agency for International Development, *Making Land Work*, 2 vols (Canberra 2008), II, 85–101. The official report on the 2009 census suggests a growth rate of only 2.7% but makes adjustments based on an acknowledged undercount to around 3%. *National Report*, 2.

or inland to the high mountains of central Guadalcanal. Poorer residents reside in the valleys. To the west, between Rove and White River, the coastal road skirts the beach and the prestigious properties along the shore, once the homes of senior public servants and government ministers. The main government buildings are clustered on both sides of and inland from Point Cruz, the much-restructured small peninsula that shelters the central wharves and port facilities.

Unlike Papua New Guinea's capital, Port Moresby, positioned on commodious Halifax Harbour, Honiara has no substantial bay, merely a curve in the coast with small Point Cruz as the central promontory. Unlike Port Vila, Vanuatu's much smaller capital set on a safe harbour replete with sidewalk cafes showing its French influence, Honiara is often caricatured as a hick town that too hurriedly became a city. It lacks the lush surrounds of Lae or Suva, or the large expatriate population of New Caledonia's Noumea. Yet for those who live there or who visit regularly, Honiara has a laidback, pleasant nature and is a likeable place – a rumbustious and ever-growing Pacific urban sprawl. On any given day, thousands of residents perambulate constantly along Mendana Avenue, the single main coastal street that stretches from Rove to Matanikau River, then, with a change of name, extends along Kukum Highway past the Central Referral Hospital, the Malaitan fishing village, Ranadi Industrial Estate and out to Henderson Airport. People walk to the central market or city offices, or take mini busses to work, school and shopping along routes that pass along the coast and snake into the hills, moving the bulk of the population about cheaply. Peak-hour traffic is now so congested that it is often quicker to walk from Point Cruz to the main market than to take a bus. It is a homely city that has long-established middle-class and elite residential areas, settlements (urban villages) and squatter areas (also urban villages). Honiara has much in common with other Melanesian cities; its village-like qualities are hard to come to terms with, but future planners must understand its hybrid links with rural areas if they are to plan wisely and cope with future flashpoints.

In the 1970s, with a population of around 15,000, it seemed that everyone knew everyone else, and although today this is no longer possible, kin networks remain strong. One has only to spend time at the docks to see the constant human traffic circulating between the provinces and Honiara, and that the urban middle classes and elites are still closely involved in this movement, looking after relatives from their original villages. People seldom arrive without contacts; every provincial village has members living in Honiara. The strength of Honiara society is imbedded in the *wantok* and *kastom* systems (see below), which depend on individual and community-level resources with limited support from or links with municipal authorities or the state. The disjunction between how settlements and relationships work in a very Melanesian manner and the way that municipal formal authority works is a key issue for the nation.

## HONIARA: A DEVELOPING WORLD CITY

Geographers and political scientists have coined ways of describing Pacific urban areas like Honiara, Port Vila and Port Moresby: arrival cities, immigrant gateways or key sites within larger circulations. Doug Saunders's concept of an 'arrival city' can be applied, with some reservations, to Honiara:

> The arrival city can be readily distinguished from other urban neighbourhoods, not only by its rural-immigrant population, its improvised appearance and ever-changing nature, but also by the constant linkages it makes, from every street and every house and every workplace, in two directions. It is linked in a lasting and intensive way to its originating villages, constantly sending people and money and knowledge back and forth, making possible the next wave of migrations from the village, facilitating with the village the care of older generations and the education of younger ones, financing the improvement of the village. And it is linked in important and deeply engaged ways to the established city. Its political institutions, business relationships, social networks and transactions are all footholds intended to give new village arrivals a purchase, however fragile, on the edge of the larger society, and to give them a place to push themselves, and their children, further into the centre, into acceptability, into connectedness.[7]

His worldwide study describes the networks that provide security and self-identity, entry mechanisms (access to housing and jobs) that enable people to survive in what is an alien environment. Social-mobility pathways provide eventual entry to permanent employment, property ownership and upwards class mobility.[8] While Saunders has listed many primary characteristics shared by Honiara (circulation and survival techniques), his examples of arrival cities – for instance Manila in the Philippines, Mexico City or the many Chinese cities drawing in rural people – are all gigantic compared with Honiara. Honiara's small size is important in understanding its dynamics; the level of urbanisation is not so great as to have become totally anonymous, and pre-urban social forms survive or have been adapted to operate in the new hybrid environment. Honiara's size, ingrained cultural aspects and hybrid forms allow it, and perhaps other Pacific cities, to operate differently from many urban areas elsewhere in the developing world.

In the 1980s, Bartram and Watters introduced the 'MIRAB' (migration, remittances, aid and bureaucracy) concept to describe Pacific small island economies. Mainly applied to Polynesia and Micronesia, it has relevance in Melanesian cities such as Honiara where government bureaucracy dominates the private economy and wages are consumed communally.[9] Other studies use the frame of the peri-urban Pacific to include the urban fringe extending beyond formal city boundaries, which

---

[7] Doug Saunders, *Arrival City: the final migration and our next world* (Sydney 2010), 11.

[8] Ibid., 20.

[9] Geoff Bertram, 'The MIRAB model twelve years on', *Contemporary Pacific*, 11:1 (1999), 105–38; Geoff Bertram, 'Introduction: the MIRAB model in the twenty-first century', *Asia Pacific Viewpoint*, 47:1 (2006), 1–13; Jon Fraenkel, 'Beyond MIRAB: do aid and remittances crowd out export growth in Pacific microeconomies?', *Asia Pacific Viewpoint*, 47:1 (2006), 15–30.

is applicable to Honiara.[10] Nigel Oram, writing on Port Moresby 40 years ago, described the similar virtually unrestricted 'spontaneous settlement' by migrants who became squatters, and pleaded that they needed to be properly integrated and included in urban planning. For many Highlanders, migration to Port Moresby was a one-way trip, not circulation.[11] Murray Chapman and other Pacific geographers and anthropologists in the 1970s and 1980s pioneered concepts of circulation between village and town. Chapman's emphasis on population movement and circulation, rather than migration, has influenced a generation of Pacific academic studies and certainly the thinking in this paper.[12] A new generation of scholarship now extends circulation and population movement arguments beyond international concepts of economic migration and slum formation in large cities to an understanding of how hybrid living spaces operate in places like Honiara.[13]

## HONIARA: URBAN CHARACTERISTICS

Honiara is surrounded by customary land and a national park. Through both British planning and Solomon Islands ingenuity, the city consists of four types of land occupancy. First, as a remnant from earlier years, is a small area of customary land reserved for canoes on the west bank of the Matanikau River's mouth, although this is now a squatter settlement. By and large, customary ownership was expunged from urban Honiara, which is quite different from urban areas like Port Moresby, where customary land is mixed with alienated land.[14] Yet 'land' below the high-water mark is still owned by customary landowners, which has implications for reclamation. The next form is registered leasehold fixed-term estate (FTE) of 75 years with

[10] Donovan Storey, 'The peri-urban Pacific: from exclusive to inclusive cities', *Asia Pacific Viewpoint*, 44:3 (2003), 259–79; John Connell, 'Regulation of space in the contemporary postcolonial Pacific city: Port Moresby and Suva', *Asia Pacific Viewpoint*, 44:3 (2003), 243–57.

[11] N.D. Oram, *Colonial Town to Melanesian City: Port Moresby, 1884–1974* (Canberra 1976), 243. See also John Connell and Richard Curtain, 'Urbanization and inequality in Melanesia', in R.J. May and Hank Nelson (eds), *Melanesia: beyond diversity*, 2 vols (Canberra 1982), II, 461–500.

[12] Murray Chapman and R. Mansell Prothero (eds), *Circulation in Population Movement: substance and concepts from the Melanesian case* (London 1985); R. Mansell Prothero and Murray Chapman (eds), *Circulation in Third World Countries* (London 1985); David Welchman Gegeo, 'Tasimauri sojourns and journeys: interview with Murray Chapman', in Judith A. Bennett (ed.), *Oceanian Journeys and Sojourns: home thoughts from abroad* (Dunedin 2015), 37–64.

[13] Anita Lacey, 'Shifting the gaze, shifting the agenda: sustainable livelihoods in urban Honiara', *Development*, 54:3 (2011), 368–75.

[14] M.E.P. Bellam, 'The colonial city: Honiara, a Pacific Islands "case study"', *Pacific Viewpoint*, 11:1 (1970), 72. The original Matanikau landowners are now living on their customary lands further upstream on the Matanikau River beyond the city council boundary. Charles Kelly (clerk to Honiara City Council), pers. comm., 23 June 2015.

rights to build permanent structures and services.[15] Rights lapse if the land is not developed. The rest of Honiara's population, the majority, are crowded into the remaining city council area and overflow onto surrounding lands belonging to the Guale (the people of Guadalcanal) and the national park. The third category is temporary occupying leases (TOLs), issued since the 1970s, allowing settlers some limited surety of tenure, for which SI$100 should be paid to the Ministry of Lands, Housing and Survey annually (but seldom is) and on which residents may live as long as they renew their licences. Although Honiara now has around 3,000 TOLs, only 168 were paid up as of 2013.[16] Temporary occupying leases can now be converted into FTEs on 50-year leases. Substantial settlement areas such as Kombito are under TOLs. These can be quite large; over a generation, a TOL that once contained only the original family house now also includes several houses built by the children.

The fourth category covers 20,000–25,000 people in more than 3,000 households (about one-quarter of Honiara's population) who live as squatters on lands occupied through no formal land title, mainly on Guale land on the peri-urban fringe or in unused crevices or government reserves in FTE and TOL areas. Squatter areas have expanded fast since the mid-2000s. Permanent structures are often built in squatter areas, and customary arrangements have been made with Guale landholders to safeguard their occupancy.[17] Fixed-term estate and TOL and squatter lands may be side-by-side. Honiara residents, asked if there are suburbs, look surprised and say that there are none in the way urban tenure is understood in Australia. To accommodate relatives, even the middle class and elites sometimes build houses from local materials alongside their substantial homes, and squatters may occupy unused land nearby. City council building codes exist, but no one takes much notice. The 2014 Honiara Local Planning Scheme uses formal language that does not acknowledge the reality of thousands of illegal residences, nor suggest how to incorporate them into the city.[18]

## HISTORY OF HONIARA'S EXPANSION

While segregation was not official, it occurred through designated types of housing and access to FTE land. In the 1950s and 1960s, Honiara was in two halves, divided by the

[15] 'New resolution reached by Lands & Housing Board on lands', Solomon Islands Broadcasting Corporation. http://www.sibconline.com.sb/new-resolution-reached-by-lands-housing-board-on-lands/ (accessed 15 Oct. 2015).

[16] 'Draft Honiara local planning scheme 2015', 14–15.

[17] Solomon Islands Ministry of Lands, Housing and Survey, 'Concept note: "Solomon Islands Urban Management Programme of Support" (SUMPS)', 2013, 269. Helen Esther Maebuta and Jack Maebuta, 'Generating livelihoods: a study of urban squatter settlements in Solomon Islands', *Pacific Economic Bulletin*, 24:3 (2009), 119; Douglas Larden and Marjorie Sullivan, 'Strengthening land administration in Solomon Islands', in *Making Land Work*, II, 307–25, particularly 316; Christine Jourdan, 'The cultural localization of rice in the Solomon Islands', *Ethnology*, 49:4 (2010), 269.

[18] 'Draft Honiara local planning scheme 2015'.

Matanikau River (Figure 2). The western side (other than at White River) and the fronts of some eastern ridges were inhabited by Europeans. All government services emanated from Point Cruz, which had some small residential areas. A strip of high covenant, mainly government, houses ran along the beach between Rove and White River, with more on the hills at Lengakiki and Vavaea. High-density housing for Solomon Islanders was established inland from the market and Fiji Quarters, spreading to Mbokonavera. Chinatown, along the Matanikau River's east bank, was a neutral zone accessed by all. Accommodation for single and married labourers was developed at Kukum inland from the beach east of the Matanikau. The new Indigenous middle class, mainly public servants, lived on the lower slopes of the ridges behind the central market. Kola'a Ridge, in the hills between the Matanikau and Kukum, developed as another middle-class area. Visiting the airport at Ranadi from 1945 until 1958 (which was still at the Fighter II strip from the war), or further out at Henderson airport once it was reconditioned, was the only reason for 1950s Europeans to visit east Honiara. Solomon Islanders shopped in Chinatown and had little need to proceed west of the Matanikau, except for trips to central market, churches and the wharves, and to work as domestic servants or for the government.[19] Kakabona village to the west and the new post-1945 Matanikau village upriver were the closest Guale settlements. White River and Vaivila Fishing Village, and to some extent Kukum, developed as village-style but modern residential areas within Honiara's boundaries.

Honiara has always had a high rate of inward migration; the population has increased fivefold since independence in 1978. The urban area has extended further along the coast to the east and inland down valleys and along ridges (Figures 3 and 4). Malaitans are the largest group of inward migrants, followed by those from Western, Guadalcanal and Central provinces. The male/female ratio has become more equal, male predominance dropping from 75% in 1959 to 58% in 1976 and 53% in 2009. The number of households has more than tripled since 1978, and the household size is bigger (see Table 1). In the 1970s and 1980s, the population was overwhelmingly young, with 39% under 14. In 1976, 75% were under 29, and another 17.1% were under 44; young couples and new families were the norm. Just under 6% were aged 45–59, with 2.1% over 60. In 1986, 92% were under 44, 5.12% were aged 45–59, and 2.1% were over 60.[20]

Many Indigenous residents cultivated gardens on the town's fringes for family food and cash crops. A 1984 survey found 62% of women had root crop gardens, and 26% had leaf vegetable gardens away from their homes. Settlement and squatter area residents still walk long distances to their sweet potato and tapioca gardens on customary land leased from the Guale.[21] When heavy rains destroy these and other gardens

---

[19] J.L.O. Tedder, 'Honiara (capital of the British Solomon Islands Protectorate)', *South Pacific Bulletin*, 16:1 (1966), 36–41, 43.

[20] Solomon Islands Statistics Office, 'Solomon Islands 1986 population census, report 1: population by sex, age and ward, final results', Statistical Bulletin 3 (1988), 5, 15.

[21] Jourdan, 'The cultural localization of rice', 270; Solomon Islands Statistics Office, 'Solomon Islands population census, report 1, supplement: summary of population by socio-economic characteristics, final results', Statistical Bulletin 12 (1988), 23, 27.

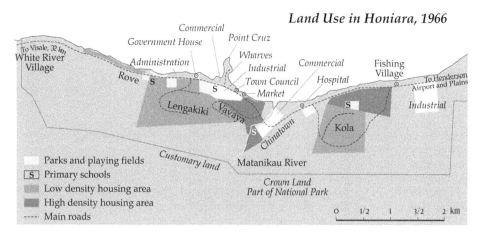

FIGURE 2:  Honiara, showing areas of settlement and land use, 1966.
Source: Peter Kenilorea, *Tell It as It Is: autobiography of Rt. Hon. Sir Peter Kenilorea, KBE, PC, Solomon Islands' first prime minister*, ed. Clive Moore (Taipei 2008), 183; based on a 1966 map by J.L.O. Tedder.

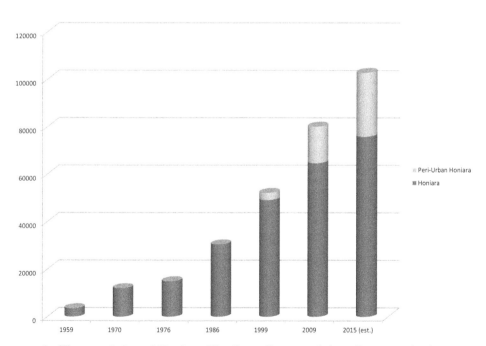

FIGURE 3:  The population of Honiara City Council area and the adjacent peri-urban population of Guadalcanal Province, 1959–2015. Based on data from 'Draft Honiara local planning scheme 2015', 13. Note: the depiction in this graph should be treated with caution. Although urban areas of Honiara outside the city boundaries do not show in statistics until 1999, they existed before then in a small way.

TABLE 1: Honiara demographic overview, 1959–2009

|  | 1959 | 1976 | 1986 | 1999 | 2009 |
|---|---|---|---|---|---|
| Population | 3,534 | 14,942 | 30,413 | 48,513 | 64,609 |
| Males | 2,685 | 8,905 | 17,293 | 27,050 | 34,089 |
| Females | 849 | 6,037 | 13,120 | 21,462 | 30,520 |
| Households | 445 | 2,734 | 4,317 | 6,921 | 8,981 |
| Average household size | n.a. | 5.5 | 7.0 | 7.1 | 7.0 |

Source: National Census, 1959, 1976, 1986, 1999, 2009.

on Guadalcanal, as occurred after the April 2014 floods, supplies to Honiara's markets are low, prices are high, and residents suffer.

Separation of Honiara's affairs from those of the protectorate government began in the late 1940s, when a six-man town board was established. The Honiara Town Council was created between 1956 and 1958, although the first full elections were not held until 1969. Public health and other social issues such as education began to be transferred to the council. All early council members were appointed by the high commissioner, with one member each supplied from the departments of the district commissioner central, public works, lands and survey and medical. The council had specific responsibilities and duties to pass bylaws (which required government approval), with only limited powers to raise revenue, relying on an annual subvention from the protectorate. The district officer for Honiara served as the council's executive officer, with duties similar to those of a clerk of council. Although a rudimentary town plan existed in the 1940s, this became more substantial in 1962. A 1968 town council ordinance allowed for future elections, with a core of appointed members. In 1969, the Honiara Town Council (Constitution of Wards) Order created 12 wards (Figure 4).

Members were elected for each ward, three others were nominated by the government, and the district commissioner central was an ex-officio member. Of the SI$121,000 budget in 1969, only SI$11,000 came from a service tax. The main expenditure was on capital works. The council created four new junior primary schools to cater to the new housing estates at White River, Mbokonavera, Tururuhu and Vura, followed by three more at Rove, Koloale and near the training college in Kukum.[22] The council took responsibility for the provision of junior primary education in Honiara. Tuvaruhu and White River schools were started in 1969, Mbokonavera School the next year, Vura School in 1971, and Koloale School in 1973. The Kukum foreshore was cleared and made into a public park, and the botanical gardens were vested in the council in 1971. In 1974, council revenues reached SI$339,000, and expenditures were $200,000, spent mainly on public health and education and on constructing a public market and an abattoir.[23]

---

[22] *B.S.I.P. News Sheet*, Mar. 1958, 31 Oct. 1971; British Solomon Islands, *Annual Report on the British Solomon Islands for the Years 1958–1959* (London 1959), 63–64.

[23] British Solomon Islands, *Report for the Year 1974* (Honiara 1975), 148.

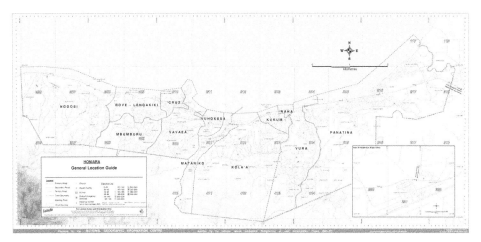

FIGURE 4: Honiara, showing the ward divisions, 2006.
Source, Solomon Islands Department of Lands and Survey, 2006.

The town council became a municipal authority in 1980. The 1999 Honiara City Act created a city council of 20 members – 12 elected, four appointed by the minister for home affairs and four places reserved for the three parliamentarians with Honiara constituencies and the premier of Guadalcanal Province.[24] In 1986 the largest wards were Panatina, Vura, Vavaea and Kola'a Ridge. As shown in Table 2, by 2009 the population of Cruz, Kukum and Naha wards had decreased, with increases of more than 50% in Nggossi, Mbumburu and Panatina. Kola'a, Vura, Panatina and Nggosi are the largest wards. Panatina, now huge, was once only a coastal education and industrial enclave but now extends inland as far as Kombito and Gilbert Camp and east as far as Burns Creek.

## HYBRID HONIARA

Long-established FTE areas such as at Kola'a Ridge, Panatina and Vura can perhaps be regarded as suburbs, but so too can White River, which began as a British-designated urban village. The TOL areas are usually described as settlements, although residents there call them villages, in recognition of traditional domicile characteristics and hybrid space. Squatter areas can be large – at Burns Creek for example – or quite small, wedged into more established areas. The settlements operate like villages with functioning local communities, plus basic municipal services for roads, water and electricity. Extended families gather for rites of passage such as funerals and marriages and maintain aspects of village authority. (The FTE areas lack this characteristic.)

Honiara's hybrid nature relates to the operation of *wantokism*, extended kinship relationships, and *kastom*. *Wantokism* is derived from 'one talk', meaning

---

[24] Honiara City Act 1999 (Solomon Islands), http://www.clgfpacific.org/images/campaign/54/file/Solomon%20Islands%20Honiara%20City%20Act.pdf (accessed 15 Oct. 2015).

TABLE 2: Population of wards within Honiara, 1986 and 2009

| Wards | 1986 population | 2009 population |
| --- | --- | --- |
| Nggosi | 3,900 | 10,068 |
| Mbumbaru | 1,350 | 3,625 |
| Rove-Lenggakiki* | 1,554 | 2,646 |
| Cruz | 545 | 232 |
| Vavaea | 4,699 | 6,954 |
| Vuhokesa | 634 | 1,191 |
| Mataniko** | 2,317 | 4,347 |
| Kola'a*** | 4,279 | 10,151 |
| Kukum | 1,654 | 1,835 |
| Naha | 577 | 356 |
| Vura | 4,830 | 9,096 |
| Panatina | 4,884 | 14,108 |

Source: Solomon Islands Statistics Office, 'Report on 2009 population and housing census, basic tables and census description', Statistical Bulletin 6 (2009), 13.
*Notes*: *also spelt Langgakiki, **also spelt Matanikau, ***also spelt Kolaa.

from the same language, and implies giving preference to kin in the expectation of a series of reciprocal obligations being fulfilled. *Wantokism* is only meaningful beyond the village situation (within which everyone speaks one language) and comes into its own in urban situations like Honiara, or in school or plantation/work sites with multi-ethnic social contexts. In urban areas, *wantokism* and closer kinship become a method of organising space, and for newcomers is a way of surviving the harsh, money-driven environment. Yet *wantokism* applies at different social depths. Finding same-language speakers means ease of communication, but some language groupings are so large (Kwara'ae from Malaita, for instance) that, beyond a level of linguistic ease, *wantokism* serves no further purpose without kin relations. Closer kinship, rather than wider *wantokism*, is often the basis of residential groupings, although general social relationships are typically more comfortable if language or shared cultural values are involved.

    *Kastom* means contemporary shared traditions and customary ways of behaving, although it is not a hegemonic ideology, and the state has had little success in harnessing *kastom* as an ideological tool. David Akin has suggested that this is partly because some of the leading Christian churches, particularly in the past, opposed all retention of what they saw as 'customary ways' and, more importantly, because the most *kastom*-conscious island is Malaita, where *kastom* emerged after World War II as an anti-government ideology.[25] *Kastom* is a fluid concept that is used selectively and is part of Solomon Islanders' coping mechanism in dealing with modernisation and change. *Kastom* varies across language groups and islands, and mixes into new combinations in Honiara. *Kastom* is situational and can be dominant or downplayed,

[25] *Kastom* also acquired such meanings on neighbouring islands involved in Maasina Rule. See David Akin, *Colonialism, Maasina Rule, and the Origins of Malaitan Kastom* (Honolulu 2013).

depending on the circumstances of the speaker and the event.[26] Solomon Islanders are inclined to speak of *kastom* as if it is a universal category, yet innumerable variations in interpretation occur, depending most basically on the provincial origins of people. Increasingly this is complicated by 'mixed marriages' across languages and provinces.

In the 1950s, town authorities encouraged three urban villages to develop: the Fishing Village, Kukum and White River. Vaivila, the Malaitan Fishing Village on the rocky reefed shore at Kukum, was settled by people from Lau and Langa Langa Lagoons on Malaita. It does not seem to have been planned by protectorate authorities, who nevertheless acquiesced to its growth. Many of the first inhabitants were employed at nearby hospitals or as house servants at the agricultural college. They made extra money from fishing, selling their catches at Honiara market. In the 1970s, 28 Vaivila households were granted FTEs, and 57 were issued TOLs, establishing the family residential patterns that continue today.[27] Vaivila village is crowded, and the houses are often poorly constructed. Originally from artificial islands, its occupants are used to living in close proximity: the Fishing Village land is divided into clans, and mirrors land divisions back on Malaita. Vaivila is a convenient fishing and trading village with access to the ocean and to commerce along the coastal roadside. Nearby Kukum is more mixed, originally containing labour barracks and cheap housing blocks.

White River village settlement on Honiara's western border also began in the 1950s and has a more diverse ethnic composition (more Micronesians and Polynesians). White River is a long-established TOL settlement but also has FTE areas. A stroll around it reveals housing compounds made of part-thatched and part-modern materials. Much of the artefact production of Honiara comes from Polynesians living at White River. Some of the early Malaitan settlers, such as the Ramosaea family, have compounds where newer family members have built houses next to their parents' original home. The same applies to most of the settlement and squatter areas. They are urban villages where strengths lie in customary relationships and market stalls are built at road junctions, providing easy access to common household needs.

White River and Kombito are different styles of urban villages at opposite ends of the city. Kombito is a large, three-stage complex of TOL housing areas, neighboured inland by Gilbert Camp. Both Kombito and Gilbert Camp sit inland from more respectable Vura and Naha FTE housing estates and are part of an ongoing extension of urban growth since the 1970s. Kombito is near Borderline, a significant road junction, which in some ways is the outer bastion of respectable Honiara life: it was once on the border with the national park before a large area was absorbed into the city area. The urban sprawl between Kukum and Gilbert Camp is by far the most substantial in Honiara and is expected to grow further.[28] The urban villages, settlement and squatter neighbourhoods change over time; leaders rise and decline; they

[26] David Akin, '*Kastom* as hegemony? A response to Baabadzan', *Anthropological Theory*, 5:1 (2005), 98.

[27] Harry Masae, pers. comm., Vaivila village, Honiara, 19 Oct. 2007; *B.S.I.P. News Sheet*, 15 Feb. 1970; Oram, *Colonial Town to Melanesian City*, 139.

[28] See maps and related discussion in 'Draft Honiara local planning scheme 2015', 13–16.

are dynamic networks of functions, not easy to discern and each different. Malaitan Michael Kwa'ioloa and anthropologist Ben Burt's *The Chief's Country* provides an excellent window into settlement life in Honiara. Kwa'ioloa lives in Kombito 3, surrounded by family and other Kwara'ae relatives and *wantoks*. He and other Malaitan leaders there operate with many of the trappings of a Malaitan bigman.

> In Honiara, although we are not at home, we understand that our tradition stays wherever we stay. If we are without our tradition, everything will be all over the place. People of different languages are involved, because our area of south-east Honiara is one community including Kobito [sic], Kofiloko, Lau Valley, and up to Gilbert Camp. Other areas have other groups. We call this a community, because everyone knows each other. We coordinate the chiefs and if there are any problems we deal with them.[29]

Kwa'ioloa described having formed a house of chiefs in Honiara, although by other accounts its scope is limited to areas around his Kombito home. His claims do not cover all Malaitan settlements in Honiara, and it is questionable how much authority 'chiefs' really hold in urban areas. In addition, an emerging group of richer, urban kin prefer to avoid obligations to poorer relatives who have migrated from provincial villages. Even in areas like Gilbert Camp and Kombito, people engage with the market economy and heed the government's promotion of individualistic behaviours rather than following provincial versions of *kastom*. At most, they are creating a modernist version of *kastom* based on their particular socio-economic context. The major ethnic component between Kukum and Gilbert Camp is Malaitan, and it is rare for anyone other than a Malaitan to win the large East Honiara parliamentary seat.[30] Thus, even from a national political perspective, the Malaitan dominance in east Honiara combines modern politics with Indigenous strengths.

Although traditional leadership remains important, the Christian denominations are more basic to Honiara than *kastom* leadership. These churches spread through all Honiara's settlements, villages and more developed urban communities, providing a stable social network and leadership in all communities.

## ARRIVAL, NETWORKS, INTEGRATION AND CIRCULATION

Although the RAMSI people's surveys[31] suggest that a growing number of Honiara's population see it as home and seldom return to the provinces and their original villages, over decades continual circulation between all islands and Honiara has

---

[29] Michael Kwa'ioloa and Ben Burt, *The Chief's Country: leadership and politics in Honiara, Solomon Islands* (Brisbane 2012), 168.

[30] Over 12 elections, five out of seven members were Malaitans, and another was part Malaitan.

[31] See 'People's survey', RAMSI, http://www.ramsi.org/media/peoples-survey/ (accessed 15 Oct. 2015).

occurred. For some this means visiting relatives in Honiara every year or so, but others circulate almost constantly between home and Honiara several times a year for family and business reasons. For the many long-term Honiara residents who have maintained their village connections, circulation means at least going home each Christmas, maintaining family obligations, checking on projects and returning with relatives who need medical care or children of siblings who need better access to education facilities.

Over the last decade, Honiara has been swamped by cheap Japanese second-hand cars. The city desperately needs a second highway, although construction will be financially and logistically difficult. Nevertheless, automobiles and now mobile phones have revolutionised transport and communications. In 2013, over 80% of Honiara residents had access to mobile phones, up from just 23% in 2009.[32] Substantial riots have occurred in the past, but future disturbances are likely to be orchestrated from mobile phones and Facebook. While 'rascal' gangs do not operate in the same way as those in Port Moresby or Lae, criminal groups are involved in opportunistic break-ins and other crimes.[33] Life is not yet lived behind razor wire, although those with the most to lose do protect themselves with guards, dogs and high fences. An Asian commercial elite combines the 'old Chinese' from colonial days and the 'new Chinese' and other 'new Asians' – Chinese, Koreans, Filipinos, Malaysians and Japanese. Most 'trade stores' are Asian owned and operated, and considerable Indigenous resentment is directed at the extent of Asian political and economic influence. Recently, Asians have begun moving into the urban transport business, which is supposed to be reserved for Indigenous Solomon Islanders.[34]

As the events of 1998–2003 and the 2006 riot make clear, the potential remains for violence to develop again in Honiara. Many of the same ingredients that created the Tension years remain: dissatisfaction with lack of development in Guadalcanal Province; continued Malaitan circular migration, particularly to Honiara; a burgeoning disaffected young population with no prospects of work; a growing Honiara constantly encroaching on Guale lands; blatant political corruption that has flourished despite RAMSI; and the possibility of misguided rogue leadership. The national government is aware of but incapable of dealing with these problems, and the Honiara City Council has no capacity to do so. When small riots occurred in May 2014 after the flash floods – over mal-distribution of relief funds – a

---

[32] '2013 SIG RAMSI people's survey report', 26 June 2013, http://www.ramsi.org/wp-content/uploads/2014/07/FINAL-Peoples-Survey-2013-1-final-111900c1-79e2-4f41-9801-7f29f6cd2a66-0.pdf (accessed 15 Oct. 2015), 60; O'Callaghan, *Rebuilding a Nation*, 45. In 2009, a new telecommunications act was passed, which broke the one-carrier monopoly held by Our Telekom (formerly Solomons Telecom) and introduced Bemobile, a PNG company with foreign backers.

[33] Sinclair Dinnen, *Praise the Lord and Pass the Ammunition: criminal group surrender in Papua New Guinea* (Boroko 1994); Sinclair Dinnen, *Law and Order in a Weak Sate: crime and politics in Papua New Guinea* (Honolulu 2001).

[34] Clive Moore, 'No more walkabout long Chinatown: Asian involvement in the economic and political process', in Sinclair Dinnen and Stewart Firth (eds), *Politics and State Building in Solomon Islands* (Canberra 2008), 64–95.

Chinese store was burnt down, and once more the Chinese community braced themselves for a larger riot that mercifully did not come.[35] RAMSI and the Solomon Islands government like to believe that the Royal Solomon Islands Police riot squad is sufficient to ensure that calm will prevail, but during major disturbances the police can do little to control crowds.

When we add the cultural qualities of *wantokism*, kinship, *kastom*, *Masta Liu* (see below) and linguistic diversity to the urban-village characteristics, the mix thickens. Back in the 1960s, M.E.P. Bellam noted that two-thirds of his Honiara informants associated mainly with kin, half lived with kin, and one-quarter worked with kin.[36] This remains true 50 years later, particularly within the majority settlement and squatter areas. Cato Berg, in his study of Honiara in the 1990s, made an interesting suggestion that Honiara's elite is not representative of the rest of the Solomon Islands. Berg concluded that its formation is based on Solomon Islands families that became prominent during the late 19th and early 20th centuries, usually through connections to Christian missions or by living near trading stations and protectorate headquarters. He suggested that the 'British Protectorate may have left behind an implicit hierarchy which today manifests itself in the composition of the urban elite'.[37] For some families, these links go back to work as labourers in Queensland or Fiji in the 19th century.[38] The grandfathers of the present elite often were labourers overseas, village or sub-district headmen or police, mission catechists, teachers or pastors, or 'boss bois' (overseers) on protectorate plantations, or they achieved some standing during World War II in the Labour Corps. It was their families who first migrated to Honiara after the war, but how much of this was British-inspired and how much was Indigenous-motivated based on these new family experiences is debatable.

Urban *wantokism* can be viewed both horizontally and vertically. Around Honiara, people of similar income levels live in settlements and 'suburbs': for instance at White River or the many other 'valley' communities. Here *wantokism* is being remade through weekend neighbourhood gatherings for sporting or church events, gardening, birthdays and many other forms of social grouping. People have horizontal ties from roughly equivalent personal circumstances. Vertical forms of *wantokism* also occur, pyramidal hierarchical styles, with big men and big women at the top, who may be superiors at work or mothers- and fathers-in-law and *tabus* (in-laws), or important people in the neighbourhood. Both horizontal and vertical *wantokism* is continually

---

[35] 'Police out in force to prevent fresh riots in Solomons capital', ABC News, http://www.abc.net.au/news/2014-05-17/an-solomon-riots/5460094 (accessed 25 May 2014); *Solomon Star*, 19 May 2014; Terrence Wood, 'From floods to flames in Honiara', Devpolicy Blog, http://devpolicy.org/in-brief/from-floods-to-flames-in-honiara-20140521/ (accessed 25 May 2014).

[36] M.E.P. Bellam, Urbanization and regional development in the British Solomon Islands Protectorate, report to the Western Pacific High Commission, 1968, Auckland, University of Auckland Special Collections, WPHC 29/II, 312/2/3, 10.

[37] Cato Berg, 'Managing difference: kinship, exchange and urban boundaries in Honiara, Solomon Islands', MA thesis, University of Bergen (Bergen 2000), 193.

[38] Peter Corris, *Passage, Port and Plantation: a history of Solomon Islands labour migration, 1870–1914* (Melbourne 1973); Clive Moore, *Kanaka: a history of Melanesian Mackay* (Port Moresby 1985).

being created, communicated, stored and used by individuals and inter-connected *wantok* groups for comfort, resistance, nostalgia and everyday advancement.

*Wantokism* also involves corruption when it interferes with legal or adminis-trative procedures, but it is culturally imbedded and so complex in its manifestations that it is easier to work with than to oppose.[39] The related term *Masta Liu*, in use since the 1970s, describes another cultural phenomenon – temporary urban resi-dents, usually male, who depend on their *wantoks* and wander opportunistically in urban space. *Masta Liu* survive partly from calling on kin obligations and partly on their wits. Other more recent related terms are *hospaep* (from 'hosepipe'), which means to suck up resources from their wider group of primary affiliation, and the graphic *nila* (to insert a needle to drain blood). Many *Masta Liu* become adept at *nila* and *hospaep* techniques, draining the financial body of dollars under the pretext of *wantokism*.[40] Another word has also recently entered the Pijin vocabu-lary: *beligas*, meaning thieves, and often with a violent edge. *Masta Liu* are just con-niving gentlemen by comparison. *Beligas* have more in common with Papua New Guinea *raskols* and are really hard-core criminals. The use of the term *beliga* is an indication that urban tensions are increasing.

Some 65–70 languages are still used in Solomon Islands (depending on who is counting), with another 50 or so dialect variations.[41] Each is probably spoken in Honiara. Solomon Islands Pijin is the overarching language that links all groups, and many use or at least understand Standard English. Most Honiara residents speak several languages and understand phrases in others; often they say they can 'hear' other languages but not speak them. This linguistic world is part of the complex-ity of Honiara. Pijin has become the major urban language, although vernacular languages are intermingled with Pijin, the content depending on the language groups involved. Speakers often begin conversations with pleasantries in their verna-culars, then retreat to Pijin. The educated elite will often begin with pleasantries in Pijin before turning to English peppered with Pijin words and phrases. Humour, casual style and good manners permeate most conversations. Solomon Islanders choose their words carefully, indicating familial relationships and showing respect,

---

[39] I am indebted to George Hoaʻau and Paul Roughan for advice and explanations of urban *wan-tokism*. See also Gordon Leua Nanau, 'The *wantok system* as a socio-economic and political network in Melanesia', *OMNES: the journal of multicultural society*, 2:1 (2011), 31–55.

[40] Ian Frazer, 'Walkabout and urban movement: a Melanesian case study', in Murray Chapman (ed.), 'Mobility and Identity in the Island Pacific', special issue, *Pacific Viewpoint*, 26:1 (1985), 185–205; Murray Chapman and R. Mansell Prothero, 'Circulation between "home" and other places: some propositions', in Chapman and Prothero, *Circulation in Population Movement*, 10; Berg, 'Managing difference', 37–59; Christine Jourdan, 'Masta Liu', in Vered Amit-Talai and Helena Wulff (eds), *Youth Cultures: a cross-cultural perspective* (London 1995), 75–98.

[41] 'Solomon Islands', Ethnologue: Languages of the World, https://www.ethnologue.com/country/SB (accessed 16 Oct. 2015); Christine Jourdan, 'Multilinguisme et Identités Urbaines a Honiara (Îsles Salomon)', in Dorothée Dussy and Éric Wittersheim (eds), *Villes Invisibles: Anthropologie Urbaine du Pacifique* (Paris 2013), 77.

even changing kin categories to fit difficult situations.[42] Language, kinship, networks, circulation and integration are all part of urban strategies for survival and success. Modern music is also an important aspect of Honiara: local country, gospel, reggae and love ballads are all available on CDs and are played on local radio stations, enabling learning and mixing of languages in enjoyable circumstances.

Add to this mix other invisible boundaries such as *tambu* (taboo), which in some Solomons cultures, particularly on Malaita, regulates gender relationships in spatial and behavioural ways. Languages also contain subtle cultural codes that help individuals negotiate relationships, and swearing or cursing via reference to offensive sexual scenarios is common among closely related Malaitans. Breaches of *tambu* codes and curses are usually compensated in cash and customary wealth items, forming another thread in the social fabric. Compensation can also be misused, with claims engineered and relying more on gullibility and fear than actuality.[43]

These aspects of Honiara life have become more complicated with more 'mixed' marriages. In the 2013 'People's survey', half of all Honiara respondents and 45% of those living in Honiara settlements had partners from a different province, triple the interprovincial marriage rates for the rest of Guadalcanal or Malaita. Here we see urban Solomon Islanders beginning to shed exclusive provincialism and become citizens of the nation.[44]

## Conclusion

Honiara is a city of villages and nascent suburbs, but its social composition is changing. While the pre-independence town had a transient quality, now almost 97% of Honiara interviewees for the 2013 'People's survey' identified the city as their permanent home.

The arrival city model does not sit comfortably over Honiara. Cultural hybridity is a better fit: urban services are basic, and much of what makes Honiara function is an extension of pre-urban societies adapted to urban ways. The city council is weak, and the national government has limited funds for urban development. Urban services favour the FTE areas and not the majority settlement and squatter areas. Partly a consequence of small size, the urban *wantok* concept remains strong, as do extended kin networks, even though visitors and extended families strain small incomes. Although Honiara's houses may be creaking at the seams, they continue to shelter and maintain their occupants. Families still manage to look after their own, despite the financial challenges. Beggars are rare in Honiara, unlike in Port Moresby, where for decades they have been common in downtown Boroko. Squatters are the most vulnerable and marginal residents. Town planning must allow for their presence and enable them to live with dignity; the government, at all levels, must fulfil its obligations to all citizens. If it does not, it will find that elements in Honiara retain the potential for volatility.

---

[42] Berg has given an example of two Rennellese brothers who met at a hotel and conducted their conversation as if they were uncle and nephew to escape the implications of the disrespect of the two meeting in that situation. See Berg, 'Managing difference', 115.

[43] Much of this paragraph is based on my observations since the 1970s. See also ibid., 176–79.

[44] '2013 SIG RAMSI people's survey report', 20–21.

# From *Taovia* to Trustee: Urbanisation, Land Disputes and Social Differentiation in Kakabona

## REBECCA MONSON

## ABSTRACT

Land in the vicinity of Honiara is amongst the most contested in Solomon Islands, and peri-urban areas were a focal point for much of the fighting during the 1998–2003 civil conflict. This paper focuses on the historical development of Kakabona, a series of hamlets to the immediate west of Honiara. In order to understand the conditions that preceded the Tension better, I draw on ethnographic fieldwork, archival research and an analysis of court records to examine some of the shifts in land tenure arrangements occurring from the 1950s onwards. While land disputes are often approached as contests over economic resources, I suggest that the arguments mobilised before the courts reveal the profoundly epistemological or ontological challenges that urbanisation raises. Understanding these challenges throws new light on the ways in which urbanisation has worked, firstly, to deepen social fragmentation and inequality and, secondly, to concentrate control over land transactions and disputes in the hands of a relatively small number of men.

Kakabona comprises a series of hamlets clustered along the Tandai Highway as it runs along the coastline to the west of Honiara (Figure 1).[1] These hamlets are densely populated and built in the narrow strip of flat land that lies between the beach and the hills that rise sharply from the ocean. The area is populated by around 1,500

*Acknowledgments*: Funding for this research came from the ANU College of Law and the Australian Federation of University Women Georgina Sweet Fellowship (2008). I thank the Guadalcanal Province and the Solomon Islands Ministry of Education and Human Resources Development for permitting me to undertake this research, and three anonymous reviewers for their comments. I am immensely grateful to the people of Kakabona, whose hospitality and generosity made this work possible.

[1] As is often the case in Solomon Islands, particular names may refer to several places, producing complex, overlapping and contested geographies. The name 'Kakabona' also refers to a specific village within the wider area that I discuss in this paper.

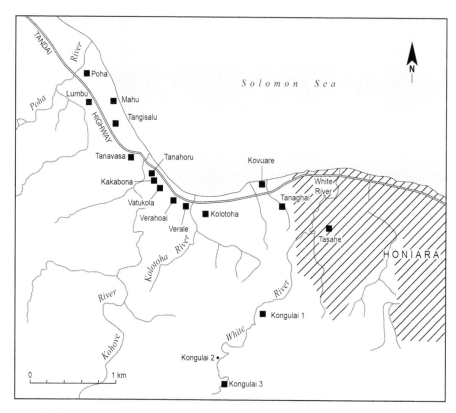

FIGURE 1: Kakabona area.

people,[2] most of whom belong to social groups with lineage narratives that connect them to a variety of places across north-west Guadalcanal. The population also includes substantial numbers of people who originate from other provinces and have married people from Guadalcanal. The majority of the population and all the churches are Roman Catholic.

Oral histories suggest that the population of north-west Guadalcanal was highly mobile and concentrated in small hamlets in the bush until well into the 19th century.[3] Settlement of Kakabona intensified following World War II, when the capitals of the British Solomon Islands Protectorate and the Western Pacific High Commission were relocated to Honiara. The effects of rural–urban migration and the commoditisation of land were increasingly felt in villages in Kakabona from the 1950s onwards. By the 1970s a number of people were selling land to migrants, often without adequate consultation of other people who claimed access

---

[2] Prima Chapa, Michelle Taylor and Jennifer Wate, unpublished report on a participatory rural appraisal workshop held in Honiara, 2008, copy on file with the author.

[3] See also Murray Bathgate, 'Movement processes from precontact to contemporary times: the Ndi-Nggai, West Guadalcanal, Solomon Islands', in Murray Chapman and R. Mansell Prothero (eds), *Circulation in Population Movement: substance and concepts from the Melanesian case* (London and Boston 1985), 83.

to the land and without distributing the proceeds of transactions to them. As a result, many of these transactions were highly contested and ultimately contributed to the grievances that underlay the civil conflict that occurred from 1998 to 2003. Kakabona was one of the focal points for violence during the Tension, and residents who were identified as 'Malaitan' (many were of mixed heritage) were threatened, intimidated and often evicted by those identified as 'Guale' (who were equally often of mixed Guadalcanal and Malaitan heritage). Armed groups of Malaitan or Guale militants established bunkers and checkpoints in the vicinity of the town boundary at White River, and shoot-outs regularly occurred in the hills surrounding Kakabona. Many residents fled the area as their homes were burned and looted, and bridges and other essential infrastructure were destroyed.[4] In order to elucidate some of the conditions that preceded the Tension, this paper draws on court files concerning two long-running and interlocking disputes coming before the chiefs and courts during the 1980s and 1990s.

## URBANISATION AND INCREASED COMPETITION FOR LAND IN KAKABONA

Kakabona and the area that surrounds it consists of a number of large territories associated with several intermarrying matrilineal groups, referred to by local residents as *traebs* (tribes).[5] Each of these groups is associated with one of two moieties, and a prohibition on intra-moiety marriage continues to be widely followed today. Evidence suggests that people have occupied this area for thousands of years, and Spanish accounts from the 1500s refer to large villages along the coastline.[6] These populations, however, appear to have declined or moved inland by the 19th century.[7] Coastal

---

[4] See Norman Arkwright 'Restorative justice in the Solomon Islands', in Sinclair Dinnen, Anita Jowitt and Tess Newton (eds), *A Kind of Mending: restorative justice in the Pacific Islands* (Canberra 2003), 177–94. See also the testimony of Claudette Liliau in Solomon Islands Truth and Reconciliation Commission, *Final Report*, vol. 4: *Annex I* (Honiara 2012), 1068–73.

[5] In contrast to communities I have worked with elsewhere in Solomon Islands, who regularly use vernacular terms for both a kin group and its territory, people in Kakabona generally refer to *traebs*, *sbutraebs* [*sub-traebs*?] and *laens* (tribes, subtribes, lines), and I consistently heard the names of particular areas of land (for example, 'Poha village') rather than a vernacular term for a group's territory (such as *puava* in Marovo).

[6] David Roe, 'Prehistory without pots: prehistoric settlement and economy of north-west Guadalcanal, Solomon Islands', PhD thesis, Australian National University (Canberra 1993); Patrick Vinton Kirch, *On the Road of the Winds: an archaeological history of the Pacific Islands before European contact* (Berkeley 2000), 134–35.

[7] This may have been owing to an increase in the impact of headhunting raids from the central and western islands associated with contact with Europeans. See also Murray Chapman and Peter Pirie, *Tasi Mauri: a report on population and resources of the Guadalcanal Weather Coast* (Honolulu 1974), 2, 16; Murray Bathgate, 'Bihu matena golo: a study of the Ndi-Nggai of west Guadalcanal and their involvement in the Solomon Islands cash economy', PhD thesis, University of Wellington (Wellington 1975), 83; J.M. McKinnon, 'Tomahawks, turtles and traders: a reconstruction in the circular causation of warfare in the New Georgia group', *Oceania*, 45:4 (1975), 290–307; Lindsay Wall and Rolf Kuschel, 'Burial customs and grave sites on pre-Christian Nggatokae, western Solomon Islands', *Archaeology & Physical Anthropology in Oceania*, 10:1 (1975), 61.

populations began to grow again during the early 20th century as plantations were established along the north-west coastline. While reports written during this period give somewhat conflicting accounts, at least one village in the vicinity of Kohove River appears to have existed from the early 1900s onwards. Oral histories indicate that the population of Kakabona remained both sparse and mobile until well into the 1930s.[8]

World War II and its aftermath marked a significant turning point in the history of the area. The seven-month battle that occurred on Guadalcanal during 1942 was concentrated on the central and western parts of the north coast. Honiara district was evacuated,[9] and the residents of a small settlement at Kohove River fled to the relative safety of Tangarare on the west coast. Once the Japanese had been driven out, US forces used parts of the north-west coast for artillery and target practice, and many of the remaining residents were relocated for safety reasons. As the local population moved elsewhere, a massive influx of foreign troops and a smaller number of members of the Solomon Islands Labour Corps flowed into north Guadalcanal, and the area around Honiara became a major transit and supply base.[10]

After the war, the capital of the protectorate was relocated from Tulagi to Honiara, and the capital of the Western Pacific High Commission was similarly relocated from Suva.[11] A mission was also established by the Roman Catholic bishop Jean-Marie Aubin at the site of a major US Marine Corp base at Tanaghai.[12] Some of the land needed for the establishment of the new capital had already been alienated to a number of colonial families, the Levers group (a large company with copra trading and planting interests) and the Catholic Church. Land in the vicinity of White River was purchased from Mamara Plantation as well as from people living in Kakabona and Mataniko who claimed to be the landowners.[13]

The relocation of the capitals of both the protectorate and the Western Pacific High Commission was associated with an increase in British aid, which contributed to a building and construction boom and the development of infrastructure,

---

[8] Bathgate has referred to a family from a named *duli* (now usually referred to in Pijin as *traeb*) living at Vatukola around the turn of the century, and this is supported by the oral histories that I collected. See Murray Bathgate, *Fight for the Dollar: economic and social change in western Guadalcanal, Solomon Islands* (Wellington 1993), 797. See also M.E.P. Bellam, 'The colonial city: Honiara, a Pacific Islands "case study"', *Pacific Viewpoint*, 11:1 (1970), 72 and 77. Yet Paravicini observed a village of 80 houses at a place he called 'Kakabona'. See E. Paravicini, *Reisen in den Britischen Salomonen* (1931), cited in Roe, 'Prehistory without pots', 23.

[9] Bellam, 'The colonial city', 72

[10] Ibid.; Bathgate, *Fight for the Dollar*, 110–11; Judith Bennett, *Natives and Exotics: World War II and environments in the Southern Pacific* (Honolulu 2009), 55, 140–41.

[11] Bellam, 'The colonial city', 70

[12] Gideon Zoloveke, *Zoloveke: a man from Choiseul* (Suva 1981), 28; Clair O'Brien, *A Greater Than Solomon Here: a story of Catholic Church in Solomon Islands 1567–1967* (Honiara 1995), 226, 229.

[13] Nigel Oram 'Land, housing and administration in Honiara: towards a concerted policy', *O'o: a journal of Solomon Islands studies*, 1 (1980), 137.

such as schools, on north Guadalcanal.[14] The people on the coast in Kakabona and Tanavasa, as well as those in the bush further inland, greatly benefitted from this development. By the late 1950s, the area around Kakabona supplied nearly all the vegetables to the twice-weekly market in Honiara.[15]

The growing township and the opportunities it offered attracted large numbers of migrants from other parts of Guadalcanal as well as from other provinces. Between 1959 and 1970, the population of the town tripled to almost 12,000 people,[16] and many migrants settled in Kakabona and other areas surrounding the town. Nigel Oram spent several weeks in Honiara in 1977 and specifically mentioned that people from Chief Moro's village on the Weather Coast were settling in Kakabona.[17] It is also clear, however, that many of the people who settled in Kakabona came from further afield. While patrilateral cross-cousin marriage had historically been very common,[18] Guadalcanal men who had migrated for work began returning to their villages with wives from other islands, often from Catholic communities on Malaita but also from other denominations in the western islands.[19] The spousal selection of Guadalcanal women also widened, not only owing to the increasing rates of in-migration to Guadalcanal but also because a small but growing number of women were leaving their villages to attend school or enter wage employment.

As marriage networks widened, so too did the range of people who could claim access to the resources within a matrilineage's territory. The broadening of marriage networks meant that claims to kinship and land were no longer confined to a relatively small network of two cognatically and affinally linked groups.[20] Furthermore, while patrilocal residence had historically been predominant, residence patterns diversified as access to employment opportunities, education, health care and infrastructure became a core factor in people's choice of where to live. Court transcripts and archival records indicate that migration to the north-central coast was already contributing to land disputes and social conflict by the 1970s. One expatriate warned protectorate officials that 'the areas from Mataniko village to Kakabona, Poha, Vura, Tabkoko and Vatusi village areas are the most touchy areas of the Sagalu Ward, as far as land is concerned'.[21] Tensions arose within communities as relatives of migrants who had married into local landholding groups sought to

---

[14] Bellam, 'The colonial city', 73.

[15] Bathgate, *Fight for the Dollar*, 129–31.

[16] Bellam, 'The colonial city', 73; see also Donovan Storey, 'The peri-urban Pacific: from exclusive to inclusive cities', *Asia Pacific Viewpoint*, 44:3 (2003), 259–79.

[17] Oram 'Land, housing and administration in Honiara', 140.

[18] Franklin Takutile, 'Mortuary feast at Vatupilei', in Peter Larmour (ed.), *Land in Solomon Islands* (Suva 1979), 23. See also Ian Hogbin, *A Guadalcanal Society: the Kaoka speakers* (New York 1964), 10.

[19] See Bathgate, 'Movement processes from precontact to contemporary times', 97.

[20] Murray Bathgate, *Matriliny and Coconut Palms: the control and inheritance of a major capital resource among the Ndi-Nggai speakers of western Guadalcanal in the Solomon Islands* (Wellington 1993), 19; Bathgate, *Fight for the Dollar*, 189.

[21] Mrs I.V. Phillips to Ngautu Village c/o Guadalcanal Council, Honiara, 2 Nov. 1974, Honiara, Solomon Islands National Archives (hereinafter SINA), BSIP LAND 1/1/1 vol. 1, 2.

settle on land. Disputes occurred regarding the sale of land to the government for a housing scheme, and a number of Malaitan and Chinese settlers were chased out of villages in Kakabona after purchasing land there.[22] Much of the land was sold by senior men within the landholding groups in the area, including Charlie Tsilivi, the government-appointed headman for Visale District.[23]

The role of *tsupu*, the customary gift exchange facilitating access to land, was also increasingly modified into more capitalist forms during this period. As had historically been the case, migrants to Honiara continued to approach senior men for permission to settle on customary land. When senior men provided migrants with permission to settle, they increasingly did so in return for cash, without consulting other members of the landholding group and without distributing the proceeds of transactions among them. These arrangements began to look more like commodity exchange and supplanted the previous gift exchanges that had ensured that a large number of people knew of such arrangements and shared in their benefits.[24] As a result of these innovations, in particular the increased individuation of transactions, the legitimacy and meaning of these land 'sales' were often highly contested and increasingly came before the chiefs and courts.

Today, Kakabona is densely populated, with most of the population living relatively close to the coastline. On the eastern side, close to the Honiara town boundary, numerous parcels of land have been registered under the Land and Titles Act.[25] These parcels are registered in the names of trustees who represent the landowning group, and all the trustees belong to a relatively small group of male leaders. Most of the land further west is unregistered and is divided into large blocks associated with particular matrilineages. During the 1980s and 1990s, a series of disputes regarding these blocks came before the chiefs and courts, largely as a result of attempts to register and then lease or sell land under part V, division 1 of the Land and Titles Act. This provides that the commissioner of lands may acquire the land (through lease or purchase) after a public acquisition hearing, at which the 'owners' of the land are identified. The land is then transferred back to the owners through a process of registration. Land may be registered in the name of up to five 'duly authorised representatives' on behalf of the landholding group, who are joint owners on a statutory trust.[26] These procedures inevitably involve the delineation of boundaries on the ground and between the groups that occupy the disputed land and surrounding areas. The process of registering land is therefore contingent upon state institutions sanctioning the claims of some people and not others to particular socio-spatial boundaries and 'ownership' of land.

---

[22] Transcript of court proceedings, copy on file with the author.

[23] See for example the following files: Namoborunga (Kongulai), SINA, BSIP LAN 2/1/67; Land lease – Kakabona – Vatukola Cooperative Society, SINA, BSIP LAND 2/1/86; Kovuara, Kakabona, SINA, BSIP LAN 2/1/92.

[24] See for example the following files: Namoborunga (Kongulai), SINA, BSIP LAN 2/1/67; Land lease – Kakabona – Vatukola Cooperative Society, SINA, BSIP LAND 2/1/86; Kovuara, Kakabona, SINA, BSIP LAN 2/1/92.

[25] Land and Titles Act [Cap 133] 1996 (Solomon Islands).

[26] Ibid., sec. 195(1).

## DEBATING THE BOUNDARIES OF BELONGING

The court files that I reviewed related to a number of ongoing and intertwined disputes concerning two large blocks of land, referred to here as Parcel A and Parcel B.[27] The transcripts of hearings indicate that the people who speak as representatives of claimant groups and as their witnesses are typically, although not always, senior male leaders. The claims mobilised in these forums revolve around highly complex, fragmented and non-linear oral histories of origin and migration, descriptions of boundaries and sacred sites, and intermarriage between groups and the birth of descendants. These stories frequently refer to displacement due to warfare with other groups or due to confrontations with colonial plantation owners; many tell of groups returning to earlier sites of settlement after periods of displacement. Many of the recorded accounts refer to shifting alliances between matrilineages and negotiations regarding land, particularly following displacement from previous sites; some tell of factions within kin groups being cast out after contravention of the prohibition on intra-moiety marriage. Disputes before the courts often revolve around competing recollections of *tsupu*, with parties describing the negotiations that occurred, the items provided, the speeches given and the people involved. These stories are indexed to and evidenced by existing or abandoned villages and gardens, sacred sites, rivers and other features in the landscape. These emplaced genealogical histories are known as *tutungu* and may stretch back for centuries, constructing a web of relationships between various individuals, groups and places across the island of Guadalcanal.

Read side-by-side, the contested and overlapping narratives contained within the court files suggest that prior to colonisation and during the early colonial period, Kakabona was occupied by a number of groups that were closely entwined through intermarriage. These groups were also relatively mobile, moving in and out of particular areas at different times. The records for Parcel A indicate that the members of three matrilineages have all sought to assert their 'ownership' of the land by constructing their maternal forebears as either the original occupants of the land or as having received the land via *tsupu* from the first settlers of the land, who are widely said to have 'died out'. By contrast, claims to Parcel B are generally indexed to two feasts that occurred in 1937 and 1986, with debate focusing on the exact nature of the 'rights' those feasts transferred and the forms of leadership they conferred upon a number of individual men. According to the court records, none of the parties to any of these disputes ever asserted an *exclusive* claim to land, nor were exclusive rights ever granted by the courts. Rather, the courts have typically identified one lineage as the 'owners' of the land and described other groups as having 'secondary' or 'usufructuary' rights. The courts have therefore refrained from awarding exclusive

---

[27] The court records that I draw upon are formally publicly available; however I have anonymised material in order to provide people with a degree of privacy vis-à-vis a broader audience. For further discussions of the ethics of using court records, see Rebecca Monson, 'Unsettled explorations of law's archives: the allure and anxiety of Solomon Islands' court records', *Australian Feminist Law Journal*, 40:1 (2014), 35–50.

rights to one group but have nevertheless imposed Anglo-American legal categories upon customary arrangements. In at least one instance, the court's imposition of a hierarchy of rights was linked to the issuing of eviction notices to all settlers in a particular area and the actual eviction of a Malaitan man married to a Guadalcanal woman as well as their 'Malaitan' sons.

The discursive and material enactment of claims to property is therefore entwined with the construction and assertion of gendered, racialised and spatialised categories and hierarchies of people and groups. Courts have sought to distinguish 'owners' of the land from 'users', and claimants have deployed their lineage histories in ways that either expand or contract their social networks, depending on the particular claims being made and the interests at stake.[28] In the dispute concerning Parcel B, one group asserted their ownership of the land by arguing that the land was held by their *sub-traeb* rather than the larger *traeb* they belonged to with their opponents, thus emphasising their differences rather than their shared heritage. Another party sought to demonstrate that they too had a claim to the land by stressing the common ancestry of the lines and foregrounding the *traeb* over the *sub-traeb*. Adjustment of social networks may also occur via extending or contracting the temporal scale of the narrative: the identification of the dominant matrilineage on the land is often reciprocally indexed to the identification of dominant men so that shifting the temporal scale may reveal or obscure an entirely different set of political relationships and claims to land. As the dispute regarding Parcel A progressed through the courts, members of two particular lines shifted their claim from one based on transfer through *tsupu* at one date to one based on original occupation at an earlier date.

*Tutungu* therefore have the potential for both expansion and contraction and may be strategically deployed so as to include or exclude particular individuals and social groups. This is a common feature of many Melanesian descent and landholding systems and has been the subject of significant scholarly debate.[29] Michael Scott has argued that some analyses of the deployment of lineage histories portray them simply as essentialised representations of sociality that emerge from colonial and postcolonial intercultural encounters.[30] Scott has questioned this approach and demonstrated that the potential for both 'cutting' and 'expansion' exist in the narratives of the Arosi people of Makira. According to Scott, when Arosi selectively affirm or deny aspects of

---

[28] Compare with Nicholas A. Bainton, 'Keeping the network out of view: mining, distinctions and exclusion in Melanesia', *Oceania*, 79:1 (2009), 18–33.

[29] See for example Marilyn Strathern, 'Cutting the network', *Journal of the Royal Anthropological Institute*, 2:3 (1996), 517–35; James Carrier, 'Property and social relations in Melanesian anthropology', in C.M. Hann (ed.), *Property Relations: renewing the anthropological tradition* (New York 1998), 85–103; Stuart Kirsch, 'Property effects: social networks and compensation claims in Melanesia', *Social Anthropology*, 9:2 (2001), 147–63; Stuart Kirsch, 'Keeping the network in view: compensation claims, property and social relations in Melanesia', in Lawrence Kalinoe and James Leach (eds), *Rationales of Ownership: transactions and claims to ownership in contemporary Papua New Guinea* (Wantage 2004), 79–89; Bainton 'Keeping the network out of view'.

[30] Michael W. Scott, 'Neither "new Melanesian history" nor "new Melanesian ethnography": recovering emplaced matrilineages in southeast Solomon Islands', *Oceania*, 77:3 (2007), 337–54.

their lineage histories, they do not 'invent' tradition but deploy *kastom* (the Pijin term for 'custom') in culturally persistent ways.[31] Debra McDougall has drawn on this approach to argue that the property narratives mobilised by Ranonggans both inside and outside the courts similarly reveal the potential for both inclusion and exclusion.[32]

Despite significant differences between the Arosi narratives explored by Scott and the Ranonggan narratives examined by McDougall, both assert a social history in which particular lineages are uniquely tied to particular places. Yet both sets of narratives also acknowledge that production and reproduction require the interaction and 'entanglement' of ontologically diverse peoples, particularly through histories of exogamous marriage and co-residence on land.[33] Scott has suggested that the need for Arosi to maintain inter-lineage cooperation as well as distinctions founded on narratives of original occupation may be understood in terms of a tension between 'forces of stability' and cohesion on the one hand and 'forces of destruction' and fragmentation on the other.[34]

The *tutungu* recorded in court records exhibit a similar potential for both cohesion and inclusion on the one hand and fragmentation and exclusion on the other. This is most obvious for Parcel A, where people's claims to land are indexed to origin narratives that construct particular matrilineages and particular places as mutually constitutive, but simultaneously acknowledge histories of entanglement with other lineages on the land. At first glance, claims to Parcel B are of a different nature: they do not depend on assertions to original occupation, and people often describe the effects of the 1937 and 1986 feasts as taking the land 'outside *kastom*'.[35] Yet the 'property stories' regarding Parcel B nevertheless draw on culturally persistent models of place-making and relatedness that assert both a privileged relationship between particular matrilineages and the land as well as the need for cooperation with other lineages. They emphasise the importance of gift exchange, the articulation of matrilineal connections to the land through the recitation of genealogies, the tracing of political authority over land through senior males within a matrilineage, and the need to marry outside the matrilineage. Notably, while claimants to land in Parcel B do not claim to be the 'original' owners of the land, they do still trace their

---

[31] Ibid., 339.

[32] Debra McDougall, 'The unintended consequences of clarification: development, disputing, and the dynamics of community in Ranongga, Solomon Islands', *Ethnohistory*, 52:1 (2005), 81.

[33] Michael Scott, 'Ignorance is cosmos; knowledge is chaos: articulating a cosmological parity in the Solomon Islands', *Social Analysis*, 44:2 (2000), 56–83; McDougall, 'The unintended consequences of clarification', 94.

[34] Scott, 'Ignorance is cosmos; knowledge is chaos'; Scott, 'Neither "new Melanesian history"'.

[35] To date this land has been registered in the names of male trustees only, and in the case of one block, the name of the father has now been replaced with that of his sons. It is possible that taking the land 'outside *kastom*' may be associated with an assertion of patrilineal inheritance, with control over land passing directly from fathers to their sons. Yet, to date, such transfers have only occurred across two generations, making it far too early to discern any shift in practices of descent and inheritance.

claim to the 'original' occupants, a matrilineage that is said no longer to exist. This effectively constructs today's claimants as the successors of the original occupants of the land.

*Tutungu* are therefore highly dynamic and may be deployed in ways that include as well as exclude particular individuals and groups. In many instances, however, the construction of a hierarchy of claims has been associated with the material enactment of reduced social networks so as to limit access to the land. This is apparent in the eviction of Chinese and Malaitan settlers as early as the 1970s and is starkly revealed by the eviction of the spouses and children of Guadalcanal landholders during the Tension. The mobilisation of *tutungu* in highly exclusionary ways has contributed to a legitimate fear of dispossession among some people and competition among groups who attempt to establish themselves as the 'owners' of the land. These claims should not be understood as purely postcolonial reifications of customary tenure, for they reproduce and revalue culturally persistent models of place-making and relatedness. They do, however, demonstrate a greater tendency to exclude than may have historically been the case, largely as a result of contemporary challenges such as urbanisation and population growth, the commodification of land, and courts' hierarchical interpretations of land tenure.

## Male Spokespersons and 'Dangerous' Disputes

My interlocutors in Kakabona frequently described land disputes as not only sensitive but potentially 'dangerous' matters and drew on metaphors of warfare that evoked comparisons to precolonial headhunting raids. Land disputes entail the construction and assertion of hierarchical relationships among groups and persons and the delineation of boundaries between people and on the ground.[36] The socially fragmenting power of land claims constructs land disputes as threatening matters[37] and is crucial to the perception of peri-urban areas as sites of instability and insecurity.

The last 60 years have seen a range of developments that threaten the relationships between lineages and the places that sustain them. The widening of marriage networks and residence patterns has been associated with a widening of potential claims to land, while the desire of many people to live close to Honiara and to access the wealth associated with land transactions has also meant an increase in the actual assertion of claims. The expansion of potential and actual claims to land in the vicinity of Honiara contributes to the perception of land scarcity and constitutes not only a material threat but also a threat to forms of social identification and relatedness that are founded on the assertion of a privileged relationship to the land. In this context, it is hardly surprising that some people are emphasising the exclusionary rather than inclusionary aspects of ancestral models of relatedness.[38]

[36] See Nicholas Blomley, 'Cuts, flows, and the geographies of property', *Law, Culture and the Humanities*, 7:2 (2011), 203–16.

[37] See also Monson, 'Unsettled explorations of law's archives'.

[38] See Scott, 'Neither "new Melanesian history"'.

The potential for increased social differentiation and fragmentation is exacerbated when claims to land are contested before the chiefs and courts. Concepts of land and identity embedded in lineage narratives have been hybridised with the conceptions of 'property' initially imported by European protectorate officials, missionaries and traders. When these forums record decisions, some interpretations of *kastom* are recorded and legitimated rather than others, and this means that not all social actors are equally positioned to gain endorsement of their claims to land as property rights into the future.[39]

The public articulation of lineage histories and matrilineal connections is 'dangerous' and akin to warfare because it threatens to undermine the essential union of ontologically different kinds of people.[40] Yet restraint in the articulation of lineage histories and the assertion of social boundaries can be equally dangerous because it may constitute a failure to assert the identity of the group in the context of mounting threats to that identity. The violent enactment of social boundaries – for example, through the eviction of migrants during the Tension – needs to be understood in the context of these perceived, if not actual, threats to ancestrally received models of identification and relatedness. Far from ensuring 'security' of tenure, state recognition of customary claims has worked to promote the potential for fragmentation that exists within ancestral models. When chiefs and courts recognise some groups and not others as 'the real landowners', they affirm some claims to a privileged relationship to the land while de-legitimating others. These processes construct land disputes as 'dangerous' matters and peri-urban areas as sites of instability and insecurity, where people are struggling to secure both their material and ontological survival. In this context, it is hardly surprising that some people in Kakabona describe themselves as being engaged in 'a struggle for survival'.

The socially fragmenting power of property narratives and land disputes has important implications for the production and re-inscription of gendered models of leadership. Prior to colonisation, masculine leadership on Guadalcanal was highly contested and revolved around the *taovia*, now often referred to in Pijin as *jifs* (chiefs) or 'big men', and *malaghai*, often referred to as 'warriors'. Scott has suggested that on Makira, this dyad of the chief and warrior embodied the tension between cohesion and fragmentation that exists within lineage narratives.[41] According to Scott, chiefs on Makira were previously 'men of peace', responsible for uniting and stabilising the multiple matrilineages co-resident on the land. If the unique claims of the autochthonous lineage were encroached upon, however, 'a remedial and even violent response could erupt in the form of a warrior or defender of the local lineage and its land'.[42]

Scott's analysis of the idealised 'men of war' and 'men of peace' provides important insights into the construction of public discussions and disputes regarding

---

[39] Monson, 'Unsettled explorations of law's archives'.

[40] See Scott, 'Ignorance is cosmos; knowledge is chaos'; McDougall, 'The unintended consequences of clarification'.

[41] Scott, 'Ignorance is cosmos; knowledge is chaos', 63.

[42] Ibid., 63–64.

land as a masculine domain on Guadalcanal. When I asked residents of Kakabona why women were less likely than men to appear as parties or witnesses before chiefs and courts, they often drew on metaphors of warriors and warfare. Many referred to the role of men in 'defending' and 'fighting' for the interests of the group in land disputes, and one senior woman explained that 'on Guadalcanal, the women must stand behind the man – this is for protection, *not* because she is secondary'. Across the course of the 20th century, ancestral models of masculine prestige were destabilised by a range of processes, including missionisation, colonisation, the cessation of feasting and warfare, and the development of the commodity economy.[43] Today the ability to 'defend' the interests of the group by speaking on their behalf has become a critical means by which forms of authority, prestige and solidarity previously associated with *taovia* and *malaghai* may be performed, expressed and reproduced. In other words, the idealised masculine roles of the chief and warrior now find their coalesced expression in the ideal representative of the group in discussions and disputes regarding land.

The reproduction of the authority of 'big men' through land disputes occurs at a number of levels. When a group is defined by land acquisition officers, chiefs and courts as the 'landowning group', the land may be registered in the names of up to five 'duly authorised representatives' on behalf of that group.[44] The names listed on land titles are, in most if not all cases, the names of those 'big men' who also appear in state forums on behalf of the successful group. People often explain that the men who are identified as 'trustees' were nominated at the time of registration because they were 'big men' and skilled spokespersons who could 'fight' for, defend and represent the interests of the group. Yet registration fixes their control over the land and the wealth that flows from it, enhancing their authority over the land vis-à-vis other members of the landholding group even further.

Under both *kastom* and state law, trustees should consult with other members of the landholding group before dealing in the land.[45] Yet evidence exists that some trustees have failed to fulfil this obligation and have abused their authority over both the land and its people. Land in Kakabona has often been sold to migrants from other areas as well as to local landholders who wish to establish new hamlets or gardens. Many of these sales have been made by trustees, although other people have also sold land. These transactions are often illegitimate in the eyes of other members of landholding groups because deals are often struck by individuals in exchange for cash, without adequate consultation of other members of the landholding group and without distributing the proceeds of sale. These arrangements look increasingly like commodity exchange and have supplanted the previous gift exchanges that ensured that a large number of people not only shared in the benefits of land deals

---

[43] See Rebecca Monson, 'Negotiating land tenure: women, men and the transformation of land tenure in Solomon Islands', in Janine Ubink (ed.), *Customary Justice: perspectives on legal empowerment* (Rome c. 2011), 169–85.

[44] Land and Titles Act [Cap 133], sec. 195(1).

[45] See for example the comments of then Chief Justice Muria in *Kasa v. Biku* [2004] SBHC 62 (Solomon Islands); HC-CC 126 of 999 (14 Jan. 2000).

but also knew of their details. As a result of these processes, the legitimacy and meaning of land 'sales' is often highly controversial and a significant source of conflict. During the Tension, many of the migrants who had 'purchased' land were chased off the land by other claimants. In numerous instances, significant anger was also directed towards the people who were alleged to have sold land. Younger members of land-holding groups resented the sale of what they regarded as their 'birthright', particularly given the perception that they will face land shortages in the future.[46]

## Conclusion

Land disputes in Solomon Islands are often treated primarily as contests over economic resources. Yet the perception of land disputes as 'dangerous' matters throws light on the epistemological or ontological challenges associated with urbanisation, in particular the ways in which urbanisation has exacerbated social fragmentation and inequality. Furthermore, the dangerous, socially disruptive nature of land disputes has implications for the gendered construction of leadership, decision-making and dispute resolution. Land disputes have become a key arena for the performance of masculine authority and prestige, and the ideal spokesperson for the group embodies not only the oratorical power of the *taovia* but also the aggression that was previously symbolised by the *malaghai*. This serves to construct men, rather than women, as the ideal spokespersons for the group. It also works to entrench the authority of a relatively small group of male leaders over land so that the roles of 'big man' and 'trustee' are mutually constitutive.

The socially fragmenting power of land claims has also been crucial to the emergence of peri-urban areas as sites of instability and insecurity. Land disputes are dangerous matters that pose a threat to long-standing models of place-making and relatedness, literally confronting people with the question of who they are and where they belong. Many people in Kakabona are profoundly aware of the new challenges they face in the 21st century and describe themselves as being engaged in 'a struggle for survival'. Yet they are also negotiating this struggle through active, self-conscious re-evaluation of historical models, and this creates immense space not only for anxiety but also for creativity, innovation and renewal.

---

[46] Tarcisius Tara Kabutaulaka, 'Beyond ethnicity: the political economy of the Guadalcanal crisis in Solomon Islands', State, Society and Governance in Melanesia Program, Working Paper 1 (2001), 14.

# Customary Authority and State Withdrawal in Solomon Islands: Resilience or Tenacity?

## DEBRA MCDOUGALL

### ABSTRACT

After a period of civil crisis (1998–2003), the Solomon Islands state was often characterised as weak and failing, but the society as strong and resilient. Such characterisations resonate with discussions of 'resilience' now prominent in international development discourse. Focusing on institutions of chiefly authority in Ranongga (in Solomon Islands' Western Province), this paper suggests that while such non-state forms of governance did help to maintain social order in a time of national crisis and economic collapse, they should not be understood as autonomous systems that have retained their identity against external disturbances. To the contrary, like other neo-traditional institutions of governance, chiefs' committees have emerged out of institutions of colonial indirect rule. Contemporary frustration about the state's absence and weakness paradoxically highlights the importance of the state in ordinary communities.

In late 2002 and early 2003, Solomon Islands was labelled a 'failed' or 'failing' state, a depiction that was influential in the decision of the Australian government to initiate what became the Regional Assistance Mission to Solomon Islands (RAMSI).[1] This

*Acknowledgements*: Research for this article was funded in part by an Australian Research Council grant (#0666652) as well as by the Social Science Research Council and the Wenner-Gren Foundation. I thank editors, co-contributors and two anonymous reviewers for comments.

[1] John Roughan, 'Pacific first: a failed state!', *Solomon Star*, 13 Feb. 2002; 'The Solomon Islands: the Pacific's first failed state?', *Economist*, 13 Feb. 2003. See also Sinclair Dinnen, 'Lending a fist? Australia's new interventionism in the southwest Pacific', State, Society and Governance in Melanesia Program (herinafter SSGM), Discussion Paper 1 (Canberra 2004); Tarcisius Tara Kabutaulaka, 'Australian foreign policy and the RAMSI intervention in Solomon Islands', *Contemporary Pacific*, 17:2 (2005), 283–308; Minh Nguyen, 'The question of "failed states": Australia and the notion of state failure', Mar. 2005, http://www.uniya.org/research/state_failure.pdf (accessed 16 Jan. 2011); Terence Wesley-Smith, 'Altered states: the politics of state failure and regional intervention',

discourse on the failed state produced a counter-discourse on the strength of Solomon Islands society. As Solomon Islands academic Gordon Nanau put it:

> 'failed states' are not the same as 'failed communities'. It was government apparatus that failed during the period of social unrest. Communities remained and indeed succeeded in acting as buffers providing the needs of their people in the absence of government services.[2]

Through the conflict years, customary land tenure and traditional subsistence practices meant that economic collapse did not lead to widespread hunger.[3] The durability of trans-local kinship meant that many who fled the conflict in Honiara and Guadalcanal had another home to which they could return. Traditional leadership, Christian church organisations, women's groups, grassroots non-governmental organisations and other non-state institutions played a critical role in maintaining social order and, many have argued, preventing the civil crisis from worsening.[4]

This paper is an ethnographic and historical discussion of one such institution: a chiefs' committee. Chiefs and quasi-formalised bodies of chiefs are now ubiquitous in the Solomons. My primary focus is Pienuna village, on the island of Ranongga in the Western Province of Solomon Islands. In describing the ways that individual men known as chiefs and the Pienuna Chiefs' Committee have mediated

in Greg Fry and Tarcisius Tara Kabutaulaka (eds), *Intervention and State-Building in the Pacific: the legitimacy of 'cooperative intervention'* (Manchester 2008), 37–53.

[2] Gordon Nanau, 'Intervention and nation-building in Solomon Islands: local responses', in Fry and Kabutaulaka, *Intervention and State-Building*, 159.

[3] Clive Moore, *Happy Isles in Crisis: the historical causes for a failing state in the Solomon Islands, 1998–2004* (Canberra 2004), 69. Despite inadequate statistics on food security, a 2004 report concluded that 'The subsistence sector continues to adequately support the majority of the population'. The steep decline in income during the conflict period had adverse effects primarily on low-income groups living in urban areas, on rural people's ability to pay for things such as school fees and on the government's ability to deliver basic services. Solomon Islands Government and United Nations Development Programme, 'Solomon Islands millennium development goals: report 2004', June 2005, 8 and 13. For another account of the health situation of the population soon after the conflict, see UNICEF Pacific Office, 'Solomon Islands: a situation analysis of children, women and youth', 2005, 10, http://www.unicef.org/pacificislands/Solomon_Island_Sitan_Latest_pdf.pdf (accessed 6 Oct. 2015).

[4] Moore, *Happy Isles in Crisis*, 20, 152–56; John Braithwaite, Sinclair Dinnen, Matthew Allen, Valerie Braithwaite and Hilary Charlesworth, *Pillars and Shadows: state-building as peacebuilding in Solomon Islands* (Canberra 2010), 13–14, 31–32, 41–45. On churches see Richard Carter, *In Search of the Lost: the death and life of the seven peacemakers of the Melanesian Brotherhood* (Norwich 2006); Debra McDougall, 'Religious institutions as alternative structures in post-conflict Solomon Islands: cases from the Western Province', SSGM, Discussion Paper 5 (2008); Dalcy Tovosia Paina, 'Peacemaking in Solomon Islands: the experience of the Guadalcanal Women for Peace movement', *Development Bulletin*, 53 (2000), 47–48; Alice A. Pollard, 'Resolving conflict in Solomon Islands: the Women for Peace approach', *Development Bulletin*, 53 (2000), 44–46.

local disputes, I provide evidence for arguments that Solomon Islands communities remained strong despite the failure of the state. At the same time, though, I want to question the broader 'weak state/strong society' framework that informs much work on informal governance in the Solomons, a framing that may lead us to downplay the degree to which the formal state has penetrated social structure and political institutions in ordinary communities.

The analysis draws on long-term ethnographic research undertaken on Ranongga for nearly two years between 1998 and 2001, with several shorter trips undertaken between 2005 and 2010. I have interviewed men and women about the work of the chiefs' committee and have observed rituals of dispute resolution. In addition to watching traditional leaders at work within communities, I have tracked ongoing efforts to articulate local customary principles in forms recognisable by outside agents, including the government and non-governmental organisations. I have sometimes assisted these efforts by recording discussions, transcribing, and translating documents. In accounting for the history of customary institutions, I draw on oral history, secondary sources and documents from Native courts and Native councils in the Solomon Islands National Archive. Few documents from the postcolonial period have found their way into the archive, but I draw on fragmentary records that were in the possession of my Ranonggan interlocutors.[5]

The paper was developed as part of a session on 'Governance gaps and local resilience' at the Solomon Islands workshop held in Canberra in November 2013. Rarely used before the mid-20th century, the term 'resilience' is now a buzzword in fields including psychology, health studies, social work, disaster management, economics and climate change.[6] The term was adopted from studies of mechanical systems into the emerging field of ecology in the 1970s to describe complex systems with multiple states of equilibrium that involve both change and stasis.[7] Since the 2000s, resilience theory has featured prominently in research focused on social and environmental systems.[8] Beyond the academy, resilience has supplanted discourses

---

[5] Research methods are described in more depth in the introduction to Debra McDougall, *Engaging with Strangers: love and violence in rural Ranongga* (forthcoming).

[6] A Google Ngram based on search terms 'resilient + resilience' in the English language corpora showed that frequency of use (as a proportion to words in the corpora in the given year) rose by 1,060% between 1900 and 2008, with the sharpest increase after 1960. See http://tinyurl.com/odwfq3o (accessed 15 Oct. 2015). In the first 60 results of a Google Scholar search on 'resilience' and 'Solomon Islands', the term was used in reference to species or ecosystems in 25 sources, in reference to socio-ecological systems in 21 sources, in reference to individuals or groups in two references, and in reference to socio-political systems in eight sources. Only one source made reference to the resilience of the bureaucracy of the formal state; all others focused on the resilience of non-state formations. See http://tinyurl.com/obu9exh (accessed 15 Oct. 2015).

[7] The most cited source from this period is C.S. Holling, 'Resilience and stability of ecological systems', *Annual Review of Ecology and Systematics*, 4 (1973), 1–23.

[8] The literature on resilience is huge and interdisciplinary. Many scholars have tracked the genealogy of the concept and outlined different disciplinary approaches. See for example W. Neil Adger, 'Social and ecological resilience: are they related?', *Progress in Human Geography*, 24:3

of sustainability to become 'the mantra of the moment' in mainstream discourse of international development actors. According to Rigg and Oven, 'From confronting the challenge of climate change to addressing financial crises, security threats and live-lihood vulnerability in poor countries, it seems that building resilience will, somehow, do the trick'.[9] They have observed that resilience has become a normative goal of much development work without challenging a neoliberal focus on economic growth. Neoliberal approaches assume that transnational market-led integration increases socio-economic resilience, downplaying evidence that marketisation and delocalisation may also increase risk and vulnerability. Neoliberal resilience is chal-lenged by what Rigg and Oven have labelled 'neo-populist' approaches, which suggest that traditional societies and local social structures are inherently resilient.[10] Such neo-populist interpretations tend to exaggerate the coherence of traditional systems. They may also provide convenient alibis for neoliberal reformers seeking to devolve responsibility for service provision from the state onto individuals or communities: if the latter are resilient enough, they should not really need state support.[11]

Resilience features in recent development-oriented literature on Melanesia. It is most prominent in work on social environmental systems, including work on climate change and natural disasters, but socio-political institutions are also characterised as 'resilient'. Some examples are Indigenous political structures, informal systems, cus-tomary law, reconciliation, peacebuilding, norms of political structures, informal economy, civil society, anti-corruption measures, the media, *wantokism* (the tendency to give preference to relatives or people from the same language group) and court institutions.[12] In much of this work, 'resilience' is deployed as a descriptive term, a

(2000), 347–64; Debra J. Davidson, 'The applicability of the concept of resilience to social systems: some sources of optimism and nagging doubts', *Society & Natural Resources*, 23:12 (2010), 1135–49; Carl Folke, 'Resilience: the emergence of a perspective for social-ecological systems analyses', *Global Environmental Change*, 16:3 (2006), 253–67; Daniel F. Lorenz, 'The diver-sity of resilience: contributions from a social science perspective', *Natural Hazards*, 67:1 (2013), 7–24. For critical analyses of the 'resilience paradigm' and 'neoliberal resilience', respectively, see Michael Fabinyi, Louisa Evans and Simon J. Foale, 'Social-ecological systems, social diversity, and power: insights from anthropology and political ecology', *Ecology and Society*, 19:4 (2014), 28; Jonathan Rigg and Katie Oven, 'Building liberal resilience? A critical review from developing rural Asia', *Global Environmental Change*, 32 (2015), 175–86.

[9] Rigg and Oven, 'Building liberal resilience?', 175; see also Davidson, 'The applicability of the concept of resilience', 1135–37.

[10] Rigg and Oven, 'Building liberal resilience?', 177–78.

[11] I thank an anonymous reviewer for suggesting this interpretation.

[12] Elsina Wainwright on behalf of the Australian Strategic Policy Institute, 'Our failing neighbour: Australia and the future of Solomon Islands', June 2003, 27, https://www.aspi.org.au/publications/our-failing-neighbour-australia-and-the-future-of-solomon-islands/solomons.pdf (accessed 16 Sep. 2015); Sinclair Dinnen, Abby Mcleod and Gordon Peake, 'Police-building in weak states: Australian approaches in Papua New Guinea and Solomon Islands', *Civil Wars*, 8:2 (2006), 88, 104; Jennifer Corrin, '*Ples Bilong Mere*: law, gender and peace-building in Solomon Islands', *Feminist Legal Studies*, 16:2 (2008), 173; Volker Boege, 'Peacebuilding on Bougainville:

metaphor or a trope rather than as a theoretical term, as is the case in some studies of social environmental systems.[13] Yet as Rumsey has argued, rhetorical tropes are often a central component of theory in ethnographic writing and are thus worthy of close attention.[14]

Whether approached as a theory or as a metaphor, the notion of resilience presumes a more-or-less coherent system that persists in recognisable form in the face of external disturbances. This formulation immediately raises questions of boundaries: where is the boundary between the system and the external disturbance? It also raises questions about the nature and scale of change: how do we distinguish between changes that are part of the normal functioning of a resilient system versus changes that constitute a complete transformation or destruction of the system?[15] Literature on resilience usually assumes that resilience is a desirable quality of a social system, but no real reason exists to assume that persistence is better than transformation in either social or environmental systems. Questions of continuity and change are particularly complicated in the context of customary institutions of Melanesia. As David Akin's study of Maasina Rule in Solomon Islands illustrates, social movements aimed at transforming society may do so in the name of ancestral tradition – the idea is not that the social system stays the same but that it is transformed according to local rather than foreign visions of a good life.[16]

Approaches that emphasise the 'resilience' of local socio-political or cultural systems often unwittingly replicate a tendency in early- and mid-century anthropology to represent societies or cultures as integral wholes that are externally bounded, internally cohesive and frozen in time – a tendency that was thoroughly (even incessantly) critiqued in the 1980s and 1990s.[17] In an incisive paper that brings the insights of contemporary anthropology to biological science-dominated approaches to resilience, Fabinyi, Evans and Foale have observed that many contemporary critiques of the resilience paradigm repeat critiques made of functionalism or neofunctionalism

---

international intervention meets local resilience', *Global Dialogues*, 2 (2013), 36–43; Braithwaite et al., *Pillars and Shadows*; M. Anne Brown, *Security and Development in the Pacific Islands: social resilience in emerging states* (Boulder 2007).

[13] Fran H. Norris, Susan P. Stevens, Betty Pfefferbaum, Karen F. Wyche and Rose L. Pfefferbaum, 'Community resilience as a metaphor, theory, set of capacities, and strategy for disaster readiness', *American Journal of Community Psychology*, 41:1/2 (2008), 127.

[14] Alan Rumsey, 'Ethnographic macro-tropes and anthropological theory', *Anthropological Theory*, 4:3 (2004), 268–69.

[15] Lorenz, 'The diversity of resilience', 11.

[16] David W. Akin, *Colonialism, Maasina Rule, and the Origins of Malaitan Kastom* (Honolulu 2013), 30.

[17] See for example Arjun Appadurai, 'The production of locality', in Richard Farden (ed.), *Counterworks: managing the diversity of knowledge* (New York 1995), 204–25; Akhil Gupta and James Ferguson, 'Beyond "culture": space, identity, and the politics of difference', in Akhil Gupta and James Ferguson (eds), *Culture, Power, Place: explorations in critical anthropology* (Durham, NC 1997), 33–51; Johannes Fabian, *Time and the Other: how anthropology makes its object* (New York 1983); Eric R. Wolf, *Europe and the People without History* (Berkeley 1982). For a critique of some of these critiques, see Ira Bashkow, 'A neo-Boasian conception of cultural boundaries', *American Anthropologist*, 106:3 (2004), 443–58.

in ecological anthropology of the 1960s.[18] They have argued that neither pre-1960s ecological anthropology nor 21st-century resilience paradigms pay adequate attention to the internal diversity of any given social system: they tend to gloss over the fact that different actors within a system benefit in different ways from its structures. Both paradigms disregard connections between a local system and broader political economic forces that have given rise to that system.

This essay reviews discussions of the contrast between the weak state and strong society in Solomon Islands. I then turn to an ethnographic and historical account of the work of chiefs on Ranongga and the institution of the Pienuna Chiefs' Committee, one of the institutions of local governance that allowed many rural residents of Solomon Islands to weather the broader national crisis. In the next section, I move away from this somewhat functionalist account of the chiefs' committee to explore a genealogy of these neo-traditional institutions of customary governance in the context of late colonial projects of indirect rule. Far from being a more-or-less autonomous system of customary governance, institutions such as the Pienuna Chiefs' Committee emerged through the expansion of state power into local areas. Metaphors of resilience tend to direct our attention away from the dramatic transformations of customary authority that are an important part of the social and political history of rural Melanesia.

The study is focused on Ranongga, but the analysis is arguably applicable in many areas of the Solomons. While many local leaders in Ranongga have a degree of authority reportedly lacking in communities heavily involved in resource extraction, their efforts to consolidate customary authority on the scale of the island have been less successful than similar efforts elsewhere in the region. Among the most prominent examples include the Isabel Council of Chiefs, which fuses customary and religious authority in this nearly entirely Anglican society and has sought collaboration with the provincial government and external support in the post-conflict era.[19] Another successful island-wide institution is Choiseul's Lauru Land Conference of Tribal Communities, founded by Revd Leslie Boseto, an influential leader in the United Church and long-serving member of parliament. The Christian Fellowship Church (CFC) of North New Georgia, discussed in this issue by Edvard Hviding, is also a remarkable institution, combining traditional and church authority.[20] All of these examples fuse Christian and customary authority in a manner that is more difficult in regions marked by

---

[18] Fabinyi et al., 'Social-ecological systems, social diversity, and power', 4.

[19] Graham Baines, 'Beneath the state: chiefs of Santa Isabel, Solomon Islands, coping and adapting', SSGM, Working Paper 2 (2014); Geoffrey M. White, *Identity through History: living stories in a Solomon Islands society* (Cambridge 1991); Geoffrey M. White, 'The discourse of chiefs: notes on a Melanesian society', in Geoffrey M. White and Lamont Lindstrom (eds), *Chiefs Today: traditional Pacific leadership and the postcolonial state* (Stanford 1997), 229–52; Geoffrey M. White, 'Chiefs, church, and state in Santa Isabel, Solomon Islands', in Matt Tomlinson and Debra McDougall (eds), *Christian Politics in Oceania* (New York 2013), 171–97.

[20] See also Edvard Hviding, 'Re-placing the state in the western Solomon Islands: the political rise of the Christian Fellowship Church', in Edvard Hviding and Knut M. Rio (eds), *Made in Oceania: social movements, cultural heritage and the state in the Pacific* (Wantage, UK 2011), 51–89.

denominational diversity.[21] Institutions of customary governance of the sort I discuss are not limited to rural areas, as is illustrated by Michael Kwaʻioloa's autobiographical accounts of his work as a chief in urban Honiara and rural Kwaraʻae.[22]

Although local political institutions, such as the Pienuna Chiefs' Committee, that are found all around Solomon Islands today appear to be resilient in the face of civil conflict and state collapse, I suggest that they are better described as tenacious.[23] If the notion of resilience evokes a system that sustains itself, the idea of tenacity calls attention to the efforts of actors within the system. In the case of chiefs' committees, this tenacity is manifest in a commitment to what is called *kastom* – ways of doing things that are seen to be grounded in local places and ancestors. But it is also manifest in active efforts over many generations to engage with the state in ways that are hoped will lead to a positive transformation of their way of life. Despite the fact that much of the work of the chiefs' committee is focused on the maintenance of *kastom* (understood as local ways of doing things), it proves difficult to draw a boundary between the local and the foreign. The chiefs' committee I discuss here has not retained a traditional shape in the face of external disturbances associated with a century of colonialism; instead it has taken shape through extensive engagement with the apparatus of colonial rule. The Native (later local) courts and councils that are the antecedents of contemporary chiefs' committees, such as the one I describe for Pienuna, were integrated into the broader system of government, albeit somewhat tenuously and very late in the history of the British protectorate. Today, institutions such as chiefs' committees function more-or-less autonomously, but that is because the postcolonial state has withdrawn support and recognition for such bodies.

WEAK STATE, STRONG SOCIETY

Both advocates and critics of neoliberal state-building in the RAMSI decade have highlighted the importance of what are variously called informal, customary,

---

[21] Just under two-thirds of Ranonggans belong to the United Church, but over the past generation United Church communities have schismed to include a range of other denominations. Approximately one-third of the island's population belong to the Seventh-day Adventist Church. Solomon Islands Government, *Report on 2009 Population & Housing Census*, vol. 1: *Basic Tables and Census Description* (Honiara 2012), 53.

[22] Michael Kwaʻioloa and Ben Burt, *Living Tradition: a changing life in the Solomon Islands* (London 1997), 144–55; Michael Kwaʻioloa and Ben Burt, *The Chief's Country* (Brisbane 2012), 15–16, 163–88. On Ranonggan leaders engaging with Malaitans, see Debra McDougall and Joy Kere, 'Christianity, custom, and law: conflict and peacemaking in the postconflict Solomon Islands', in Morgan Brigg and Roland Bleiker (eds), *Mediating across Difference: Oceanic and Asian approaches to conflict resolution* (Honolulu 2011), 155–8.

[23] If 'resilience' is on the rise, 'tenacity' seems to be on the decline. An Ngram with terms 'tenacity + tenacious' showed a steady decline from about 1890, with a 55% decrease in frequency of use between 1900 and 2008. 'Tenacity + tenacious' was overtaken by 'resilient + resilience' in 1984. See http://tinyurl.com/odwfq3o (accessed 15 Oct. 2015).

traditional or Indigenous political structures – part of the strong society that endured in the face of state weakness and failure. Scholarship on state-building in the Solomons has not been dominated by the language of 'resilience'; nevertheless these 'weak state/ strong society' discourses resonate with ideas of resilience, because customary institutions are seen as coherent systems that persist despite external disturbances.

Proponents of neoliberal state-building tend to depict the strength of Indigenous political structures as a problem to be overcome with the expansion of a stronger state. For example, the Australian Strategic Policy Institute report that made the case for regional intervention depicted the modern nation-state as a shallow overlay:

> In the South Pacific, the introduced institutions of the modern nation-state have been overlaid on top of a multiplicity of indigenous political structures. The latter have proven to be remarkably adaptable and their resilience in the face of colonial and post-colonial transformations provides the broader basis for the continuing weakness of the state.[24]

Later, Francis Fukuyama acknowledged that *wantok* networks and customary land tenure provide a degree of security for Solomon Islanders but argued that they also thwarted the development of modern nationalism and impeded the formation of a modern state.[25] In such approaches, Indigenous political structures are figured as both cause and consequence of state weakness.

Critics of neoliberal state-building depict the resilience of local institutions as a strength to be harnessed. A substantial body of work has critiqued such state-centric approaches for overlooking the positive strengths of local society. Kabutaulaka described Solomon Islands as a 'plural society where the state will always share and compete for power with other organizations'; rather than seeking to strengthen the state at the cost of those other organisations, he argued, 'both state and non-state entities must be strengthened'.[26] Morgan and McLeod argued that RAMSI's effectiveness was 'severely constrained by the pervasive belief that "culture gets in the way"'.[27] Dinnen also critiqued state-building operations that seek to impose models from wealthy donor nations onto less wealthy recipient nations without questioning the 'universality of state structures and the technology of institutional transfer'.[28] Writing of policing, Dinnen and Allen have argued that while a serious need exists to enhance the capacity of the state in policing, it is also essential to recognise the

---

[24] Wainwright, 'Our failing neighbour', 28.

[25] Francis Fukuyama, 'State-building in Solomon Islands', *Pacific Economic Bulletin*, 23:3 (2008), 21–22. For a critique see Morgan Brigg, 'Wantokism and state building in Solomon Islands: a response to Fukuyama', *Pacific Economic Bulletin*, 24:3 (2009), 148–61.

[26] Kabutaulaka, 'Australian foreign policy and the RAMSI intervention', 284.

[27] Michael G. Morgan and Abby McLeod, 'Have we failed our neighbour?', *Australian Journal of International Affairs*, 60:3 (2006), 423.

[28] Sinclair Dinnen, 'A comment on state-building in Solomon Islands', *Journal of Pacific History*, 42:2 (2007), 259–60; see also Sinclair Dinnen, 'Beyond state-centrism: external solutions and the governance of security in Melanesia', in Fry and Kabutaulaka, *Intervention and State-Building*, 102–18.

role that non-state community-based actors have played in ameliorating conflict.[29] Braithwaite et al. have recognised that RAMSI became more responsive to local circumstances as the mission progressed but have characterised it as a 'generic' state-building operation that paid little attention to the specific circumstances of the conflict and the Solomons, an approach that was 'blind to the strengths of the Solomon Islands state and society'.[30]

The RAMSI years produced substantial interest in and research on informal, traditional, localised forms of governance. A prominent example is 'Justice delivered locally', an initiative undertaken by the Solomon Islands' Ministry of Justice and Legal Affairs and supported by the World Bank's Justice for the Poor project.[31] The 'Justice delivered locally' initiative sought to document both the causes of conflict throughout the Solomons and the means through which Islanders were able to seek justice. The final report of this program depicts the justice systems of the Solomon Islands as multiple, overlapping and intersecting, and documents the ongoing importance of non-state systems of justice, especially those involving the authority of traditional leaders and (to a lesser degree) church leaders.[32] While non-state systems have demonstrated flexibility and adaptability, they are under considerable strain. The report notes that they appear unable to deal with land disputes arising in the context of resource extraction and with disruptive behaviour caused by forms of substance abuse.[33] Ordinary people value non-state systems even as they desire a more robust engagement with state structures and services. Many feel that the government has withdrawn support for local authorities.

During a five-year period of civil crisis, people were able to eat and shelter themselves because most of their needs were fulfilled through subsistence agriculture on ancestral land that had never been fully transformed into modern forms of property; they were able to maintain social order because of more-or-less self-sustaining institutions of dispute resolution that were not tightly coupled with the formal state. Work that emphasises such strengths of local society in Solomon Islands – especially in rural areas and especially in areas minimally dependent on the formal economy – underlines the limits of neoliberal resilience discourses.[34] My account of the work of

---

[29] Sinclair Dinnen and Matthew Allen, 'Paradoxes of postcolonial police-building: Solomon Islands', *Policing and Society*, 23:2 (2012), 224.

[30] Braithwaite et al., *Pillars and Shadows*, 4, 163.

[31] Justice for the Poor aims to approach 'justice reform as a cross-cutting issue in the practice of development' and operates in East Asia, the Pacific and Africa. 'Justice for the Poor: promoting equity and managing conflict in development', World Bank, http://go.worldbank.org/IMMQE3ET20 (accessed 23 July 2015).

[32] Matthew Allen, Sinclair Dinnen, Daniel Evans and Rebecca Monson, 'Justice delivered locally: systems, challenges, and innovations in Solomon Islands', World Bank research report, Aug. 2013, http://www-wds.worldbank.org/external/default/WDSContentServer/WDSP/IB/2013/09/27/000356161_20130927130401/Rendered/PDF/812990WP0DL0Se0Box0379833B00PUBLIC0.pdf (accessed 16 Sep. 2015). I was involved in this project as a peer reviewer for this and other interim reports.

[33] Ibid., 13–22.

[34] Rigg and Oven, 'Building liberal resilience?'.

Pienuna chiefs during a period of state withdrawal and crisis also speaks to the importance of maintaining local systems that are only loosely coupled to state systems, especially in a context where the state has been unreliable in consistently serving the interests of the rural population. Yet like the Justice for the Poor report, my research also reveals that local actors are frustrated by their lack of engagement with the institutions of the state. Furthermore, when viewed from a historical perspective, it becomes clear that an institution such as the chiefs' committee is not an identifiable local system that has retained a distinct identity in the face of external disturbances, but rather emerged out of colonial-era Native courts and councils and postcolonial local courts and councils. Even prior to the conflict of 1998–2003, neoliberal restructuring and downsizing eliminated financial support for local government. The work of chiefs was never fully, or even mostly, encompassed within the formal institutions of the colonial and postcolonial state, yet this history signals the shortcomings of approaches that envision neo-traditional leadership as a discernibly bounded, resilient local system that has retained its identity in the face of external disturbances.

## THE ORDINARY WORK OF CHIEFS IN EXTRAORDINARY TIMES

Much of my own ethnographic research was undertaken during a period of economic crisis and state collapse in Solomon Islands. Cash was short, and state services contracted, but subsistence agriculture provided for most people's basic needs. Local leaders solved most disputes that arose. This was certainly a more 'resilient' society than the one in which I had grown up or in which I live today (the urban United States and Australia, respectively), where a failure of the state and economic collapse on the scale experienced by Solomon Islanders in the early 2000s would have had far more devastating consequences. In this section, I describe some aspects of the highly localised work of individual leaders and the institution of the chiefs' committee, focusing in particular on problems that are trans-local in nature.

In Ranongga, dispute resolution is called *varivatuvizi*, which can be translated as 'causing to be straight'.[35] The work is often spoken of as 'mending', 'stitching together' or 'tying back together' broken relationships. Church leaders also straighten conflicts, and customary authorities invoke Christian narratives and values. Despite such intersections, local people distinguish clearly between Christian and customary forms of dispute settlement: Christian authorities reconcile people through prayer alone, whereas customary authorities also oversee the exchange of money or traditional values, called *ira* (compensation) in Ranongga.[36] As will be seen, Ranonggans have been engaged in codifying customary rules and formalising dispute resolution procedures, part of the long attempt to integrate local content into the apparatus of

[35] Similar metaphors are common throughout the Pacific. See Geoffrey M. White and Karen Ann Watson-Gegeo, 'Disentangling discourse', in Karen Ann Watson-Gegeo and Geoffrey M. White (eds), *Disentangling: conflict discourse in Pacific societies* (Stanford 1990), 3–52.
[36] McDougall and Kere, 'Christianity, custom, and law', 148–49.

government law. Despite such efforts at formalisation, dispute settlement remains embedded in social relationships, and the authority of men settling disputes comes not from an institutionalised position but from relationships with the disputants. Formalised rules tend to be quickly put aside in the interest of finding an amicable solution.[37]

The first example I discuss illustrates the intersection between formal politics and informal dispute settlement, as well as the way that what people call 'the problems of town' return to rural villages. After provincial elections held in June 2009, a Ranonggan villager returned from the provincial capital of Gizo drunk and angry that people had failed to support his uncle's bid for a seat in the provincial assembly of Western Province. He tore through the community, destroying property, insulting people and swearing against individuals, chiefs and clans. Throughout the Solomons, swearing is a serious offence; in the past, I was told, it was considered equivalent to murder. No one could mediate the dispute because he had offended everyone, and the community was plunged into a period of heaviness when no one participated in communal work. After many weeks, the village chief's spokesman – who was, at the time of the offence, living with his wife's family in Isabel Province and was not himself directly involved – was summoned. He travelled all the way home to collect compensation from the offender and distribute it to those he had offended, actions that ended the period of malaise. When I visited in 2010, this man and his uncle (the one who had lost the election) were active members of the community.

A majority of 'straightening' rituals that I witnessed in Ranongga involved illicit sexuality, including incest, adultery or elopement. No hard and fast line occurs between solving disputes and the ordinary negotiation of marriage: betrothals are always fraught because taboos between brothers and sisters mean that brothers must be compensated when they hear that their sisters will be married. It is worth describing one case in detail to convey the tone of such rituals and the work involved in dispute settlement.

In late 1999, word came to Pienuna village requesting that Samuel Samata come to straighten a problem arising from a sexual affair between cousins in a neighbouring village.[38] The village had been founded, generations earlier, by people of Pienuna. Samata was the 'left-hand' of current village chief John Pavukera, and his paternal grandfather (John Pavukera's maternal grandfather) was the last precolonial chief of Pienuna; his matrilineal clan held the larger territory encompassing both Pienuna and the village where the incest had occurred. Because of these relationships, he had some responsibility for the moral wellbeing of those in the territory. More directly, Samata was a collateral relative of the young man who had committed the offence.

---

[37] This point is also made by Akin, *Colonialism*, 79–86.

[38] While I disguise the identities of people involved in disputes so that only local people who already know the circumstances of disputes could identify them, I use the real names of people involved in solving disputes except in cases in which their actions are controversial or may reflect poorly on themselves or their families. In previous work, I used pseudonyms and other methods of anonymising my data, and this approach was roundly critiqued by most whom I had represented in such a way. I have obtained permission to use names in these contexts.

We set off for the village in the early evening, stopping at several points to pass the news and wait out rain showers. It was pitch dark when we arrived at the kitchen of the grandmother of the young man who had committed the offence (she had organised the 'straightening' ritual). Samata would speak for the side of the young man; John Pavukera had already arrived and would speak for the young woman's side (he was related to both offenders through his father). We waited for several hours, a delay caused in part by the perceived need for an equal exchange of valuables between the two sides. The young man's side had a *bakia*, a large ring of fossilised clamshell that is the traditional valuable of the western Solomons. Although they have not been manufactured since the late 19th century, *bakia* continue to be necessary in transactions involving marriage, warfare and land. The young woman's side did not have a *bakia* and were scrambling to collect an appropriate amount of cash.[39]

It was nearing midnight when everyone gathered together. The offenders sat silently, heads down, throughout the proceedings. The village pastor (also the young woman's mother's brother) began with prayer, noting that everything that is 'straight' on earth is also 'straight' in heaven. Samata said that offenders were 'rotten' (the local term is *nyete*, referring to rotten *Canarium*) but that the point of the work was to ensure that their younger siblings would not follow the crooked path they had forged. Then the two sides began discussing compensation. The man who brought the *bakia* wanted to present it, saying that while cash just melts away, the *bakia* remains forever as a reminder of the seriousness of the offence. The young woman's side wanted to know the prices of the *bakia*, but John Pavukera said that this was being settled through the church as well as custom, and they could not set a price for a fine. Samata said that it was better not to present the *bakia* if the other side didn't have one; even though chiefs had established a monetary equivalent for *bakia* a few months earlier as part of a workshop aimed to compile a comprehensive book of 'custom law', he explained that it was impossible to put a price on *bakia* because in the past it was substituted for the life of a person condemned to death. In the end, the young man's side was allowed to present the *bakia* with the young woman's side giving cash, on the condition that the young man's side would not complain later that they had given too much. (Those present justified the imbalance by musing that it was, after all, the boy who did the 'work'.) With the *bakia* and cash exchanged, both Samata and John Pavukera sternly warned that if such an offence should recur, they would send the offenders directly to the court, where the cost would be extremely high. Finally, Samata said,

> Now the mending is done … Think of the image of Jesus Christ tied to the cross. When he died on the cross, he mended the sins of the sort that these two have committed. If he had not come, people would have died. Jesus's coming joined back together the lives of people. They are once again siblings.

The pastor concluded with a prayer of thanksgiving.

---

[39] On the relationship between cash and shell money, see David Akin and Joel Robbins (eds), *Money and Modernity: state and local currencies in Melanesia* (Pittsburgh 1999).

In addition to marriage and sexuality, Pienuna chiefs were constantly engaged in negotiations around land and property. As with marriage, most of the work of 'straightening' occurs outside formal disputes. Ranongga's land-holding clans are matrilineal, but rights to property often pass from father to children and other affinal relatives. In funerals and other rituals, people often simultaneously assert individualised control over plots that their fathers have cleared or planted while affirming an ongoing relationship with original matrilineal owners who continue to hold the territory. Such rituals allow a great deal of flexibility and adaptability but are seen as problematic in situations requiring clearly delineated property rights. Minor disputes over property, involving the right of a person to clear a small area for settlement or gardening or planting a crop, are often linked to deeper disagreements about the ultimate clan ownership of large territories.

In 1998 the Pienuna Chiefs' Committee was called to mediate a dispute involving a small block of land in southern Ranongga – it was referred to as a 'hearing' (*paraparanga*, literally a 'talking'). It involved a typical scenario: one man had planted sago palms on land that another man claimed; the second man pulled out the palms, saying that the first had failed to ask permission. The committee was tasked with judging the evidence and making a decision about the veracity of the claims, but as in the incest case, the task was framed as mending a social fabric that had been torn. The logic of the two cases is parallel: engaging in sexual relationships or fighting over land is antithetical to the moral obligations of kinship, so engaging in these activities destroys the kin relationship. Thus, at the opening of the hearing, the chairman of the Pienuna Chiefs' Committee told the disputants to 'remember that they were not different people' and referred to them repeatedly as 'those two brothers' (they were related through their fathers); he pointed out that he and other committee members were also related to the disputants so that everyone assembled was kin to one another. The chairman entreated the disputants to 'keep things small' by discussing only the destruction of the sago palms and the boundaries of the small 'block' where they were planted.

The hearing was not a success. One of the disputants objected, saying that he did not realise this was a 'court' (he used the Pijin term *kot*). He thought that the matter of the sago palm had been resolved and that this gathering was for him and his 'brother' to sit down and work out the real story of this area of land so that their children and grandchildren would know it. He did not want to 'fight about property', just tell the true story. Unfortunately (but typically), 'just telling the story' would open an unresolvable disagreement about the mythical charters for the clan ownership of the land itself, which is precisely what the committee chairman had hoped to avoid by exhorting them to 'keep things small'. In this case and many others I have encountered, a foreign clan had arrived and acquired land from the original matrilineal clan, but whether the foreign clan had purchased the land or whether they were mere guests of the original clan was uncertain.[40] Despite the conciliatory tone of the disputant in the sago palm case, his proposal to tell stories about clan ancestors

---

[40] Burt has noted that in contemporary Kwara'ae land disputes, productive ambiguity of histories of clan territories are increasingly understood as deceit. Ben Burt, 'Land in Kwara'ae and development in Solomon Islands', *Oceania*, 64:4 (1994), 330.

was understood as an aggressive move.[41] As he began to name the dead ancestors buried in the area, he was cut off mid-sentence by the committee chairman. The hearing was quickly ended, and the Pienuna delegation went home with the sense that the problem had not been resolved.

Ten years later, the area under dispute in 1998 became the headquarters of Ranongga's single and ill-fated logging operation.[42] Predictably, the disagreement about clan ownership resurfaced in more pernicious ways. This time, rather than being mediated by a chiefs' committee, young men confronted one another in the bush with machetes, and senior men faced off in legal courts. When a High Court decision forced the claimants to prove their 'tribal' ownership of the land before contesting the legality of the process through which the defendants acquired timber rights and contracted the logging company, the Pienuna Chiefs' Committee was called to adjudicate the issue it sought to avoid in 1998 – whether the foreign clan or the original clan really owned the land. It may be tempting to imagine that these bitter conflicts over logging would not have arisen if the smaller dispute over planting sago palm had been more conclusively resolved. Yet prior to logging, solving property disputes did not involve a conclusive determination of clan ownership: the chiefs' committee exhorted the disputants to see one another as brothers. All the legal processes involved in acquiring timber rights or contesting logging operations require claimants to articulate the divisions among themselves, speaking as members of clearly bounded and distinct 'tribes'.

In all cases of dispute resolution discussed here – swearing after an election, incest, a property dispute – local leaders sought to mend relationships and restore moral order. Chiefs drew on local knowledge and their own relationships with parties to the disputes. At the same time, in all the cases, we see that the problems are not simply localised, nor are the institutions through which these senior men work. The government court is always present as an encompassing level of justice; sometimes the work of chiefs is understood to be part of formal government (the 'court'). The dispute that arose in the context of logging illustrates the limits of the 'customary' authority of chiefs with regard to the domain in which they are assumed to have most knowledge and power: land. While processes such as the chiefs' committee hearing are often able to solve disputes around property use by reminding disputants of their kinship ties, large-scale resource extraction virtually forced disputants to divide themselves into clearly bounded clans that exclude non-members. Most chiefs no longer have that kind of power.[43]

---

[41] Scott has made this argument in reference to Makira. Michael Scott, 'Ignorance is cosmos; knowledge is chaos: articulating a cosmological parity in the Solomon Islands', *Social Analysis*, 44:2 (2000), 56–83; Michael W. Scott, *The Severed Snake: matrilineages, making place, and a Melanesian Christianity in southeast Solomon Islands* (Durham, NC 2007), 244–47.

[42] This case is discussed in greater detail in Debra McDougall, 'Church, company, committee, chief: emergent collectivities in rural Solomon Islands', in Mary Patterson and Martha Macintyre (eds), *Managing Modernity in the Western Pacific* (St Lucia 2011), 121–46; McDougall, *Engaging with Strangers*, ch. 6.

[43] Interestingly, Fukuyama notes that customary land has almost never been converted to modern property without coercion or fraud. Fukuyama, 'State-building in Solomon Islands', 22.

## HISTORIES OF CUSTOMARY AUTHORITY

The contemporary work of Ranonggan chiefs at the end of the 20th century might be viewed as evidence that traditional forms of social organisation are resilient enough to adapt to external pressures without disintegrating or losing their basic identity. In this section, I consider a longer history of customary authority in Ranongga to argue that the Pienuna Chiefs' Committee should not be considered in isolation from the broader structures of the colonial state and capitalist economy that have had a profound influence on Ranongga for more than a century.

Anthropological literature on chiefs in contemporary Pacific societies has explored the complex ways in which older forms of authority have been transformed in the context of missionisation, colonial rule and postcolonial nationalism.[44] Two features of colonial- and postcolonial-era chiefly leadership are important in considering the relationship between informal non-state and formal state authority. First, since colonial pacification, chiefs have not had the right to exercise legitimate violence.[45] Second, linked as it is to ancestral traditions, the authority of customary chiefs has been divorced from the primary source of supernatural agency through Christianisation. Customary authority is not secular: some chiefs are thought to continue to wield various forms of ancestral power, and as we have seen, chiefs tend to frame the realm

---

[44] See a number of edited volumes, including Michael R. Allen (ed.), *Vanuatu: politics, economics and ritual in island Melanesia* (Sydney 1981); Robert J. Foster (ed.), *Nation Making: emergent identities in post-colonial Melanesia* (Ann Arbor 1995); White and Lindstrom, *Chiefs Today*. On Vanuatu and New Caledonia, see Bronwen Douglas, *Across the Great Divide: journeys in history and anthropology* (Amsterdam 1998), chs 1–2. On Fiji, see Peter France, *The Charter of the Land: custom and colonization in Fiji* (Melbourne 1969); Martha Kaplan, *Neither Cargo nor Cult: ritual politics and the colonial imagination in Fiji* (Durham, NC 1995), R.R. Nayacakalou, *Leadership in Fiji* (Melbourne 1975). Within Solomon Islands, see Geoffrey White on Santa Isabel: *Identity through History*; 'The discourse of chiefs'; 'Chiefs, church, and state in Santa Isabel, Solomon Islands'; Edvard Hviding on Marovo: *Guardians of Marovo Lagoon: practice, place, and politics in maritime Melanesia* (Honolulu 1996), 72–74; 'Re-placing the state'. Studies of chiefs in Malaitan societies (urban and rural) include Akin, *Colonialism*, esp. 50–55 and 171–86; Roger M. Keesing, 'Chiefs in a chiefless society: the ideology of modern Kwaio politics', *Oceania*, 38:4 (1968), 276–80; Roger M. Keesing, 'Killers, big men, and priests on Malaita: reflections on a Melanesian troika system', *Ethnology*, 24:4 (1985), 237–52; Roger M. Keesing, 'Tuesday's chiefs revisited', in White and Lindstrom, *Chiefs Today*, 253–63; Kwa'ioloa and Burt, *Living Tradition*; Kwa'ioloa and Burt, *The Chief's Country*.

[45] Pacification occurred swiftly in 1899–1900 in New Georgia. Hviding, *Guardians of Marovo Lagoon*, 79–130; John M. McKinnon, 'Tomahawks, turtles and traders: a reconstruction in the circular causation of warfare in the New Georgia Group', *Oceania*, 45:4 (1975), 290–307; Geoffrey M. White, 'War, peace, and piety in Santa Isabel, Solomon Islands', in Margaret Rodman and Matthew Cooper (eds), *The Pacification of Melanesia* (Ann Arbor 1983), 109–40; Martin Zelenietz, 'The end of headhunting in New Georgia', in Rodman and Cooper, *The Pacification of Melanesia*, 91–108. Elsewhere, including both Malaita and Choiseul, warfare lasted into the 1920s. Judith A. Bennett, *Wealth of the Solomons: a history of a Pacific archipelago 1800–1978* (Honolulu 1987), 21–44, 112–15; Akin, *Colonialism*, 36–49.

of 'custom' within an encompassing Christian moral universe. Yet despite these inter-sections, customary authority and Christian authority are understood as distinct.

The British protectorate in the Solomons was established in 1893, but decades passed before serious efforts at administration commenced. Initially, the government intervened in 'Native affairs' primarily in cases of violence committed against Europeans; the most intensive interventions occurred in areas such as the western Solomons, where intergroup warfare interfered with the expansion of plantation capitalism. The first Native Administration Regulation came into effect in 1922, with policies of direct rule through government-appointed headmen. Through the 1930s, debates occurred between Solomon Islands-based resident commissioners and their superiors in Fiji about the feasibility of implementing forms of indirect rule, including Native courts and councils staffed by local leaders. Colonial authorities worried that these institutions should not be established without first codifying customary rules, a project thought impossible for the diverse and fragmented polities of Solomon Islands. Throughout the 1930s, colonial officers worked through Native headmen to adjudicate an increasing number of disputes, and beginning in the 1940s, the administration supported the establishment of Native courts, which lacked legal status until 1942. They were established in earnest only after World War II.[46]

Policies of indirect rule, implemented in the Solomons a half century after they were formulated in British Africa as well as Fiji, established the category of 'custom'. Significant differences occur in how Solomon Islanders from different regions have engaged with the notion of 'custom', especially in the degree to which it is opposed to government law. Nevertheless, across the country the 'customary' became the realm over which Islanders themselves could exercise control. Akin has argued that 'indirect rule was set down on Malaita as an empty vessel, and Malaitans seized the opportunity to fill it with "customary" contents to their own liking'. According to Akin, for the people of Malaita, post-war attempts to set up government courts and councils and to expand the delivery of medical and educational services were 'much too little and far too late'; they rejected government courts and councils and created institutions fully in Indigenous control. In the context of Maasina Rule, *kastom* came to include everything that was seen as 'moving forward in a Malaitan way' under the control of Malaitans rather than Europeans.[47] People of the western Solomons were more enthusiastic colonial subjects than most Malaitans, an attitude derived in part from their more privileged position in the colonial political economy. Rather than establishing autonomous *kastom* institutions, most appear to have embraced government courts and councils in the 1940s. Interestingly, the local men involved in Native courts during the era seem to have rarely invoked the notion of 'custom' as distinguished from government law. One of the few references

---

[46] Akin, *Colonialism*, 86–93, 128–31, 50–63; Bennett, *Wealth of the Solomons*, 281; H. Ian Hogbin, 'Native councils and Native courts in the Solomon Islands', *Oceania*, 14:4 (1944), 257–83; H. Ian Hogbin, 'Notes and instructions to Native administrations in the British Solomon Islands', *Oceania*, 16:1 (1945), 61–69.
[47] Akin, *Colonialism*, 6, 163, 210.

to 'custom' in court returns from the Vella Lavella District in the late 1940s appears to have been added by a district officer, who wrote the phrase 'and native customs' to the clerk's description of an offence as 'had connect with mouth of girl which is forbidden in law'.[48] The court returns, prepared by local clerks, made extensive reference to the rule of law and the fact that people were now living in the era of government.

During the post-war period in Ranongga, a new kind of neo-traditional 'customary' authority was consolidated in the interstices of colonial government, missions and commerce. Like Maasina Rule chiefs in Malaita during the same period, the men who embodied this authority were agents of radical change in social life, economic activities and even settlement patterns; their projects were not uncontested but could not have been accomplished without the broad support of the population. Three men dominated the post-war scene on Ranongga: Simion Panakera of Pienuna, George Hilly of Kudu and Niqusasa of Mondo. Panakera and Hilly were among the earliest students of the Methodist mission school of Roviana; Niqusasa was educated through the Seventh-day Adventist mission. Niqusasa and other Seventh-day Adventist leaders relocated residents from settlements on the treacherous west coast to the more accessible (and previously depopulated) northern peninsula of Ranongga, eventually establishing Buri, which is now Ranongga's largest village. George Hilly also undertook a major reconfiguration of the island's population after the earthquake of 1952, resettling many residents of two Methodist villages on the western coast to a new settlement on alienated land that had been leased to a European planter prior to the war. Hilly acquired rights to the land from the district administration on behalf of a cooperative society established for the export of copra.[49] Like Hilly, Panakera was an energetic entrepreneur who acquired rights to large areas of coastal land for copra plantations, which were run with the cooperation of relatives as well as some labourers hired from the eastern Solomons. Both men bought copra from other smallholders, transported it using ships they owned, and ran retail stores described to me as larger than any of the shops in Gizo in the late 1990s. These ventures declined in the 1960s as the government began to support smaller cooperative ventures, and Hilly and Panakera found themselves indebted to Chinese merchants in Gizo. All three men, along with a number of others, including village chief Toribule of Pienuna, held senior positions in the Native administration and Native court for the Vella Lavella District and, after 1957, a separate Ranongga and Simbo court and council. They remained important 'customary' authorities throughout their lives.

The next generation of men who became 'customary authorities' in the 1980s faced changed economic circumstances. Copra was overtaken by timber as the main export commodity of the province and protectorate. While chiefs – refigured as tribal landowners – could capture a greater share of royalty money, logging overall

---

[48] Case no. 5 of 1947, Honiara, Solomon Islands National Archive (hereinafter SINA), British Solomon Islands Protectorate, Office of the District Commissioner for Western District, General Correspondence 1943–1970, Vella LaVella Native Council, BSIP 7/1/DCW/124-127.

[49] Note on Emu Harbour Cooperative Scheme, 13 Jan. 1954, SINA, British Solomon Islands Protectorate, Office of the District Commissioner for Western District, General Correspondence 1943–1970, Emu Harbour Scheme, BSIP 7/1/DCW/130.

undermined the moral authority of chiefs, who became embroiled in bitter and pro-tracted land disputes. A bifurcation also occurred between rural residents and an edu-cated elite able to engage with the state and multinational capital. Small, steep and densely populated, Ranongga was excluded from the frenzy of activity. Relatively uninvolved in the dirty politics of logging, local chiefs retained much of their moral authority, but this moral authority was no longer backed by the ability to make things happen economically.

In some ways, the authority of colonial-era leaders was carried into the national arena as their sons rose to prominence in politics. This is especially notable in the case of George Hilly's son, Francis Billy Hilly, who served as a member of parliament for Ranongga and Simbo for most of the period between 1978 and 2010 and who was prime minister in 1993–94, leading a reform-oriented government.[50] On the local level, though, the 'customary' authority of chiefs and the authority of democratically elected representatives became bifurcated. Local area councils, with elected counsellors, were established in 1981 as the lowest level of government under the provincial government. The explosion of logging on custom-ary land in the early independence period meant that these institutions hardly had the chance to get off the ground. Charged with approving timber rights applications, area councils were quickly swamped with work and compromised by conflicts of interest. Local courts, formerly 'Native courts', were similarly overwhelmed with land disputes. Given that national regulation of logging was severely lacking, a strong argument could have been made for bolstering these institutions. Instead, in the late 1990s, in the context of the Asian economic crisis and pressures from the donor community to cut back state expenditure and undergo a period of structural adjustment, both local courts and local area councils were defunded and eventually eliminated. By the time I first visited Ranongga in 1995, local courts were rarely meeting, and local area councils were not functioning.[51]

One unsuccessful attempt to lessen the pressure on the formal justice system by relying on customary authority is especially interesting to us here because it marks the origin of the Pienuna Chiefs' Committee: the Local Court (Amendment) Act

---

[50] The pattern is evident elsewhere. For example, prominent Guadalcanal politician Ezekiel Alebua is the son of colonial headman Dominiko Alebua. His biography is recounted in Tarcisius Tara Kabutaulaka, *Footprints in the Tasimauri Sea* (Suva 2002).

[51] On forestry, see Judith A. Bennett, *Pacific Forest: a history of resource control and contest in Solomon Islands, c. 1800–1997* (Cambridge 2000); Peter Dauvergne, 'Corporate power in the forests of the Solomon Islands', *Pacific Affairs*, 71:4 (1998–99), 524–46; Ian Frazer, 'The struggle for control of Solomon Island forests', *Contemporary Pacific*, 9:1 (1997), 39–72; Tarcisius Tara Kabutau-laka, 'Global capital and local ownership in Solomon Islands' forestry industry', in Stewart Firth (ed.), *Globalisation and Governance in the Pacific Islands* (Canberra 2006), 239–35. On the demise of area councils, see John Cox and Joanne Morrison on behalf of AusAID, 'Solomon Islands provin-cial governance information paper', Oct.–Nov. 2004, https://www.academia.edu/6746443/Cox_J._and_J._Morrison._2004._Solomon_Islands_Provincial_Governance_Information_Paper (accessed 8 Oct. 2015); Debra McDougall, 'Sub-national governance in post-RAMSI Solomon Islands', State, Society and Governance in Melanesia Program, Working Paper 3 (2014).

1985.[52] The act required claimants to attempt to solve grievances through the mediation of chiefs before approaching the local court. An oft-noted problem with this legislation is that decisions of the chiefs were almost inevitably appealed to the local court. Less attention has been given to the fact that *chiefs were the local court* and had been since the late 1940s. Correspondence among Indigenous members of the Ranongga–Simbo Local Court in the years after the 1985 act reveal their confusion about how the procedures or personnel of the supposedly customary chiefs' councils differed from the procedures and personnel of the local court, which had always been tasked with hearing cases involving 'custom'.[53] A decade after the 'customary' authority of chiefs was disentangled from the formal structures of the state, the formal system was defunded. The Pienuna Chiefs' Committee was the residue of a history of attempts to invoke and structure customary forms of authority within the formal state.[54]

The withdrawal of state support and recognition did not end the work of men who had been involved in local courts and councils. Building on the legacy of their fathers, senior men continued to mediate disputes, as described above. They also sought recognition and relationships with extra-local forces, not only a relatively weak and withdrawing state but also non-governmental organisations that emerged as important actors in the 1990s. Among the latter was WWF (World Wide Fund for Nature), which sought to consolidate customary knowledge for purposes of community conservation and development.[55] In Ranongga, WWF hired an Australian consultant in 1999 to hold a series of meetings to produce a book of 'custom law' and create a 'peak body' of customary authorities, named the Ranongga Simbo Custom Council. The following year, Western Province leaders issued a unilateral declaration of independence to establish the province as a sovereign state. (Though never formally rescinded, the independence of Western Province has not been recognised by the central government or any international actors.) This 'new state' sought to recognise and bolster the customary power of chiefs in rural areas. The Ranongga Simbo Custom Council had not met since it was constituted by WWF; indeed, administrators and elected members of the newly constituted state did not know of its existence until I put administrators in touch with WWF staff to organise a meeting with members of the Ranongga Simbo Custom Council, provincial and state officials, and WWF staff. At that meeting, state officials encouraged the custom council to be self-sufficient, but the questions from the chiefs focused on how they could get recognition and support from the government. One chief from Simbo said that the

---

[52] Also discussed in White, 'The discourse of chiefs', 231.

[53] Chiefs' hearings (partial correspondence of the Pienuna Chiefs' Committee), 1986–90, folder in possession of author.

[54] On the transition from indirect rule to state withdrawal in the realm of policing, see Dinnen and Allen, 'Paradoxes of postcolonial police-building', 225–27.

[55] Ben Burt and Michael Kwaʻioloa, *Falafala Ana Ano 'I Kwaraʻae = The Tradition of Land in Kwaraʻae* (Suva 1992); Michael Kwaʻioloa and Ben Burt, *The Chief's Country*, 49–56; Debra McDougall, 'The unintended consequences of clarification: development, disputing, and the dynamics of community in Ranongga, Solomon Islands', *Ethnohistory*, 52:1 (2005), 81–109.

colonial government recognised chiefs and appointed them as headmen, but since national independence in 1978, politicians have taken the real power and are antagonistic to chiefs. He and others argued that today chiefs are chiefs in name only, without money or power to do their jobs. To my knowledge, that was the last meeting of the Ranongga Simbo Custom Council. Some leaders are aware of the book of 'custom law', but as noted in the discussion of the incest case above, the rules intended to be definitive are often discarded in practice.

By 2006–07, when I returned for further research, the Pienuna Chiefs' Committee was increasingly moribund. Panakera's son Geoffrey Panakera had died in 2005, and a few older men were becoming less active. Jebeti Toribule (son of Pienuna's previous chief Toribule and 'spokesman' for the current chief, John Pavukera) complained that the next generation showed little interest in taking up the work of their fathers; younger men were unwilling to accompany him and learn the art of dispute resolution. The only person who was keen to be mentored was Geoffrey's sister and replacement, Marina Alepio. The WWF project had moved away from attempting to reconstitute customary authority and was focusing on providing technical assistance in monitoring marine resources. Jebeti was working on the rules codified through WWF-sponsored workshops, which he hoped could be registered with the Western Province government as village 'by-laws'. He had also attended some workshops on human rights led by RAMSI. He was, however, weary and struggling to support his own family. Not long after my research trip concluded, Jebeti moved with his entire family to his wife's home on the island of Santa Isabel. In April 2007, a devastating earthquake uplifted Ranongga by several metres. Many older men and women died in the six months following the earthquake, including Samuel Samata, who was healthy, active and not yet 70 when a sudden illness led to his death.

When I returned again to Ranongga in 2010, I was thus surprised to find that a reinvigorated committee was holding a series of day-long meetings to formalise its structure and codify its rules. In a May 2010 meeting, it had been renamed the 'Pienuna Chiefs' Trust Board', officer positions were designated, and 'tribal chiefs' (representing all matrilineal clans of the village) were chosen to be signatories to the bylaws they would enact. I am not entirely sure what caused this reinvigoration: some members had attended workshops in previous months organised by prominent citizens of Gizo with the help of the provincial government. These men had formalised the governance structures and drawn up development plans for their own communities in Marovo Lagoon and were eager to encourage other communities around the province to do the same. Internal community dynamics were also important: the son of one of the most active members of local courts in the previous generation was re-engaged with the work of the community, after nearly a decade of disengagement because of a dispute about the WWF project; an energetic daughter of the former village chief had returned to Pienuna after many years of residence in Honiara.

In the 2010 meetings I attended in June and July, the chairman (Samata's brother Luke Irapio) brought with him to the meetings a 1979 local court handbook as well as a thick folder of material from a meeting of regional chiefs a few months earlier in Gizo, which included development proposals from the so-called 'trust boards' of other communities. Debates concerning the appropriate amount of compensation for various offences and the cash value of *bakia* continued. The tribal chiefs were seen as part of a hierarchy of authority – from the family, to church, to tribal chiefs, to the chiefs' committee, to ward chiefs, and finally to provincial and government law.

A striking feature of these 2010 meetings was the increasing involvement of women as tribal chiefs of their extended families and considerable discussion of issues concerning 'gender equity' and the 'rights of the child'.[56] Women were excluded from customary authority during the colonial period but found opportunities for collective action and leadership through the church;[57] this church leadership has now facilitated their increasing involvement in what had been established as a male realm. Such developments are encouraging insofar as they signal the progressive movement of such 'customary' organisations in rural areas away from the neo-traditional patriarchy of colonial-era customary institutions. It is also possible that women are able to become more involved in customary realms of authority because men no longer see it as an efficacious path to broader influence and authority.[58]

Viewed in light of ongoing attempts by local people to tap into the authority of the state, the chiefs' committee (now chiefs' trust board) is difficult to characterise as resilient. Rather than emphasising the integrity of this system and its ability to absorb change, I have sought to emphasise the tenacious efforts of actors to transform their local communities by gaining recognition and resources from the state and other trans-local actors. The chiefs' committee might be depicted as a resilient traditional institution, but it can also be seen as the result of many years of frustrated attempts to transform the community through engagement with the trans-local institutions.

## Conclusion: The Deep Roots of the Shallow State

Today, throughout the Solomons, one can find a palpable sense of nostalgia for the late colonial era. Like nostalgia in the post-socialist world for the old USSR, nostalgia for colonialism in Solomon Islands must be approached with caution, more as a

---

[56] Elsewhere, men identifying as traditional chiefs have objected to what they see as outsider-driven projects of gender empowerment. See for example Kwa'ioloa and Burt, *The Chief's Country*, 273.

[57] See especially the following articles within Bronwen Douglas (ed.), 'Women's Groups and Everyday Modernities in Melanesia', special issue, *Oceania*, 74:1–2 (2003): Bronwen Douglas, 'Christianity, tradition, and everyday modernity: towards an anatomy of women's groupings in Melanesia', 6–23; Regina Scheyvens, 'Church women's groups and the empowerment of women in Solomon Islands', 24–43; Alice Aruhe'eta Pollard, 'Women's organisations, volunteerism, and self-financing in Solomon Islands: a participant perspective', 44–60; Debra McDougall, 'Fellowship and citizenship as models of national community: United Church Women's Fellowship in Ranongga, Solomon Islands', 61–80.

[58] Debra McDougall, 'Tired for nothing? Women, chiefs, and the domestication of customary authority in Solomon Islands', in Margaret Jolly and Hyaeweol Choi (eds), *Divine Domesticities: paradoxes of Christianity in the Asia Pacific* (Canberra 2014), 199–246.

critique of the present than a real desire to return to the past. The nostalgia is possible, in part, because the colonial administration that people today remember is not the administration that shelled their villages in the late 19th century or extracted head taxes without providing services in the early 20th century. After World War II, the colonial administration was finally beginning to put resources into service delivery, to establish schools and health clinics, and to expand the possibilities for Islander engagement in their own government. Such changes were a response to new directives from London but also, as Akin has argued, a response to Solomon Islanders' own mobilisation to demand government that would serve them, a mobilisation that began in the 1930s and culminated with the post-war Maasina Rule movement of Malaita and the south-eastern Solomons.[59] Even in areas where such protest movements were less influential, the post-World War II era was a time of relative optimism about possibilities for societal transformation.

Since Solomon Islands gained independence in 1978, dramatic transformations have occurred but not in ways many people hoped. Politicians are criticised as corrupt, interested only in monopolising power and wealth. The state is understood as oriented towards international donors and multinational corporations instead of its own citizens. This dissatisfaction is not limited to individuals outside the state. Civil servants and provincial politicians express frustration with the centralisation of government resources in Honiara and the expansion of politician-administered constituency development funds.[60] Allen has suggested that part of the reason for the violent conflict that began in 1998 was Guadalcanal people and Malaitans 'reaching the limit of their historical frustration with the state'.[61] The problem with 'resilience' as a metaphor for understanding state/society dynamics is that it directs our attention away from this frustration.

Even in its postcolonial absence, the state shapes expectations about what the socio-political order ought to be. Observers have depicted the modern state in Solomon Islands as an 'overlay' on top of 'resilient' Indigenous institutions – a sort of veneer that can be, for better or worse, easily peeled off. I have argued that modern forms of bureaucracy and the overarching authority of the state is no mere overlay. Somewhat paradoxically, the persistent desire for state recognition of customary authority and widespread frustration about the state's absence points to the importance of the state in communities. Discussing what he has aptly dubbed 'the deep roots of the shallow state', Thiago Opperman has noted that scholars have long documented the 'upward colonisation' of the state by segmentary lineages and other Indigenous socio-political formations. Less attention has been paid to the ways in which formal bureaucratic structures of state government have colonised the life worlds of ordinary villagers in Melanesia. As Opperman has discussed in a case study from Bougainville, even though the state is experienced as an external (if not entirely absent) force in their lives, villagers enact the function of the state in myriad para-state organisations in their

---

[59] Akin, *Colonialism*, 150–63.
[60] Debra McDougall, 'Sub-national governance'.
[61] Matthew G. Allen, *Greed and Grievance: ex-militants' perspectives on the conflict in Solomon Islands, 1998–2003* (Honolulu 2013), 179.

own communities. The fact that they often feel that they are 'faking it' should not detract us from the profound transformation of socio-political relations that has occurred.[62]

Critics of the state-centric assumptions intrinsic to projects of neoliberal state-building are right to point out the strengths of local socio-political institutions. I have argued here that these institutions should not be understood as hitherto more-or-less autonomous entities only beginning to be integrated into the state but as structures that have emerged over generations of engagement with the state apparatus. Pointing out this history of entanglement does not diminish the importance of the work that individuals and groups such as the Pienuna Chiefs' Committee do, nor does it contradict local understandings that they are customary. Far from being part of resilient, more-or-less self-contained systems that have maintained their shape against external forces, customary authorities in the Solomons and elsewhere in the Pacific have tenaciously sought to harness the power of the state and have, in the process, incorporated its modes of organisation into local lives.

[62] Thiago Opperman, introduction, Australian National University, 2014 State of the Pacific Conference, session on 'New forms of local governance and justice', 18 June 2014; Thiago Cintra Oppermann, 'Fake it until you make it: searching for mimesis in Buka village politics', *Oceania*, 85:2 (2015), 199–218.

# Big Money in the Rural: Wealth and Dispossession in Western Solomons Political Economy

## EDVARD HVIDING

## ABSTRACT

This paper discusses the multiple ways in which rural economic wealth in the New Georgia islands of the western Solomons has been built up in both ephemeral and enduring ways through several decades of intensive industrial logging on customary lands. The scale of wealth accumulation in the rural western Solomons and the often associated process of dispossession of communal natural resource rights are rarely taken into account in discussions of political economy in early 21st-century Solomon Islands. Through this paper, changing configurations and trajectories of accumulation and dispossession are traced. The comparison of two distinctly different processes whereby collective social agency over customary land is weakened, ultimately for accumulation in the hands of a few, involves a discussion about the centralisation and disintegration, respectively, of customary chieftainship in New Georgia. This leads to a more general assessment of how authority over customary land in Melanesia can be the subject of large-scale dispossession.

## LAND TENURE, LEGISLATION AND FORMS OF LAND GRAB IN MELANESIA

While the Pacific Islands region may lend itself to views of smallness, remoteness and insularity, alternative perceptions of interisland relations and global connectedness have gained analytical force.[1] In fact, nothing is inherently small or isolated about a vast maritime region of historically, socially, culturally and economically connected

*Acknowledgements*: I am grateful to four anonymous readers, to the JPH editors and to the guest editors of this collection for insightful critical comments.

[1] See for example Epeli Hau'ofa, 'Our sea of islands', in Eric Waddell, Vijay Naidu and Epeli Hau'ofa (eds), *A New Oceania: rediscovering our sea of islands* (Suva 1993), 2–16, reprinted in *Contemporary Pacific*, 6:1 (1994), 148–61; Edvard Hviding and Knut M. Rio (eds), *Made in Oceania: social movements, cultural heritage and the state in the Pacific* (Wantage, UK 2011); Nicholas Thomas, *Islanders: the Pacific in the Age of Empire* (New Haven 2011).

islands and continental margins.[2] At the Pacific Islands region's south-western edge of Melanesia, where the majority of Pacific Islanders live, cultural diversity and rapidly accelerating global connections of political economy, with high financial stakes, falsify any notion of 'smallness'. In Melanesia, intense processes of 'compressed globalization' – whereby diverse, large-scale connections of global scope are initiated and engaged in locally by few participants on the ground – generate new forms of inequality in interaction with the global political economy in the starkest sense.[3]

From this starting point, I examine present processes of 'accumulation by dispossession'[4] in a corner of the world perhaps most notable in political terms for its socially generous distribution of various forms of entitlements to productive resources, particularly land. With recent examples from New Georgia in the western Solomon Islands, I discuss how large-scale economic wealth in rural Melanesia can be built up in both ephemeral and enduring ways through sustained global connections with logging companies. I compare two different local trajectories towards weakened collective social agency over customary land, culminating in accumulation of such agency in the hands of a few. This leads to a discussion about centralisation and disintegration, respectively, of customary chieftainship in New Georgia. While the western Solomons situation is of course one of specific configurations, the examples I give invoke more general arguments about how authority over customary land in Melanesia, though not necessarily the land itself, is the subject of increasing large-scale dispossession.

In Melanesia, territories of land and groups of people have shared histories and generate each other. The land is held by small groups of rural people related through diverse forms of kinship as their inalienable ancestral estate, a privilege that is not just historically conditioned but also, in the legislation of the independent nations of the region, to some degree constitutionally enshrined. Papua New Guinea and Solomon Islands demonstrate particularly dense and complex political economies grounded in natural resource wealth with a particular emphasis on the large but rapidly diminishing stands of rainforest trees that provide the basis for a transnational logging economy.[5] With reference to national legislation and to diverse localised customs that are variations on shared underlying themes, such, then, is the idealised

[2]See for example Paul D'Arcy, *The People of the Sea: environment, identity, and history in Oceania* (Honolulu 2006); Hau'ofa, 'Our sea of islands'; Marshall Sahlins, 'Cosmologies of capitalism: the trans-Pacific sector of "the world system"', *Proceedings of the British Academy*, 74 (1988), 1–51; Marshall Sahlins, 'Goodbye to *tristes tropes*: ethnography in the context of modern world history', *Journal of Modern History*, 65:1 (1993), 1–25.

[3]Edvard Hviding, 'Compressed globalization and expanding desires in Marovo Lagoon, Solomon Islands', in Signe Howell and Aud Talle (eds), *Returns to the Field: multitemporal research and contemporary anthropology* (Bloomington 2012), 203–29. See also Deborah Gewertz and Frederick Errington, 'Why we return to Papua New Guinea', *Anthropological Quarterly*, 70:3 (1997), 127–36.

[4]David Harvey, *The New Imperialism* (Oxford 2003).

[5]For the Solomons, see for example Peter Dauvergne, 'Corporate power in the forests of the Solomon Islands', *Pacific Affairs*, 71:4 (1999), 524–46; Ian Frazer, 'The struggle for control of Solomon Islands forests', *Contemporary Pacific*, 9:1 (1997), 44–52.

Melanesian condition: the Indigenous people themselves control nearly all land, as well as constituting the legislative and state powers. But many recent reports from Papua New Guinea detail alarming rates of transformation of title to customary land, as well as of the land itself and the resources that grow on it and are located under its surface. This is referred to as the Papua New Guinea 'land-grab' situation.[6] Corrupt and/or defunct national and local government, financially strong multinational resource extraction corporations, the complicity of national police with corporate capitalist powers, and local land-holding groups in different states of political disintegration and social disarray provide the fuel for increasingly large-scale dispossession of resources on customary land in parts of Papua New Guinea. Dispossession not only of the natural resources but also of control over the land itself is the further result of new, insidious schemes of land lease that disempower customary landholding groups.

   This bleak picture is in part a function of scale, given that, among the Melanesian nations, Papua New Guinea has by far the largest state apparatus, with associated similarly large-scale forces of military and police. With the forces of state and capitalist corporations joining hands, constitutionally enshrined local privileges over customary land are hollowed out. The undermining of local control over customary land is further exacerbated when representatives of landholding rural groups themselves engage in complicity with external resource-grabbing agents or succumb to the windfall cash offered to them in return for gaining access to the land and its resources.[7] A multiplicity of agents, including Melanesian landholders themselves, thus contribute to what in some cases amounts to massive dispossession of land that has for many generations constituted the very foundation of independent and resilient rural ways of life. The complexities involved suggest forcefully that contemporary Melanesian relations to and contestations over land and natural resources are not so much about the apparently simple, although diverse, colonial construct of 'land tenure' but rather about highly complicated interactions between socialities and materialities of local and global scales. Present-day dispossession in Melanesia, then, takes on both directly material and more opaque non-material forms.

## ACCUMULATING RURAL AGENCY IN THE LOGGING ECONOMY

In order to expand comparatively on the study of forms of dispossession concerning customary land in Melanesia, it is the nation of Solomon Islands I discuss here, with a particular focus on lands on which extensive logging continues to be carried out after several decades of such operations in the New Georgia group of the western Solomons. I start with a by-now standardised anecdote from the rural

[6]See for example Colin Filer, 'The new land grab in Papua New Guinea', paper presented at the International Conference on Global Land Grabbing, University of Sussex, 7 Apr. 2011.
[7]See for example Andrew Lattas and Knut M. Rio, 'Securing modernity: towards an ethnography of power in contemporary Melanesia', *Oceania*, 81:1 (2011), 1–21; Edvard Hviding and Tim Bayliss-Smith, *Islands of Rainforest: agroforestry, logging and eco-tourism in Solomon Islands* (Aldershot 2000).

Melanesian hinterlands of the Solomons, where people have never really seen government investment in infrastructure, and where the feeling of being left out from access to good things of the modern world remain strong. The short anecdote, told by Solomon Islanders to refer to an iconic, small, standardised event, goes like this (although not entirely, because it is so much more incisive in Solomon Islands Pijin): 'A middle-aged man says to his teenage son, "Drink, son, drink beer, drink as much as you like, for I am LO"'.

Although sustained beer drinking in the remote rural Solomons is in any event quite a new thing worthy of note, it is the 'LO' designation that I wish to highlight. LO emerged as a popular term in Solomon Islands during the so-called 'logging boom' of the 1990s when the largely uncontrolled export of round logs became the mainstay of the national economy,[8] and also had some of its roots in the events surrounding the Australian-operated Gold Ridge mine on the island of Guadalcanal. Quite simply, LO stands for land owner. From being an acronym associated with individual signatures on agreements whereby collectively held customary land was opened up for large-scale resource extraction by foreign companies, LO soon became a derisory term to refer to the tendency of many who made such signatures on behalf of their entire kin group of collective holders of customary land rapidly to forget their relatives when money started coming in. Such strategic omissions of the social collective first occurred in the monopolisation of easy-to-appropriate 'signature' payments from Asian logging companies, and then escalated as increasingly contested royalty payments channelled directly into the bank accounts of a few signatories (or LOs) for each shipload of round logs sent to Asia.

Quite simply, then, what the 'Drink, son' anecdote refers to is the widespread feeling of limitless access to cash for consumption among those few who have swindled the majority of their fellow land-holders, those who for some time called themselves LOs without realising the emerging parallel connotation of ridicule and harsh social critique. It is for this reason, and to highlight the mutually constitutive roles of inalienable customary land and the people attached to it through history, that I replace the term 'land owners' with 'land-holders' throughout this paper, except in those cases where I invoke the scathing commentary invented by Melanesians themselves for those who appropriate the common good.[9] The 1990s concept of LO has faded somewhat, and in more recent times it is not so much money that is being appropriated in a centralised fashion as it is the very control over customary land itself. On the other hand, the LO concept also gained additional currency in the late 1990s, as the island of Guadalcanal was vernacularised as Isatabu and was seen by its customary land-holding groups as having been egregiously taken over in stages by the colonial power, the post-colonial state and labour migrants and other settlers from the neighbouring island of Malaita. The civil unrest, which from 1998 escalated into localised armed skirmishes and a coup in 2000 that brought the

---

[8]See Judith A. Bennett, *Pacific Forest: a history of resource control and contest in Solomon Islands, c. 1800–1997* (Cambridge and Leiden 2000); Hviding and Bayliss-Smith, *Islands of Rainforest*.

[9]This analytical use of 'land-holder' for the Solomons is more widespread, as also seen in Bennett, *Pacific Forest*. Also see Monson in this issue.

Solomon Islands state to collapse and the national economy to a near standstill, was grounded in underlying resentments focused on the perceived dispossession by exogenous agents of major parts of the island of Isatabu/Guadalcanal.[10]

In the Solomons, customary land amounts to about 87% of the total land mass. This is less than PNG's 97% but still overwhelmingly significant. The remaining 13% consists of a few urban centres and a small number of sizeable forestry plantations and intensive agriculture areas established by the colonial government on land that had been unpopulated since the deadly climax of inter- and intra-island warfare in the late 19th century. An estimated current Solomon Islands population of 570,000 and a total land mass of 28,370 square kilometres give a population-to-land ratio of only about 20 per square kilometre. Yet this figure is misleading in many actual cases of relationships between customary land and its customary holders: for example, a land-holding kin group in New Georgia that I know well has about 250 residents on about as many square kilometres of land.

Large-scale logging has been the foundation of the Solomon Islands economy since the 1990s. Timber exports in the form of round unprocessed logs from customary land earns up to 80% of foreign exchange in any given year, despite the fact that illegal tax exemptions have been rife.[11] Round-log exports are, moreover, widely known to be underreported by their largely Asian exporters, which also influences the already low timber royalty rates paid by logging companies to the customary 'owners' who have given them access to the land and its trees under the national government's so-called Standard Logging Agreement. Nevertheless, the royalties that do emerge invariably amount to what for most rural villagers are astronomical sums. In one stark example that I recorded, the routine everyday horizon of economic aspiration among the people of a particular small kin group of about 200 persons in the Marovo Lagoon increased over six years by a factor of about 3,000. This extraordinary multiplication represented the celebration in pre-logging times (1996) of what was then seen as a profitable effort of several days of communal work, and – six years later – the legal engagement post-logging (2002) of representatives of that kin group in the contested stakes of a timber royalty account temporarily frozen by the High Court. For these Solomon Islanders, the horizon of financial expectation rose over this period from SI$700 in 1996 to more than 2 million of that currency in 2002. They are certainly not alone among Melanesians to experience such staggering expansive transformation of economic desire.

No wonder, then, that the operations in Solomon Islands of Asian logging companies that – despite a remarkable level of continuous economic swindling – generate royalties to customary landholders of several million dollars from only one or two log shipments are often warmly received locally. After all, the 82% majority of Solomon Islanders who still live in villages without access to much in the way of

---

[10]Jon Fraenkel, *The Manipulation of Custom: from uprising to intervention in the Solomon Islands* (Wellington 2004); Clive Moore, *Happy Isles in Crisis: the historical causes for a failing state in the Solomon Islands, 1998–2004* (Canberra 2004); Matthew Allen, *Greed and Grievance: ex-militants' perspectives on the conflict in Solomon Islands, 1998–2003* (Honolulu 2013).

[11]Dauvergne, 'Corporate power'.

modern infrastructure have never seen any meaningful local contribution from the state. Instead, since the 1990s it has been logging royalties that have in the rural Solomons funded churches and schools, rural water supplies, innumerable outboard motors and much rapid, conspicuous consumption of very large sums of cash. It is the latter that has received the strongest attention, usually through the unscrupulous (and, some would say, antisocial though cunning) manoeuvring of LOs. It is fair to say that, with a few major exceptions, the greatest proportion of the quite extraordinarily large sums of money represented by royalties paid by logging companies to land-holder representatives in Solomon Islands has in fact disappeared rather quickly on LO-led urban hyper-consumption. These developments have contributed to a combination of social disruption, surprising and sometimes surreal connections between Islanders and capitalists of Indigenous and foreign kinds, a centralisation of decision-making power over land, and a form of dispossession that, I shall argue, applies most of all to the level of collective social agency.

The situation summarised above, with real and quick consumption of unreal sums of money, social conflict and rapid transformation of political economy, is of quite a general nature in the Solomons. It constitutes a rather gloomy example of what I have elsewhere referred to as 'compressed globalization and expanding desires',[12] which has been so characteristic of the Marovo Lagoon area of New Georgia where I have carried out fieldwork intermittently since 1986. Much grievance on the local level tends to receive little attention on the national level, though.

A significant exception to this lack of national political voice against logging is the vibrant popular music scene in the Solomons, which experienced massive expansion during the 1990s and into the 21st century, and which has attained a large following also in Papua New Guinea and elsewhere in the region. Performing and recording artists, mainly from those areas in the western Solomons where logging and its associated ills reached the highest levels, have provided scathing social commentary on both the rural and urban scenes where logging money flows. In veteran musician Ian Roni's particularly well-known song 'Mama karae' from the late 1990s, perceptive and at the time provocative lyrics have 'daddy' engaging in a combination of domestic abuse and high spending outside the household, in blatant defiance of customary family obligations. And so 'mama' can only cry for the way she is beaten by her husband, the children are ignored and the social collective is destroyed – despite the money that appears to be available to an only intermittently employed 'daddy' (it may be surmised he has access to logging money from his rural customary land). Probably the best example of direct (and hugely popular) musical critique of the destruction of both land and social relations through the logging economy is the 2007 song 'Why' by Ronnie Riti (sometimes known as Paeva) from the Marovo Lagoon. The song is mainly a heavy reggae dub with a ranting commentary in English and vernacular about the sorrowful engagement of Solomon Islanders in fights over land and money, but it opens very differently, with a line sung twice a capella in the artist's own vernacular, firmly directed at his relatives back home: '*Kagu omia ra mineka – pa kogu dola gua. Vinarajai puava gete, gete va susua!*' (I cannot see unity – as I look at the

---

[12]Hviding, 'Compressed globalization and expanding desires'.

lagoon. Fighting over land abounds, in excess!) Such songs by politically committed artists, with dirge-like content but upbeat, listener-friendly arrangements, see constant radio play and dense sharing as MP3 files. They have long provided important public commentary in a context where national and provincial politicians and government are seen as largely complicit with the logging industry.

Back, then, to the question of accumulation by dispossession. It is not the land as such that is subject to dispossession under these circumstances – so far, no external powers have been able to evict any Solomon Islanders from their ancestral customary land. Unlike the 'resource owners' of rural Papua New Guinea (or indeed the customary holders of prime coastal land in Vanuatu), their counterparts in the Solomons have not experienced much in the way of violation of rights by police and paramilitary forces paving the way for corporate transgression onto customary land. Rather, what is being lost through a particular process of accumulation centralised in the hands of a few is the local agency of collective organisation, underpinned by the principles of tradition and, indeed, of 'customary land tenure' held jointly across an entire kin-based land-owning group. As transnational logging corporations gain access to customary land, the very foundations of customary land management in the Solomons are eroded and centralised in the hands of those select few.

## THE DISPOSSESSION OF COLLECTIVE AGENCY IN NEW GEORGIA

In his model of accumulation by dispossession, David Harvey builds on Rosa Luxemburg and Karl Marx and notes how Marx's model of primitive accumulation 'suggests some lacunae that need to be remedied'.[13] He further proposes that 'primitive accumulation … entails appropriation and co-optation of pre-existing cultural and social achievements as well as confrontation and supercession'.[14] Although Harvey proposes this expanded argument for diverse contexts of working-class formation, the appropriation of 'cultural and social achievements' applies equally well to present-day developments in Melanesia. In the following account, I examine how certain non-material 'achievements' of socially corporate customary agency – indeed the very core of Melanesian sociality – are the objects of accumulation by dispossession. It is the agency over customary land and the resources on and in it, held and exercised collectively by kin groups, that concerns us here.

Over the past 20 years, I have been observing the development of two very distinct but totally contrasting scenarios for the dispossession of collective agency in New Georgia: one connected to the wholesale disappearance of customary chiefs and the fragmented disorganisation of land-holding cognatic kin groups called *butubutu*, and another connected to the unprecedented elevation of customary chieftainship and consequent intense centralisation of power over the combined lands of many different *butubutu*. The results of both processes as they can be encountered on the ground today are more or less the same, though: a severely diminished capacity

[13]Harvey, *The New Imperialism*, 146.
[14]Ibid.

of the actual land-holding groups to wield collective influence over their lands and the resources therein. Where the two processes differ is in the social distribution of financial income from the logging that takes place. And so a general pattern is discernible, whereby the land and its resources remain in local hands and apparently under customary control, while the social distribution of political power over land has been subject to quite radical transformations. Since the 1990s, the power to manage customary land collectively has been subject to centralised accumulation in the hands of a few, amounting to the dispossession of the larger public of the agency that since precolonial days has engaged the members of land-holding groups collectively in the use and management of their customary land.

'Accumulation by dispossession' may thus not be such a contrived concept after all in the rural Solomons, where rural people's own collective control over customary land is a principle enshrined in the national constitution and where social borders between the public and the private seem not to exist as such. It is not generally assumed that tribal people in Melanesia engage in privatisation for the accumulation of capital. Yet this scenario certainly has its own trajectories in New Georgia, where accumulation (of the financial benefits brought by large-scale logging) has a non-material origin in several distinct forms of centralised appropriation of land-holding agency.

This is, in turn, grounded in implications for the cosmological mechanisms of New Georgia's regionally remarkable, strong institutions of social rank, hierarchy and hereditary chieftainship – institutions that have remained at the core of the social politics of land controlled by kin groups through custom. A non-material channel for accumulation by dispossession is suggested, in the sense that what is accumulated is social potential, closely connected to customary land but not of a directly material form. Unlike in most other parts of Solomon Islands, where patri- or matrilineal forms of descent and inheritance dominate, kinship in much of New Georgia is bilateral, and genealogies of descent and succession are usually cognatic.[15] Through much inter-island exchange, including marriage, sociality is generated and power is accumulated from a variety of external and internal sources simultaneously. This fluidity of the social builds a fundamental premise for the chief as the one who mediates the connections and holds them together in a sea of travel, movement and exchange, and open-ended sociality. The chief mediates between the realms; he manages the required flow of continuous traffic into the local of things, people and ideas from other shores, a traffic that in precolonial times also involved a prescribed cycle of feasting and of predatory raiding and headhunting to overseas destinations.[16] Herein lies the New Georgian chief's traditional position of social elevation, perpetuated by

[15]Edvard Hviding, 'Disentangling the *butubutu* of New Georgia: cognatic kinship in thought and action', in Ingjerd Hoëm and Sidsel Roalkvam (eds), *Oceanic Socialities and Cultural Forms: ethnographies of experience* (Oxford 2003), 71–113.

[16]For an analysis of the inter-island history of New Georgia societies, see Edvard Hviding, 'Across the New Georgia group: A.M. Hocart's fieldwork as inter-island practice', in Edvard Hviding and Cato Berg (eds), *The Ethnographic Experiment: A.M. Hocart and W.H.R. Rivers in Island Melanesia, 1908* (Oxford 2014), 71–107.

primogeniture in a system of hereditary succession, thus building a social cosmology where historically generated chiefly lineages have remained in a privileged position into the present.

New Georgian chiefs are thus the social hubs of the New Georgians' expansive inter-island world. Their powerful presence and organisational effort are in capacities of dedicated, knowledgeable caretakers of otherwise potentially chaotic socialities of far-reaching inter-island relations and bilateral kinship. Typically the hereditary chief of a New Georgian *butubutu* emerges as a knowledgeable central actor on occasions of funerary gathering, at which participants arrive from near and far. In the oratory of high speech, the chief will give a detailed exposition, on behalf of the hosts from whose group the deceased was, of why everyone is there. This, in effect, becomes a particularly strong statement of the bilaterality of kinship ordered in relation to the deceased person, to his or her *butubutu*, to the land in question and to the combined history of (homonymous) territory and people. But the New Georgian chief does not work on his own, and a narrow centralisation of power has not been generally characteristic of the chiefly institutions. Since the old days of warfare and headhunting and into the 21st century, the chief of any *butubutu* has exercised his given power over land and people (the latter being relatives of descent and affiliation as well as affines) in close cooperation with a set of spokespersons, work organisers, and religious and secular functionaries, and, notionally, in constant support-giving dialogue with every household head of the resident *butubutu*.

In this sense, customary land-holders are traditionally obliged to forge and maintain a sustainable collective of land managers, headed by the chief but with widely shared responsibility mostly among the male members of each *butubutu*, to the degree that a wayward chief may be corrected and in some cases replaced, usually by one of his brothers deemed by the *butubutu* to be more responsible. It is this complex mosaic of power in a fundamentally hierarchical social system that has been impacted by the saturation of social life by logging. While the colonial administration in the Solomons made some half-hearted efforts to appoint Africa-style headmen, the group-type leadership characteristic of the land-holding *butubutu* level was not significantly affected.

I now discuss in more detail the two contrasting processes that I am observing through regular field visits to the western Solomons. The contrasts are rather clearly arranged over religious division, in the patterns wrought by a hundred-year-old history of interactions among Christianity, mission and Indigenous social orders.[17] Notably, the Marovo Lagoon is a stronghold of Seventh-day Adventism (SDA) in the Pacific Islands. The SDA faith, with its fundamentalist tenets and egalitarian institutions, was initially introduced to Marovo Lagoon in 1916 during intense rivalry with the Methodist Mission, which had arrived there a few years earlier. The preferences of local power wielders also played an important role: offering English as a school language and promising a later Marovo Bible translation, the SDA missionaries efficiently gained supremacy over their Methodist counterparts, who relied on the

---

[17]Edvard Hviding, *Guardians of Marovo Lagoon: practice, place, and politics in maritime Melanesia* (Honolulu 1996), 118–24.

vernacular language of the neighbouring Roviana Lagoon, a Methodist stronghold since 1902. The SDA faith was taken on rapidly by a lagoon-wide network dominated by the last warrior chiefs of the notorious coastal-dwelling head-hunters of Marovo. Regional social life across the Marovo Lagoon then developed according to a dual structure with SDAs and Methodists (later United Church) leading separate lives reinforced by mutual distrust and regional endogamy.

In the 1950s, the Methodists of New Georgia split with the emergence of the Christian Fellowship Church (known as the CFC), a prophetic movement that under its mantra of 'new life' and its complex social model of 'fellowship' led a secretive communalist life in remote parts of New Georgia until quietly moving into central economic and political positions in the late 1990s when the nation was in a situation of government collapse.[18] This deft move was masterminded by the original CFC prophet's son and successor, the Revd Ikan Rove KBE, who until his death in 2014 was designated both as a high customary chief, with supreme control over the combined lands of all *butubutu* who follow the church, and as the CFC's very own 'Spiritual Authority', actually seen as the earthly manifestation of the Holy Spirit.

The two dominant churches can be looked at from the vantage point of the logging boom of late 20th-century New Georgia and by examining the divergent implications of logging: for the CFC areas, massive financial accumulation and durable hierarchical organisation, and for the SDA areas, little economic gain and the fragmentation and erosion of customary forms of authority. The SDA church, once the pre-eminent modernist movement in Marovo Lagoon, at times rivalling the 'industrial mission' of Methodist strongman Revd J.F. Goldie, has today fallen into institutional obscurity, with very few, if any, major rural projects under its own management. An even worse decline has been experienced by the United Church, which in its past form as the Methodist Mission was once the epitome of a well-organised association, oriented towards large-scale rural development and sensitive to local world views, but which is today hardly present in the rural organisational field outside the interconnected village churches. Meanwhile the CFC, once denigrated as a cult with heathen proclivities, now successfully pursues unprecedented large-scale development agendas across rural New Georgia.

For a comparative understanding of the present-day SDA areas of central and southern Marovo Lagoon, I propose an inverted play on Roger Keesing's old article 'Chiefs in a chiefless society', in which peculiar circumstances of leadership among the egalitarian Kwaio of Malaita were discussed.[19] I suggest the concept of 'chieflessness in a chiefly society' from the historically contrasted case of the western Solomons, where ranked cognatic descent groups, hereditary chiefs, and large-scale inter-island systems

[18]Edvard Hviding, 'Re-placing the state in the western Solomon Islands: the political rise of the Christian Fellowship Church', in Edvard Hviding and Knut M. Rio (eds), *Made in Oceania: social movements, cultural heritage and the state in the Pacific* (Wantage, UK 2011), 51–89.

[19]Roger M. Keesing, 'Chiefs in a chiefless society: the ideology of modern Kwaio politics', *Oceania*, 38:4 (1968), 276–80. For comparative materials on chieftainship in Oceania, see Geoffrey M. White and Lamont Lindstrom (eds), *Chiefs Today: traditional Pacific leadership and the postcolonial state* (Stanford 1997).

of exchange and warfare have been the dominant social order. In a context where the privilege of chiefly position is to be conferred by an ageing chief on his heir, increased present-day disruption of such prescribed succession has led to many cases of resource-holding kin groups with weak, even minimal, leadership and a loss of capacity to deal collectively with the onslaught of transnational logging companies.

In the wider New Georgia area, such erosion of chiefly authority in the context of large-scale resource extraction has also led to massive acceleration of disputes over land among different claimants to influential membership in land-holding *butubutu*. Despite such challenges, a great number of logging operations commenced on SDA land during the 1990s. With the majority of the involved land-holding groups having no resident chief, however, since most younger chiefs had become members of an absentee urban elite, a lack of planning and overly loose agreements have resulted in a chaotic picture, where almost every single land-holding SDA group has engaged its own company from among the plethora of trans-nationals and national subsidiaries on the scene. This social and economic chaos is topographically and ecologically inscribed on the SDA lands of the Marovo Lagoon, where a dense and confused pattern of logging roads and shipment ponds mar the hills and coastlines. In 2005 I observed approximately one log shipment pond for every four kilometres of coastline in the Bareke hills of central Marovo, whereas in the CFC areas of northern Marovo, the log shipment ponds were up to 20 kilometres apart, and the logging road network appeared much more orderly.

In most cases without chief, a small number of entrepreneurial individuals, not necessarily with chiefly connections in the internal hierarchy of their *butubutu*, have come forth and signed the logging agreements with the company and in turn have obtained control over the bank accounts into which contract-signing payments and timber royalties are paid. The majority of their *butubutu* relatives have seen little economic benefit beyond some conspicuous consumption, outboard motor purchases and permanent house building. Instead they have experienced land erosion, destruction of garden land and other side effects of logging. In many cases I have noted how this neglected rural majority laid surprisingly little claim to decision-making power, not interfering in the often ruthless manoeuvres of their mostly urban-based entrepreneurial relatives. A large amount of power over customary land (and its economic benefit) then accumulates in the hands of a few, effectively dis-possessing the majority of their collective agency.

This pattern is strikingly dissimilar from the large tracts of land in northern and western New Georgia controlled by the CFC, where centralised hereditary leadership has continued, grounded in deep structures of local cultural heritage adapted to the present.[20] What are the sources and courses of these diverging paths in recent western Solomons history? The Indigenous CFC – whose history now exceeds 50 years – succeeds in looking after its members 'from before they are born until after they are dead', as is commented locally. Its consolidation of fragmented kin-based authority organises customary land-owning groups in large-scale ways

[20]Hviding, 'Re-placing the state in the western Solomon Islands'.

that lack parallels elsewhere in the Solomons. The financial system of the CFC manages flows of logging-generated resource revenue from the periphery of customary land-holding *butubutu* to the centre of church leadership. A range of self-initiated economic development projects are operated by the various arms of the CFC organisation, through an approach that avoids collaboration with NGOs and refuses most outside aid and instead relies on its own funding in the form of accumulated logging royalties. One logging operation – and the CFC has over the years managed a great deal of them – routinely generates SI$2–3 million in royalties to the customary land-holding group(s) under contract.

The 'secret of the CFC', church leaders point out, is not just the widely reputed higher-than-usual royalty rates negotiated. More significantly, all of the royalty money is kept outside the village economy. The CFC runs a complicated system of redistribution, where centrally accumulated wealth from royalties accruing to constituent land-holding *butubutu* is used to provide educational, health and administrative services to church members and their villages. But this well-oiled Indigenous machine, with its deeply centralised leadership model and a leader elevated to god-like status, has not been entirely beneficial for the sustainability of collective agency concerning the land. In fact, the lack of initiative, and fear of doing something that may anger the Spiritual Authority (who was notionally entitled to veto any proposed activity on the lands of the CFC and who was considered also to possess strong malevolent powers), has caused collective agency to evaporate, although in a manner entirely different from the way it has evaporated among the SDAs. With the long sickness of the Spiritual Authority, and his death on 8 June 2014, new configurations of power have been developing in the CFC, including the growth of a somewhat secretive group of 'advisers' who surrounded the ailing Revd Rove and a somewhat debilitating conflict between this group and the Revd Rove's politically influential younger brother, Job Dudley Tausinga, a 30-year veteran member of parliament since 1984. It remains to be seen how the transition of spiritual and economic power to the late Revd Rove's two designated sons will develop from the present Weberian-like crisis in the succession of charismatic authority, and whether the factional split will endure. In any case, the CFC cornerstones of centralised leadership and financial management, including subsistence-based rural self-reliance, do not appear to be contested, and no large-scale return of decision-making power over land to the 'ordinary people' is envisaged.

CHIEFS AND DISAPPEARING COLLECTIVITIES

From these New Georgia examples, we should aim to understand Melanesian forms of chieftainship as being concerned with much more than the organisation and redistribution of material production. When the chief is in fact seen as the caretaker of the social, the significance of that role surpasses the concerns of economy and underpins the foundations of rural social life with many connections to the urban. A proper chiefly performance promises to generate, as it were, social ontology itself. And so, while the 'fellowship' of the CFC approximates total relationality subsumed in the accumulated agency of centralised leadership to the degree where collective land-holding power is usurped, the enduring role of any New Georgian chief in upholding the circumstances for relation-making provides a rationale for chieftainship in terms of managing sociality itself. Conversely, when and where no chief exists, collective agency over land can be usurped by unscrupulous relatives not necessarily entitled to its supreme control, who then deploy the agency that they have accumulated in the service of personally profitable projects that channel money away from the rural.

Economics notwithstanding, what work could be more important than maintaining and developing the very foundations of society? This, in essence, is the problem when chiefless land-holding *butubutu* in New Georgia are challenged to deal directly with logging companies. Without a legitimate organiser of collective social responses, someone to speak for and about the land and the people at the highest level, that level of collectivity is easily lost. Power is soon centralised in the hands of a few who have expertise in dealing with companies – but who have little or no obligation to act on behalf of the *butubutu* as a collective. Conversely, circumstances that allow for an extraordinary strengthening of chiefly control over land through centralisation, as in the case of the CFC, also lead to the accumulation of collective agency by its dispossession from the majority. Among the members of the CFC, matters of the land and its resources are no longer in the hands of the customary chiefs of land-holding *butubutu* but are encompassed by the power of one central, pan-*butubutu* leader whose authority is religiously sanctioned. In both cases, however, large sums of money flow, but in highly different social circumstances – among the CFC remaining within the rural social movement, and among the other denominations of New Georgia largely channelled towards the urban scene.

As a relatively small but globally well-connected Melanesian place, New Georgia exemplifies two distinct paths of accumulation by dispossession of wider relevance to the region. What is material and non-material in these complex entanglements over land, persons, natural resources, power, sociality and money is not clear, and the interrelations among such fuzzy categories continue to be transformed as ever-new responses are developed locally to the challenges – and opportunities – represented by globalisation. What is clear, though, is that the collective agency, grounded in relations of kinship that characterise the ways in which Melanesians hold communal lands, is faced with new challenges as the forests on those lands have become global commodities. A sinister scenario is that of a large-scale undermining of the collectivities of land and people – represented by such totalising concepts as the New Georgian *butubutu* – that have for so long provided lifetime social security for the people of Melanesia. Collective social agency, a long-standing Melanesian safety net against material dispossession, and a way of connecting people, land and state that has few parallels in the world is under siege. The land loses its caretakers, and the Melanesian social collective loses the land. With a final reference to David Harvey, the cultural and social achievements built up over centuries by present and ancestral collectives are appropriated and accumulated by a few to the ultimate detriment of the dispossessed majority. A bitter irony exists in the present time, as demonstrated by the examples from the western Solomons, of retaining legal rights to one's customary land while in practice being robbed of its financial potential and seeing its more widely productive potential being threatened.

COMMENT

# Maasina Rule beyond Recognition

## DAVID AKIN

### ABSTRACT

While researching a recent book about the post-war Maasina Rule movement in the Solomon Islands, I was struck by the amount of misinformation that historians, anthropologists and others have published about it over the past 60-plus years. This paper highlights some key themes in this history of errors and traces their origins to colonial misunderstandings, archival obstruction, purposeful misrepresentation and theoretical muddles.

In 2013, I published a study of Maasina Rule, a movement that dominated politics in the south-eastern British Solomon Islands Protectorate (BSIP) from soon after World War II into early 1953, particularly on the island of Malaita where it began.[1] More has probably been written about Maasina Rule, over a longer period and by a more diverse collection of authors, than about any other Melanesian movement except John Frum on Tanna, which remains active. The corpus of relevant material is enormous. My book references some 70 books and articles fully or importantly about Maasina Rule, by historians, anthropologists, political scientists, Solomon Islanders, missionaries and active or former colonial officers. Many others have written about the movement within other topics, and newspaper articles, dissertations and unpublished manuscripts also exist. Moreover, archives hold thousands of

*Acknowledgements*: I dedicate this paper to Jim Tedder, 1926–2014, a district officer and district commissioner in the BSIP from 1952 to 1974, and to Hugh Laracy. This paper owes much to comments by Andrew Shryock, Gillian Feeley-Harnik, Terre Fisher, Raymond Grew, Esau Kekeubata, Jan Rensel, Farina Mir, Clive Moore, Ben Burt, Thomas Trautmann and this journal's reviewers. I thank Matthew Allen and Sinclair Dinnen, the *JPH* editors and Brett Baker for help in bringing it to press. An earlier version I gave as a talk at the East–West Center in Honolulu in March 2014, sponsored by the University of Hawai'i's Center for Pacific Islands Studies, the departments of anthropology and history and the University of Hawai'i Press.

[1] David W. Akin, *Colonialism, Maasina Rule, and the Origins of Malaitan Kastom* (Honolulu 2013).

pertinent documents, including writings by Maasina Rule adherents and wonderfully in-depth reports submitted by officers battling the movement.[2] Beyond all of this material, we have first-person oral accounts of the period from Solomon Islanders and Europeans. Maasina Rule challenges the researcher, not to exhume data but to avoid being buried by it.

From this, one might guess that little was left to say about Maasina Rule, that it was pretty well figured out by the time I started my book. Nothing could be further from the truth – while writing, I was astonished by the amount and degree of misinformation written about the movement over the decades. My own book digests a good deal of material, and no doubt I made blunders of my own that others will correct. But I refer here not to mistakes of detail – dates, names or specific events, though a plethora of those exist – but rather to sweeping errors of depiction. Some of these had become entrenched in the accepted history of the movement. The subject of this paper is what went wrong.

Briefly, Maasina Rule started in southern Malaita in 1944 and by the end of 1945 had spread throughout the island, and it soon extended in various forms to neighbouring islands.[3] Its founding substantive agenda was radically to transform local society through the elevation of new leaders who would head an integrative political structure, to codify rules that would form the basis for an Indigenous legal system, and to pursue communal economic endeavours to earn money needed to develop communities. The population, including thousands who lived in small mountain hamlets, relocated to large coastal villages and planted expansive gardens nearby. Malaitan society had long been divided by segmentary rivalries and religious difference, and the movement strove to reintegrate the populace to live and work together. Movement adherents – estimated at one point at 95% of Malaitans – declined to work on the protectorate's plantations and vowed to redirect workers to improving their home communities. At first, some colonial officers worked with Maasina Rule, but in mid-1947 the government decided to end it by imprisoning its leaders and forbidding all movement activities. On Malaita, in particular, this was followed by several years of police raids, mass arrests and general oppression. Unrelenting police actions left Maasina Rule's grander social engineering projects impossible to pursue, and the movement turned its energies to concerted popular and civil resistance and a refusal to resubmit to colonial control. This all culminated in a late-1952 agreement between the government and movement leaders.

This paper is not intended as a comprehensive overview of Maasina Rule, which showed considerable diversity, and at times contradictions, in different places and over time. Instead, I will highlight ways in which fundamental aspects of the movement's history have been misrepresented or largely ignored in the scholarly record. I have encountered some who have assumed that because I am a cultural

---

[2] For a sampling of writings by followers, see Laracy's edited collection of archival documents: Hugh Laracy (ed.), *Pacific Protest: the Maasina Rule movement, Solomon Islands, 1944–1952* (Suva 1983).
[3] I focus in this short paper on Malaita, since I know it best. Though the colonial government and most Solomon Islanders continued to portray Malaita as the movement's centre, it sometimes developed quite differently on other islands (see note 25).

anthropologist, I have relied on oral histories that I have collected to correct the written record in ways others could not have, but although my book does draw extensively on oral accounts, in this essay I build my arguments mostly on written documents, except where indicated. It is also important to note that Solomon Islanders' oral histories of Maasina Rule, valuable as they are, sometimes come with their own distortions, on a wide variety of topics, which would require another paper to address properly. I will start with some of the processes through which distortions in the written record were produced and then briefly address four problematic themes found in various writings about Maasina Rule: portrayals of the movement as (1) violent, (2) a men's movement in which women took no part or (3) a delusional cargo cult or mystical endeavour; and (4) the almost unanimous conclusion that it collapsed under government suppression and was a political failure. I am not interested here in cataloguing instances of colleagues making these mistakes; anyone familiar with the Maasina Rule literature will recognise them as I discuss them. I committed some of them myself before I seriously studied the movement. What I want to do instead is look further back to find their origins and to understand how and why they subsequently permeated and were perpetuated by the literature.

Maasina Rule is not unique in being misconstrued, of course. Similar patterns of distortion are found in European accounts of other Melanesian movements that were fought against, documented, studied and written about in similar ways and contexts, and some of them are found in accounts of grassroots reform movements well beyond Melanesia. This makes it all the more vital to understand where such faulty history comes from. Furthermore, young Malaitans who engaged in recent political conflicts in the Solomons have cited Maasina Rule as inspirational (as Guadalcanal people have the later Moro movement), and so have contemporary political groups (for example, the Malaita Ma'asina Forum), and for this reason it seems doubly important for scholars and especially Solomon Islanders to have an accurate picture of the movement's history.[4]

The sources of errors in Maasina Rule's history fall into a few basic categories. The most obvious is that government officials tried to hide what happened, both during and after the movement, in several different senses. First, many of the most important Maasina Rule files were classified secret and sealed. Researchers were not to see them until the late 1990s or later. Anyone who does read them sees why: many expose ineptitude, failure and sometimes deception. Someone gave me access to the files in the late 1980s, and at least one historian and an anthropologist who

---

[4] See Matthew G. Allen, *Greed and Grievance: ex-militants' perspectives on the conflict in Solomon Islands, 1998–2003* (Honolulu 2013). One reviewer of this paper charged me with telling Solomon Islanders how to understand their own history. I suppose anyone who writes about Pacific history (or any history) could be so accused, unless they write only for non-Indigenous audiences. My view is that because Solomon Islands students and scholars, some of them also emerging political leaders, have for some time been consuming misinformation that academics have produced about Maasina Rule (as well as much that is valuable), it is incumbent upon researchers – both Melanesian and not – to make what they believe is corrective information they uncover as available to them as to non-Melanesian colleagues. What they do with it is outside my purview.

wrote about the movement saw at least some of them before that.[5] But they have been unsealed for many years now, and even without them one can piece together a truer picture of the movement than the literature presents, so secreted files cannot by themselves explain the problems.

Another sort of concealment occurred: while the government was trying to suppress the movement from 1947 to 1952, senior colonial officials worried not about researchers but rather the European press and negative public reactions to their policies. Maasina Rule was, importantly, a labour strike, and the idea that thousands of labour movement members were being jailed might have caused problems abroad. Also, as time went on, the movement's tenacity despite years of intense suppression exposed a woefully failed government policy. Things had to be presented as otherwise, and some officials fed the press depictions of the movement as the work of delusional fanatics and cargo cultists. For one example, in 1950 the high commissioner's chief secretary G.D. Chamberlain told an Australian Associated Press 'special representative' that Maasina Rule was dying out because the movement had predicted,

> In September 1947 Liberty ships crammed with goods would appear off the Solomons; The skin of all the natives would change from black to white; European houses, complete with refrigerators and bathrooms, would be distributed free to the natives; and never-ending supplies of food, drink, and comforts would be handed to the natives,

and 'when these things did not materialise "Marching Rule" suffered a setback'. BSIP Resident Commissioner Gregory-Smith, too, told the press, among other fictions, that the movement was 'caused by fantastic propaganda about floods of American gift-goods'. Chamberlain, living in distant Fiji, may not have known the degree to which this caricature, parts of which were taken from classic European 'cargo cult' models constructed in New Guinea, misportrayed what the government was battling in Maasina Rule, but Gregory-Smith certainly did. Other common themes in public-targeted statements were false claims that Maasina Rule was rapidly fading, was a commotion by an intractable minority or had little impact beyond Malaita.[6]

Some falsehoods were intended to deceive not the public but higher-ups in the colonial administration. Most striking are mid-1947 reports and telegrams that Resident Commissioner Owen Noel and Malaita's district commissioner Roy

---

[5] See Roger Keesing, 'Politico-religious movements and anti-colonialism on Malaita: Maasina Rule in historical perspective', *Oceania*, 48:4 and 49:1 (1978), 241–61, 46–73, 244 n. 2; Laracy, *Pacific Protest*, vi. Many telegrams about the movement were written in code.

[6] Chamberlain quoted in 'Fanatical Native cult aims to drive British from islands', *Sydney Herald*, 23 Apr. 1950, 5; Gregory-Smith quoted in 'Marching Rule is wound up', *Fiji Times & Herald*, 8 Aug. 1950, 1. For the movement's labour aspects, see Ian Frazer, 'Maasina Rule and Solomon Islands labour history', in Clive Moore, Jacqueline Leckie and Doug Munro (eds), *Labour in the South Pacific* (Townsville 1990), 191–203; Akin, *Colonialism*, 231–37. On European caricatures of cargo cults (including Melanesian fixations on acquiring refrigerators and bathrooms), see Lamont Lindstrom, *Cargo Cult: strange stories of desire from Melanesia and beyond* (Honolulu 1993).

Davies composed to convince High Commissioner John Nicoll to approve, and send warships to assist, their planned crackdown on Maasina Rule, which was given the telling code name 'Operation Delouse'. The suppression campaign began that August with Nicoll's support, and across the years that followed, one finds an ongoing pattern of officers reporting resistance in sharp decline or the movement on its last legs. Some of these claims were sincere, born of gross misunderstandings of the movement and its dynamics. Others, one can only conclude, were knowingly deceptive.[7]

The reports of most officers, especially those of lower ranks, were candid, with key exceptions. This raises a difficulty in appraising the errors in archival documents: it is sometimes impossible to tell whether they express officers' honest views of Maasina Rule or are concoctions intended to mislead. One is often unsure because – against the extensive literature describing 'colonial knowledge' and its hegemonic power – most officers in the Solomons were woefully ignorant about local societies. Although some had taken anthropological courses prior to arrival, they received little formal training about the contemporary Solomons scene once they got there, and none who dealt with Maasina Rule learned a local language. Officers had long been socially isolated from much of the populace in the protectorate's south-eastern islands, but this became acute during Maasina Rule, especially on Malaita, where the movement was most intense. In particular, once the suppression campaign began, many people moved inland to places where officers and government headmen rarely or never ventured, and Maasina Rule people – the great majority of Malaitans – often shunned government officials. Further, loyalists sometimes fed officers false information.[8]

Officers' isolation is clearest in their misunderstandings of what was happening inside Maasina Rule. At times I have dismissed as disingenuous propaganda an officer's far-fetched assertion about the movement only to later find evidence that he really did believe the claim. The miscomprehensions are far more troublesome for the researcher than are the lies, since the latter are often transparent and typically limited to higher-level documents or communications, while the former can permeate the colonial archive from top to bottom. So, for instance, one can readily discern the disinformation in an annual report if one has read dozens of documents that contradict it written throughout the previous year (some by the annual report's author). But if an officer genuinely believed that, say, Maasina Rule's leaders secretly ruled by terror, then this fallacy warped most everything that he wrote and, consequently,

---

[7] See Akin, *Colonialism*, 249–66, 278–80.

[8] It is essential to stress that knowledge and isolation varied greatly between officers and over time. A key variable was their empathy towards Islanders. Regarding three notable officers on Malaita: District Commissioner G.E.D. Sandars toured the coast and worked with Maasina Rule leaders during 1945–47, though some aspects of the movement remained an enigma to him. Michael Forster patrolled almost continuously while a district officer in 1945–47 and district commissioner in 1948–49, and before the government attacked Maasina Rule, he interacted often with its leaders and followers in sometimes positive ways. Tom Russell while district officer at Malu'u in 1949–50 toured widely and wrote impressively detailed, candid reports about the movement in the north. The reports of all three are crucial sources for anyone studying the movement.

what his superiors and colleagues were likely to believe and write. Adding to the challenge of distinguishing fabrication from ignorance is that key officers were highly resistant to reconsidering faulty analyses even as the policies they generated dragged them into one political disaster after another. Some refused to reassess even decades later, and one surmises that when misconceptions were later recognised, they were sometimes perpetuated nonetheless in order to preserve policy or face. In any case, the researcher will search in vain for corrections here. Scholars of Maasina Rule have sometimes drawn upon or quoted distorting or mendacious documents as evidence for their own misreadings of the movement.

The flawed scholarly history of Maasina Rule also grew out of accounts of the movement written later by a few protectorate officers who – intentionally and not – seeded the record with misinformation. Most important here was Colin Allan, who held several BSIP postings prior to 1949, at which time he became the district officer in charge of north Malaita, where he oversaw the arrest of well over 1,000 Maasina Rule men. He then attended a Devonshire Course at Cambridge where, supervised by Reo Fortune, he wrote an anthropology thesis about Maasina Rule, parts of which later appeared in *Corona* and *South Pacific*. Upon returning to the Solomons, Allan served as Malaita's district commissioner from June 1950 to February 1952, charged with defeating the movement. He then held various positions in Honiara until 1959 and later served as the protectorate's last governor from 1976 to 1978. After retiring from the Colonial Service, Allan held visiting positions at the Australian National University and the universities of Auckland, Otago and New South Wales, and published academic articles about Maasina Rule and related topics that influenced many people's perceptions of the movement.[9]

Allan was on Malaita during the height of the futile attempts to end Maasina Rule and, it becomes clear from reading his reports over time, developed a grave antipathy toward Malaitans in general, and Maasina Rule in particular. Even his higher-level reports written as district commissioner sometimes descend into frustrated rants against the populace. His Malaita annual report at the end of 1951 dismissed compromise and said the police were teaching Malaitans the lesson, 'This Government would not tolerate the open flouting of the law and that whether passive resistance to authority continued for twenty years, nothing would persuade it from adhering to the course of its policy'. He also told the high commissioner that he would soon launch new 'prosecutions and large scale police operations' across the island to punish Maasina Rule tax resisters. But this was not to be, and in February he departed Malaita a defeated, exhausted man. It was left to his successor Valdemar

---

[9] Colin H. Allan, 'The Marching Rule movement in the British Solomon Islands Protectorate: an analytical survey', MA thesis, Cambridge University (Cambridge 1950), available from Canberra, Pacific Manuscripts Bureau (hereinafter PMB), 1189/111; Colin H. Allan, 'Marching Rule: a nativistic cult of the British Solomon Islands', *Corona*, 3:3 (1951), 93–100, reprinted in *South Pacific*, 5 (1951), 79–85. See also 'Pacific Manuscripts Bureau newsletter', series 5, no. 19, June 2005, 8, http://asiapacific.anu.edu.au/pambu/pambu/Pambu19%2005Jun.pdf (accessed 13 Oct. 2015). For Allan's 1960–89 publications on Maasina Rule, see Akin, *Colonialism*, 449.

Andersen and a new high commissioner, Robert Stanley, to forge an agreement with resistance leaders near the end of 1952.[10]

Some of Allan's writings perpetuated the idea that Maasina Rule could be understood primarily as a cargo cult, while in others he greatly exaggerated the movement's decline during his tenure on Malaita. Most influential regarding the cargo cult view was his 1950 thesis; William Davenport, who advised the government during the 1960s and interacted with many officers, told me it 'became sort of the official version of the movement to subsequent administrators in the Protectorate'. In early 1952, Allan left a copy in the Malaita district office with a recommendation that his successors read it along with '[Roy] Davies's excellent political section in the 1947 [Malaita] Annual Report', a work that laid out Davies's own severely misleading portrayal of Maasina Rule.[11]

When it comes to the historical picture that formed of Maasina Rule, Allan's personal communications to others may have been more important than his writings, and several authors explicitly acknowledged his guidance. The potential of someone like Allan to shape subsequent officers' understandings of the movement can only be grasped within the larger context. While working in the archives, I was struck by the lack of historical knowledge across generations of officers, including many astute men. As with cultural matters, they seem to have received no formal historical training and were often poorly informed or misinformed concerning even recent events before their arrival. Officers learned much of what they knew about Maasina Rule from reports by, or informal talks with, their predecessors, and in this way misperceptions and misrepresentations could be passed along for years or decades. For just one conspicuous example, High Commissioner Stanley, who in late 1952 spearheaded the government's settlement with Maasina Rule (then sometimes called 'The Federal Council'), in his memoirs portrayed the movement crudely as a cargo cult and credited Allan for his information.[12]

For this and other reasons, what I say here should not be read as criticism of district officers as a group. Some wrote sincere portrayals of Maasina Rule, factual to their best knowledge and useful to researchers. One case in point is officer William

---

[10] Colin Allan, Malaita annual report, 1951, PMB 19989/113, 16; second quote from Colin Allan to secretary to government, 'top secret' telegram, 14 Dec. 1951, Honiara, Solomon Islands National Archive (hereinafter SINA), file 4/SF108/I/2, 4. Allan's biography has been confused. For example, Wikipedia credits him with Stanley and Andersen's accomplishment, apparently drawing from an obituary that claimed: 'His patient persuasion resulted in the formation of a properly organised first Council of Malaita. It marked the end of the movement's influence and was his most notable early achievement'. See 'Colin Allan', Wikipedia, http://en.wikipedia.org/wiki/Colin_Allan (accessed 3 June 2014); Kenneth Bain, 'Obituary: Sir Colin Allan', *Independent*, 13 Apr. 1993.

[11] William Davenport, pers. comm., 1988; Akin, *Colonialism*, 291, 429 n. 83.

[12] Robert Stanley, *King George's Keys: a record of experiences in the overseas service of the Crown* (London 1975), 172–75. Stanley had just arrived in the protectorate in 1952 and knew little of the movement he parleyed with; he contributed a resolve and licence to compromise, but Valdemar Andersen deserves the bulk of the credit for hammering out the settlement and making it work to the extent that it did.

Marquand, who attended the Devonshire Course with Allan and who from 1947 into 1949 had also arrested many Malaitans. Marquand's course paper, long ignored, is a sometimes-insightful and scathingly frank critique of the government's anti-Maasina Rule policy that he had helped to implement. But even better writings like Marquand's are often marred by errors drawn from a protectorate well of information tainted by colleagues or predecessors. This problem was apparent at the highest levels. For instance, BSIP annual reports through 1974 summarised Maasina Rule as having been a cargo cult that 'needed a show of force to control it'.[13]

Another officer who published on Maasina Rule was Cyril Belshaw, who dealt with the movement briefly as a cadet in 1946 and later became a well-known anthropologist. Like Allan, he presented the movement as at base irrational and helped secure it a place in anthropology's cargo cult literature. One 1950 Belshaw article portraying Maasina Rule as 'a strange native cult' fitting a general type was that year circulated to protectorate officers. Both Allan and Belshaw were sources for Peter Worsley's influential book, *The Trumpet Shall Sound: a study of 'cargo cults' in Melanesia*.[14]

Other flawed analyses of Maasina Rule have come from its being interpreted through theoretical models inappropriate to it, especially by anthropologists. Each of these models has, in turn, deformed the picture scholars have built of the movement. Most obvious here are cargo cult models of the 1950s–70s, which led some to portray Maasina Rule as in essence a mass delusion. Also problematic were analyses, both

---

[13] Wilfred Marquand, Community development in the BSIP with particular reference to the Marching Rule, 1949/50, PMB 1189/116. In contrast to Allan's widely read thesis, I have found only one academic citation of Marquand's paper, and that only in passing. The resident commissioner received a copy that ended up in a restricted file (SINA 4/S108/VII/4), but I have no evidence that it was deliberately suppressed. In 1975 the annual report shifts radically, describing Maasina Rule as 'the most successful experiment in local government so far', which 'in many ways was more effective than the colonial administration'. British Solomon Islands, *Report for the Year 1975* (London 1975), 150–51. Two useful books by former Malaita officers are Tom Russell, *I Have the Honour to Be* (Spennymoor 2003); James Tedder, *Solomon Island Years: a district administrator in the islands, 1952–1974* (Stuarts Point 2008).

[14] See Akin, *Colonialism*, 217–19, 291, 406–07, 429. Worsley was apparently prevented from conducting research in the BSIP. Roger Keesing, pers. comm., 1979. Curiously, Worsley thanked Allan as a consultant, calling him at one point 'the best authority'. See Peter Worsley, *The Trumpet Shall Sound: a study of 'cargo cults' in Melanesia* (New York 1968), 9, 173. He listed Allan's thesis and *Corona* article in the bibliography, but he cited neither. He drew also on *Pacific Islands Monthly* and the BSIP 1949–50 annual report, but though he repeated some of their misconceptions, he rejected reductionist, cargo cult portrayals of Maasina Rule that both promulgated. David Trench, in charge of the mass arrest campaign on Malaita during 1947–49, wrote that 'cults astonishingly similar' to Maasina Rule existed in New Guinea and that, because government policies there were different, BSIP policies could not be blamed for the movement – he roundly dismissed the idea that Islanders could have legitimate, rational complaints against the colonial government. Memo to Resident Commissioner Owen Noel, 31 Dec. 1947, SINA, BSIP file 12/I/2/7. See Akin, *Colonialism*, 265. For Belshaw's altercation with Maasina Rule, see Akin, *Colonialism*, 217–19, 406–07; Cyril Belshaw, *Bumps on a Long Road* (Vancouver 2009), ch. 1.

colonial and academic, that misunderstood *kastom* – the name of the movement's core ideology – as simply a Solomon Islands Pijin gloss for 'custom', 'culture' or 'tradition' rather than as the dynamic political ideology that it was and remains today. As I detail in the book, this was a source of ongoing confusion for colonial officers who conceived of Solomon Islands societies as relatively ahistorical and unchanging. From their perspective, only authentic, pre-European ways were 'genuine customs', and Maasina Rule advocacy of *kastom* ideas and practices that were innovations was therefore fraudulent. Some anthropologists into the 1970s and 1980s held analogous views and sometimes discussed whether this or that *kastom* or related idea or behaviour in the Pacific was 'real' culture or instead 'spurious' or 'invented'. But for most people in Maasina Rule, no pedigree was required for something to qualify as *kastom*. The concept broadly indicated Islander ways of doing things, including some valued, older practices and ethical attitudes thought to be eroding but also things everyone recognised as new. *Kastom* became a label for the entire Maasina Rule program, including resistance to unwanted government interference in people's lives, new leadership and political structures, innovative social and legal rules, dramatic social engineering projects and the labour strike. The movement forbade many older Indigenous practices that might spark conflicts or hamper its agenda, and for the most part followers embraced these *kastom* prohibitions enthusiastically. The most important way in which *kastom* ideology hearkened to the past was its advocacy of a return to Islanders controlling their own affairs according to their own sensibilities.

*Kastom* in Maasina Rule, then, was radically different from European concepts of 'custom', and colonial and later scholarly failures to realise this led to serious misreadings of the movement and its goals. Its emphasis on *kastom* led many officers and some other writers to caricature it as backward looking, with its followers yearning for a return to some idealised past. Some writers today still criticise specific *kastom* ideas of Solomon Islanders as being distortions or illegitimate on the grounds that they are modern.

Let me turn now to some specific problematic themes in the literature. The first is one of the most egregious: portrayals of Maasina Rule as violent in nature or action. A primary justification for the government's decision to suppress the movement was that it was violent or soon would become so, or afterward that it would have been without the crackdown. The underlying grounds for this were sometimes simple: Melanesians, and Malaitans in particular, were said to be inherently violent and, it was sometimes added, prone to 'hysteria'. In fact Maasina Rule was neither violent nor hysterical, but one would never know this from some of what has been written about it.[15]

---

[15] Former Malaita officer Tom Russell, notable for not holding the bigoted views some of his colleagues and other Europeans did, believes violence was a possibility, and points out that officers conducting the suppression campaign could not really know if any threat of violent response was real. Tom Russell, pers. comm., 2012 and 2013; Akin, *Colonialism*, 303. Indeed, even now we cannot know what particular individuals may have considered, or fault officers for caution. For one potentially violent situation the government never knew about, see Akin, *Colonialism*, 260. But the many Maasina Rule veterans I interviewed all insisted the movement was non-violent;

Some writers merely implied violence with references to unspecified 'Maasina Rule militants' or Maasina Rule 'terrorism'. Others gave more specific examples. Zoleveke wrote, 'Inevitably the police were brought in to maintain order, violence broke out and lives were lost'. Belshaw credited the establishment of Native courts and councils on Gela in 1948 to the fact that, there, 'political discontent did not reach the peak of violence that it has reached in other areas'. Guidieri asserted,

> For the first time, violent political conflict between colonized and colonizer became inevitable. The chronicle of the Maasina Rule that ended in the violent suppression of the movement around 1948 was marked by deaths, by military expeditions on the part of the colonial administration, by bloody suppressions and prison.

Allan titled a section of his thesis 'Terrorist tactics' but mentioned there nothing of the sort except for passing falsehoods concerning open threats to British life and property and 'mass meetings accompanied by mass-hysteria'. Here and elsewhere, Allan included in this 'mass-hysteria' civil and even amicable meetings movement followers had with officers at 'Aoke and claimed that during every such meeting 'rioting had been narrowly avoided'. Later, Allan asserted that Maasina Rule's leaders were arrested owing to 'evidence of bodily injury sustained by a number of people', which is also untrue. Those making such claims cite no sources, and so who told them these things is a mystery.[16] The truth is, to the great credit of both Islanders and officers, violence was remarkably absent despite five years of intense repression and resistance and deep unhappiness and frustrations on both sides.

But the distortion is worse than that because, not only was Maasina Rule not violent, through 1948 and 1949 (and in less dramatic but quite effective ways after that), it was an organised civil disobedience movement. Thousands peacefully awaited officers scheduled to come to arrest them for refusing to pay the head tax, submit to a census or tear down fences erected around movement villages.[17] They

violence would have contravened movement policy; only one isolated, seriously violent incident occurred in eight years (a confused situation in which a soldier killed a Maasina Rule man in self-defence). Akin, *Colonialism*, 303. Certain officers clearly concocted violence or threats of violence to justify suppression. In any case, most of the examples I cite here are claims not that violence was a possibility but that it actually occurred.

[16] Gideon Zoleveke, *Zoleveke: a man from Choiseul* (Suva 1980), 44; Cyril Belshaw, 'Native politics in the Solomon Islands', *Pacific Affairs*, 20 (1947), 190; Remo Guidieri, 'Two millenaristic responses in Oceania', in Remo Guidieri, Francesco Pellizzi and Stanley Tambiah (eds), *Ethnicities and Nations* (Austin 1988), 189; Colin Allan, 'The Marching Rule movement', 26, 59–61; Akin, *Colonialism*, 282–83, 426 n. 61. Belshaw referred here to an incident at 'Aoke on Malaita in June 1946, detailed in my book, in which the greatest threat of serious violence came not from Maasina Rule followers but from government personnel who had to be restrained from shooting into a crowd of demonstrators angry because 39 Langalanga men had been arrested and summarily sentenced to hard labour prison terms for activities they thought legal. Akin, *Colonialism*, 221–22.

[17] Most (though not all) 'fences' were double-rails of bamboo with widely spaced posts, which did not physically prevent people coming or going. Some government reports and academic accounts

overflowed government prison camps and manned work gangs watched over by iso-
lated guards carrying cudgels, and did not try to escape. Many went to jail multiple
times, and in much of northern Malaita most able-bodied men did so at least once.
Some, eager for arrest, crossed the island to places where raids were planned.
Maasina Rule prison labour built much of Malaita's early post-war infrastructure.
The majority arrested were Malaitans, though many Makirans went to jail also.

A bewildering aspect of the Maasina Rule literature is the degree to which it
ignores this. Methodical civil disobedience, particularly in the northern half of the
island where most suppression efforts were focused, was long the movement's main
resistance strategy and the main focus of government efforts to end it, yet few
writers seem to have been aware of this, and none has recognised its crucial importance. Some have said large numbers were arrested, but have left out the coordinated
campaign, suggesting either widespread disorder or that officers simply rounded
people up. While the government hid much of this from the press, it is heavily documented in the archives, and researchers might have talked to some of the many
Solomon Islanders who had been involved (some of them as government police).[18]

A second common distortion is the presentation of Maasina Rule as exclu-
sively a men's movement. Some colonial reports, including annual reports, implied
that the movement treated women as virtual slave labour, but in most academic
work the error has been one of omission, in that few writers mention women at all
or express curiosity as to where this half of Malaita's population was during these
years. Women are generally seen, when seen at all, as having been apolitical or
opposed to the resistance because jailed men could not work gardens. But women
had roles in the movement early on, and titled women's leaders oversaw communal
garden projects and also held meetings (sometimes with men) to instruct young
women on movement rules. Anglican missionary Charles Fox was alone in observing,
'Women were in the movement as strongly as the men'.[19] In many places, women
were also active in the later resistance, if not always in such a civil manner as the
men. In parts of Malaita, crowds of women pelted with rocks and cursed soldiers
who were arresting men, or raucously urged men to disobey their orders. If
someone wants to dig for evidence that Maasina Rule was violent, they might point
to these women, though there is no record that they injured anyone, and officers
never cited them to portray the movement as dangerous. Be that as it may, women
acted in ways for which, had they been men, they would have been incarcerated
for long terms. But very few women were arrested, and their actions and thoughts
are mostly invisible in archives.

This omission was calculated: J.D.A. Germond was from late 1947 the div-
isional officer for the southern Solomons and, after that, acting resident commissioner,
and he directed much of the suppression campaign through the years. In 1948 he

---

labelled all fenced settlements 'fortified villages', implying military preparation, but they were part
of a symbolic, not martial, conflict. See Akin, *Colonialism*, 273–84, 287.

[18] See ibid., 272–90.

[19] British Solomon Islands, *Annual Report on the British Solomon Islands for the Years 1949–1950* (London
1950), 38; Charles Fox, *Kakamora* (London 1962), 131.

ordered his officers to arrest no women: 'The female population do not and must not come into the picture at all. We have no quarrel with the women folk for this is a "game" which does not fall within their province'. To drop this fiction and begin arresting women would have inflamed the situation, and if Germond's superiors had heard of women filling protectorate jails, they most likely would have reined him in. The façade he erected exploited the enduring European stereotype of Melanesian women as docile, non-political drudges working under domineering men. It left a historical record mostly devoid of women. Alas, details of this aspect of the movement are the hardest to recover now, since one must rely mostly on oral history, and the last Maasina Rule veterans are rapidly dying away.[20]

A third distortion, which I have already raised, is portrayals of Maasina Rule as a 'cargo cult'. A quote from a *Sydney Herald* story of the time will illustrate one variation:

> Marching rule is similar to the New Guinea cargo cult. The natives believe that ships laden with goods and food are due to arrive shortly, and that they will then enjoy a Utopian life with everything free and no work. The difference is that in New Guinea they think the ships will be manned by their own dead ancestors, while the marching rule adherents expect them to be manned by Americans – they regard the shipments as a magic form of Marshall Aid ... There were a number of similar cults among the North American Indians when the palefaces moved into their territory.[21]

Ugly yellow journalism, yes, but as I have said, officers of high rank fed such depictions of Maasina Rule to the press, and some officers understood, or at least portrayed, the movement in terms only slightly less crude. As I have described in my book, rumours about 'cargo' were in fact in circulation, and in certain cases some people acted on them, and not only later after suppression began, as some have written. But, on Malaita at least, those episodes were transitory and had only a secondary impact on the movement's main ideas or its development. I should emphasise that my intent here is not to disparage more sophisticated 'cargo cult' analyses that anthropologists have carried out, or to argue that they have nothing to offer regarding ideas that some people held during periods of Maasina Rule, or to say that no movement members' beliefs (depending on how defined) ever had mystical elements or that ideas of 'cargo' were never important anywhere. Nor do I mean to imply that all movement followers were always hyper-rational political actors – they were, after all, human beings. The problem in the literature that I am critiquing here is reductions of the movement to one largely understandable as mystical or delusional

---

[20] On women in Maasina Rule, see Akin, *Colonialism*, 172, 205–06, 280–82. Parts of a book I am writing will examine this more closely.

[21] *Sydney Herald*, 26 Aug. 1951, 2. The idea that Maasina Rule people wanted everything in life to be 'free' was often stressed in such portrayals to impart that they had no inkling of natural human economic relations and thus could not be parleyed with as rational actors (and, of course, they echoed the age-old smear that 'Natives' were lazy).

or a 'cult' in ways that, intentionally and not, obscured or overtly denied more prac-
tical political goals and actions that were central to the movement throughout its existence. When some academics, too, opted to focus their primary analytical attentions on
the movement as mystical, this extended the problem and contributed to an ignoring
of fundamental aspects of the movement such as those that I highlight in this paper.

It is notable that most officers who dealt most personally and intensely with
Maasina Rule people made little or no mention of such cargo ideas in their detailed
reports, or explicitly dismissed their importance, such as Tom Russell, who thought
them 'always a peripheral element in the movement'.[22] Others, such as Allan,
Belshaw and Davies, at times portrayed cargo or related mystical ideas as the movement's essence. Some did so at least partly in an attempt to discredit Maasina Rule,
but for officers who could not fathom Islanders' discontent, reductionist cargo cult
models were also simplifying and liberating. They offered an explanation for
Maasina Rule that obscured the political and ethical grievances behind it and
morally justified the suppression campaign as saving people from their own foolish-
ness, while also accounting for that campaign's ineffectiveness. And if Maasina Rule
was grounded in economic delusions, they could not be expected to deal with it as
a labour movement. Unfortunately for the administration, cargo ideas were far
more important to certain officers than to most Maasina Rule followers, at least on
Malaita, and this prevented those officers and those they reported to from grasping
core concerns and goals of the people. As a result, they were ineffective or much
worse in their efforts to quell the rebellion. Another result was twisted accounts of
the movement, which scholars later drew upon.[23]

Starting in the late 1970s, Roger Keesing and Hugh Laracy wrote badly
needed correctives to this perspective and challenged the idea that Maasina Rule
could be understood in such terms.[24] Today, nobody familiar with the literature,
and in particular the archival record, would portray Maasina Rule as simply 'a
cargo cult'. Once this is understood, however, it should not obscure that some followers of Maasina Rule did nurture mystical expectations, or something else that
many Maasina Rule adherents did embrace from the movement's earliest years:
hopes that Americans would come to their aid and perhaps oust the British, whom

---

[22] Russell, *I Have the Honour to Be*, 46.

[23] My critical reading of Allan's, Belshaw's and Davies's portrayals of Maasina Rule as a cargo cult
are grounded not just in their exaggerations of cargoism. Their writings about a variety of aspects of
the movement are highly inaccurate in ways that are transparent to anyone who has read the many
archival files that roundly contradict them, some written by these same officers. (I laid out many
examples in my book.) Officers who had more personal, extended interactions with the movement
on the ground but did not paint the movement as primarily mystical in nature – most notably
Forster, Russell and Marquand – also present, I think not coincidentally, more nuanced and
complex accounts of the movement writ large, even though Russell and Forster, and for a time Marquand, were no friends of Maasina Rule and were heavily invested in forcefully putting it down.
Finally Allan, interestingly, rarely mentioned cargoistic aspects of Maasina Rule in his many administrative reports on the movement from the field.

[24] Keesing, 'Politico-religious movements'; Laracy, *Pacific Protest*, 33, 150–51.

they perceived as intent on keeping Islanders backward and under thumb. Nothing necessarily irrational or mystical informed these hopes: Maasina Rule began while World War II was ongoing, and people based these ideas on their or their fellows' personal interactions with American soldiers, some of whom disliked and at times openly disrespected the British Labour Corps officers under whom Islanders worked, and who sometimes counselled Islanders politically and even told them that the United States might maintain a post-war presence in the Solomons (a possibility discussed in the US Congress).[25]

Few Solomon Islanders in the 1940s knew much of global politics or the irrelevance of soldiers' thoughts and actions. But many so urgently wanted American help partly because they did recognise one fundamental reality: the events of the war had made it obvious to most Solomon Islanders that they were not yet prepared to go it alone in the world and required a benefactor. Some Americans had seemed ready and willing to fill that role, and hopes that they would do so inspired many Maasina Rule followers and helped energise movement activities. Rejection of portrayals of Maasina Rule as fundamentally a matter of mystical dreams of cargo delivery should not distract attention from how important hopes for American political liberation were for some people from the movement's beginnings (less so after c. mid-1950). These quite different ideas are easily conflated and are difficult to disentangle in the archival record because some officers perfunctorily suffixed 'cargo' to 'American' whenever they referred to hopes for American assistance. Others clearly understood the difference.[26]

A final and most prolific flaw in accounts of Maasina Rule is the virtually undisputed assertion that the government successfully suppressed it and that, as a political movement, it largely failed. In the common scenario, arrests gradually wore down the movement until it petered out, except for resurging 'pockets of resistance' that soon faded as well. In fact, in the agreement that Stanley signed with the movement in late 1952, the government gave in to numerous demands that Malaitans had been making, and the government emphatically refusing, for years. These concessions have sometimes been portrayed as mild, conciliatory ones or as rewards for giving up

---

[25] I cannot address here areal variations in such beliefs (or in Maasina Rule generally), but for a study of hopes for and fears of American arrival in parts of Makira, where both the wartime experience and Maasina Rule were in some ways quite different from Malaita, see Michael Scott, *The Severed Snake: matrilineages, making place, and a Melanesian Christianity in Southeast Solomon Islands* (Durham 2007), ch. 3. For Maasina Rule on Santa Isabel, see Geoffrey White, *Identity through History: living stories in a Solomon Islands society* (Cambridge 1991), ch. 9. How Maasina Rule unfolded on Guadalcanal and Gela has yet to be explored and would be a fertile research topic. For the war's impact on Islanders, start with writings by Lamont Lindstrom and Geoffrey White, such as *Island Encounters: black and white memories of the Pacific War* (Washington, DC 1990); Judith Bennett, *Natives and Exotics: World War II and environment in the southern Pacific* (Honolulu 2009); Akin, *Colonialism*, ch. 4.

[26] For a discussion of the topic, see Akin, *Colonialism*, 290–99. Laracy, too, has noted that desires for American allies must be considered 'quite apart from the hope of cargo'. Laracy, *Pacific Protest*, 150. For a discussion of the American/cargo relationship, see Keesing, 'Politico-religious movements', 63–70.

the movement. Some later officers believed that their predecessors had defeated Maasina Rule in this way. Academics appear to have taken such claims at face value, or at least many have repeated them, and none has seriously challenged them.[27]

When one considers Maasina Rule's long battle with the government as a whole, it is in fact simplistic to declare either side a victor or a loser, and the reality is far more complex than I can properly present here. Both attained some of their goals but failed in others, and both pursued complex agendas that changed considerably over the years. Furthermore, the movement had no unanimity regarding some issues, and the same was true on the government side. So, for example, the 1952 agreement left unsatisfied those Maasina Rule adherents who had wanted absolute autonomy from the colonial government or for Americans to remove it (though by then almost everyone had long given up on the latter), or who had hoped to win a high (£12 per month) wage for labourers. But the settlement also galled certain key government officers (and many of the protectorate's European residents), who had toiled for years to reimpose European domination over a relatively compliant Native population and felt their colleagues had surrendered to the enemy camp. In the final analysis, though, few people on either side were unhappy to see the conflict end (and some of the same Europeans soon came to accept the settlement as having been the right move).

Throughout Maasina Rule, despite many changes in goals and tactics over eight years, followers maintained two basic objectives, particularly on Malaita. One was a resolve to refuse and block a reimposition of the pre-war system of colonial rule, which they saw as demeaning and unjust and which interfered in people's daily lives in oppressive ways. The years of mass arrests and bullying after 1947 convinced many that the colonials' attitudes had, if anything, worsened, and thus the suppression campaign only stiffened their determination to prevent a return to government rule on its old terms. A second sustained movement goal was to win Islanders a significant role in their own governance. In fact, Maasina Rule achieved important measures of both goals at the movement's centre of Malaita, and to a degree for other Solomon Islanders.

To start with the second goal, the agreement that High Commissioner Stanley sealed in 1952 included most importantly the establishment of a long-

---

[27] In June 1950, Resident Commissioner Gregory-Smith, desperate for Malaitan cooperation, released the movement's 'head chiefs' from prison on condition they work with the government. This has often been presented, including in BSIP annual reports, as a game-changing gambit that was the beginning of the end for Maasina Rule, but in fact, when chiefs advocated the government agenda, most of their communities rejected them and continued resistance. For details see Akin, *Colonialism*, 304–08. One reviewer suggested that I cite specific writers who were thus misled by government misinformation. I choose not to cite specific scholars here because no one writing about Maasina Rule has really challenged the verdict that the movement was mostly or completely a political failure, and thus singling out individuals from the crowd seems to me neither fair nor useful. I will point to myself, since I held mostly to this view until I conducted in-depth research. The same can be said regarding across-the-board failures to forefront the organised civil disobedience campaign or discuss women's roles in the movement.

demanded and long-forbidden popularly selected Malaita Council, with its own head-quarters inland, separate from the government's Auki station, and a Malaitan president elected by the council. Of the council's 35 members, at least 26 of them and its first president were former resistance leaders (eight members were government-nominated). It was agreed that this body would collect and administer future taxes on Malaita and assume a number of other tasks formerly carried out by colonial officers. To appreciate the significance of these and other concessions, one must understand that the government had for years relentlessly declared that it would grant Malaitans nothing or (until Andersen replaced Allan in early 1952) even seriously negotiate with them until *all* Malaitans had *fully* capitulated. As 1952 began, and as Colin Allan left, the government's position on Malaita, contra assertions by later officers and scholars, was in many ways worsening. Resistance, especially the organised refusal to cooperate in any way with any government undertaking, was more entrenched across a broader area than when arrests had started five years earlier. The things Malaitans won later that year were not granted to them because they stood down. Shortly before Stanley's arrival, Andersen had decided reluctantly to 'revert to a policy of force', conducting 'massive raids' with 'maximum force' across all of Malaita, essentially returning to Allan's plan and the government strategy that had failed since August 1947. Andersen made this decision owing to a declining situation and his failure – despite six months of good-faith efforts on his part – to make any real progress. Into this situation stepped Stanley, an outsider untainted by bad history and determined to end the five-year standoff: 'I had decided on a conciliatory approach as the only one likely to succeed', he later reported,

> and if there was to be any chance of success I had to reduce any conditions I felt it necessary to impose on the acceptance of the Federal Council's representations ... to what I considered to be the minimum essential to ensure recognition of my own authority as well as obedience to the laws of the Protectorate.[28]

While most academics have concurred that the government overcame Maasina Rule, officers who were on Malaita or involved in forging the 1952 agreement saw it otherwise, and their comments are telling. Acting Resident Commissioner Peter Hughes complained that the conditions being agreed to were 'suspiciously like the demands [Maasina Rule] made' in 1946, and the district officer for north Malaita condemned the settlement as a Malaitan 'political coup d'etat'. At the end of 1953, Andersen wrote, 'Apart from the wish to be independent the only major aim of the Marching Rule ... which has not been achieved is an increase in the basic wage'. Though I think Andersen overstated this, these remarks indicate how officers understood the settlement, and I have been unable to find any who were involved in making it – as opposed to some who were on Malaita before or after – who portrayed it as anything like a government victory over Maasina Rule.[29]

---

[28] Cited in ibid., 321 and 322.
[29] Ibid., 327.

This all speaks to the formal gains of the movement. Just as important, in my view, was a change the Maasina Rule experience instilled in the attitudes of state officials. The long ordeal in coming to terms with the movement left all but more reactionary officers with a strong sense of the futility of trying to control Solomon Islanders through suppression and intimidation. This was most obvious on Malaita, where, as I have said, some people were unsatisfied with the 1952 settlement. After years of oppression, many remained suspicious of the government, and though overt hostility was now muted, people continued some of the very behaviours that before had so outraged officers and instigated the suppression campaign, such as running their own *kastom* law courts and refusing to pay taxes or to census. But now officers responded with attempts at persuasion rather than police actions and were loath to make political arrests. On other islands too, political challenges were met more with engagement than aggression. For example, Davenport told me that when the Moro movement on Guadalcanal worried the government in the 1960s, High Commissioner Robert Foster declined to arrest the leaders, as some urged him to, and 'citing early mistakes made during Maasina Rule ... he directed Honiara administrators to invite Moro and his aides to come to Honiara and set up a sort of "headquarters" Custom House'.[30]

In conclusion, historians and anthropologists have faced obstacles to learning what happened during Maasina Rule, including an archival record plagued by misinformation. Yet the question remains of why so many scholars proved so amenable to flawed government portrayals of a movement that the government itself battled so long and bitterly. I cannot properly delve into this here, but a few observations may encourage further discussion. One obvious problem is that researchers have given too much credence to higher-level government documents such as annual reports. This is where distortions are extreme, and it is in more quotidian reports and correspondence, especially confidential materials that were often sealed until recent decades, that something closer to truths is found. Second, surprisingly few oral histories of Maasina Rule were collected from Islanders,[31] and many aspects of the movement only emerge when one studies the oral and written records together in a dialogic manner. But of course historians know these things, and as I said earlier, I have relied in this particular paper, unlike in my book, primarily on the written record and chiefly writings of colonial officers themselves, rather than on Solomon Islander oral histories.

I think perhaps the biggest problems in the Maasina Rule literature have resulted not from poor methodology per se but rather from a restricted chronological focus. There has been a relative lack of interest in, or at least much less research on

---

[30] William Davenport, pers. comm., 1988. See also Akin, *Colonialism*, ch. 9. In later years, penalties were reinstated for refusal to pay a tax collected by the Malaita Council.

[31] One exception is the autobiography of Jonathan Fifiʻi, *From Pig-Theft to Parliament: my life between two worlds*, trans. and ed. Roger Keesing (Suva 1989). This most valuable book does contain distortions in places, such as omitting Fifiʻi's extended ostracism from most of his Kwaio community once he tried to push the government agenda as stipulated as a condition for his June 1950 release from prison. He presented the imprisoned head chiefs' meeting with Resident Commissioner Gregory-Smith and their release as if it that essentially ended the movement.

and writing about, what happened once the suppression campaign began and the movement's original topmost leaders (the 'head chiefs') were imprisoned, something apparent in the fact that published histories are notably more accurate for the three years leading up to August 1947, when Operation Delouse began, than for the five years that followed.[32] This even though the archives hold much, much more material, of far greater detail, from the latter period – a long suppression campaign produces mountains of paper, in this case countless court records, letters, telegrams and exhaustive reports. I would venture that their quantity itself encouraged a reliance on higher-level, summary reports. Most of the historical errors I have highlighted in this paper involve the later period: the neglect of civil disobedience actions, the invisibility of women in the resistance, the belief that suppression quashed resistance and Maasina Rule accomplished little, and also many of the fictions about violence and pervasive cargo cultism. The imbalanced coverage is also problematic because the period after the leaders were arrested reveals fundamental aspects of the movement not fully apparent from the early years alone, such as the extent to which Maasina Rule was a popular, bottom-up movement driven not by powerful 'chiefs' but by the movement rank-and-file (something colonial officers long failed to grasp, to their great disadvantage). This leaves us with the question of why scholars have so favoured the earlier period rather than fully investigating the movement across its full lifespan, and to this I confess I have no satisfactory answer.

---

[32] Burt's portrayal of Maasina Rule in Kwara'ae, Malaita, is one of the best, partly because it is more attentive to the later period since the 'Federal Council' phase of 1949–1952 was importantly based in Kwara'ae. Ben Burt, *Tradition and Christianity: the colonial transformation of a Solomon Islands society* (Langhorne 1994).

# Urban Land in Honiara: Strategies and Rights to the City

## JOSEPH FOUKONA

### ABSTRACT

Urban Honiara is increasingly a space in which the poor and even the 'middle class' are excluded from both market and regulatory orders. This paper discusses the strategies that urban residents employ to access land in the face of these multiple exclusions. Drawing upon the work of Henri Lefebvre and recent case studies of urban spaces in the global south, I apply the 'right to the city' framework as a heuristic with which to analyse these strategies. I demonstrate that both settlers from other islands and Indigenous people from Guadalcanal deploy identity narratives – underpinned by claims to moral legitimacy – in their struggles over Honiara's urban space. The paper is in three parts. The first part discusses the right to the city framework and how it has been productively applied in other urban contexts. The second part examines how the history of land alienation in the Honiara area contributed to its contemporary conditions of exclusion. The final part discusses the strategies that people use to access urban land in Honiara and suggests that these might be best understood in terms of the claims to moral legitimacy that are central to the right to the city framework.

The rapid growth of settlements in Pacific towns and cities has caused the supply of urban land to become increasingly limited.[1] Much of the literature on urbanisation in the Pacific highlights informal settlement as a critical dimension of contemporary

*Acknowledgements*: I am grateful to my PhD supervisor, Chris Ballard, for his time and guidance throughout the process of writing this paper. Siobhan McDonnell and Tarcisius Tara Kabutaulaka also provided insightful comments on an earlier version of this paper. Thanks also to the guest editors, Matthew Allen and Sinclair Dinnen, as well as two anonymous reviewers, who provided invaluable suggestions for the form this paper should take.

[1] Paul Jones, 'Searching for a little bit of utopia – understanding the growth of squatter and informal settlements in Pacific towns and cities', *Australian Planner*, 49:4 (2012), 331. See also John Connell, 'Elephants in the Pacific? Pacific urbanisation and its discontents', *Asia Pacific Viewpoint*, 52:2 (2011), 121–35.

urban land problems, including their potential to contribute to violent disputation.[2] The key areas of disputation concern land access issues and the policies and legislation or custom that regulate land rights. Some scholars place the debate on rights of access to land in Melanesia within a broader analysis of an ideology of landownership and a politics of exclusion.[3]

This paper examines the strategies people use to claim and access urban land in Honiara, Solomon Islands. These strategies have the potential to translate into various forms of illegality in the context of poor planning and the maladministration of urban land. I argue that many lower- and middle-class inhabitants of Honiara deploy identity narratives strategically to claim and access urban land as a response to exclusionary market and regulatory orders. I use Henri Lefebvre's notion of the 'right to the city' as the theoretical basis for discussing these strategies. The right to the city is a form of human right that city inhabitants draw on 'to reshape the processes of urbanisation'.[4] Urbanisation is driven by capitalism, which produces class struggles in the contemporary context of 'accumulation by dispossession, where things are taken away and commodified'.[5] These things, which include urban land, are usually controlled by affluent individuals and private interests. As a result, class struggle becomes an ongoing urban issue. Central to this struggle is the creation of social movements as a collective force in reaction to urban experiences of exclusion, which can translate into violent contestations. One way to understand these struggles, as Harvey has pointed out, is through a right to the city as a political ideal that focuses on the relationship between urbanisation and capitalism.[6] Building on Harvey, I use right to the city as a moral framework to analyse the connection between strategies that Guadalcanal landowners and settlers from other islands use to access urban land and contestations due to urbanisation.

This paper has three parts. First, I introduce the 'right to the city' framework and briefly outline its usage and application in various contexts. I move on to examine

---

[2] See Paul Jones, 'Placing urban management and development on the development agenda in the Pacific Islands', *Australian Planner*, 44:1 (2007), 13–15; Paul Jones and John P. Lea, 'What has happened to urban reform in the island Pacific? Some lessons from Kiribati and Samoa', *Pacific Affairs*, 80:3 (2007), 473–91; John Connell, 'Regulation of space in the contemporary postcolonial Pacific city: Port Moresby and Suva', *Asia Pacific Viewpoint*, 44:3 (2003), 243–57; Connell, 'Elephants in the Pacific?', 121–35.

[3] Matthew G. Allen, 'Land, identity and conflict on Guadalcanal, Solomon Islands', *Australian Geographer*, 43:2 (2012), 163–80; Siobhan McDonnell, 'Exploring the cultural power of land law in Vanuatu: law as a performance that creates meaning and identities', *Intersections: gender and sexuality in Asia and the Pacific*, 33 (2013), http://intersections.anu.edu.au/issue33/mcdonnell.htm (accessed 1 June 2014). See also Gina Koczberski and George N. Curry, 'Divided communities and contested landscapes: mobility, development and shifting identities in migrant destination sites in Papua New Guinea', *Asia Pacific Viewpoint*, 45:3 (2004), 357–71.

[4] David Harvey, 'The right to the city', *New Left Review*, 53 (2008), 23.

[5] Matt Mahon, 'Interview with David Harvey', The White Review, http://www.thewhitereview.org/interviews/interview-with-david-harvey/ (accessed 28 July 2015).

[6] Harvey, 'The right to the city' (2008), 40.

Honiara's historical development from its initial alienation to its present-day urban landscape and how this provided the conditions for exclusion. Next, I discuss strategies people use to access urban land by locating this within a right to the city framework. I conclude with some reflections on the efficacy of this theoretical framework for understanding the contemporary political economy of land in urban Honiara.

## Right to the City, Exclusion and Identity

Lefebvre developed the right to the city framework in the late 1960s. He defined it as 'like a cry and a demand' that is 'formulated as a transformed and renewed right to urban life'.[7] Peter Marcuse has explained that the 'cry' is of those experiencing alienation, and the 'demand' is of those experiencing exclusion.[8] The right to the city in this context refers to the 'rights of all city dwellers to fully enjoy urban life with all its services and advantages'.[9] It is 'a moral claim founded on fundamental principles of justice, of ethics, of virtue, of the good – not as a legal claim enforceable through a judicial process'.[10] This definition of right to the city has been interpreted, used and applied in writings on urban citizenship, urban social movements, evictions of the urban poor and urban land development policy.[11] The right to the city has been used to imagine new notions of citizenship that resist the global forces of capitalism. The traditional notion of citizenship is based on nation-state membership. The new form of citizenship articulated through the right to the city framework 'bases membership on *inhabitance*'.[12] That is, anyone living in the city should be entitled to a right to the city. These new notions of citizenship are 'pursued by social movements that emerge out of the poorer half of the global city ... rooted in the politics of identity and difference'.[13]

[7] Henri Lefebvre, *Writings on Cities* (Oxford 1996 [1968]), 158 and 174.

[8] Peter Marcuse, 'From critical urban theory to the right to the city', *City*, 13:2–3 (2009), 185–97. See also David Harvey, 'The right to the city', *International Journal of Urban and Regional Research*, 27:4 (2003), 939–41; Eugene J. McCann, 'Space, citizenship, and the right to the city: a brief overview', *GeoJournal*, 58:2 (2002), 77–79; Eugene J. McCann, 'Race, protest, and public space: contextualizing Lefebvre in the U.S. City', *Antipode*, 31:2 (1999), 163–84.

[9] Edésio Fernandes, 'Constructing the right to the city in Brazil', *Social & Legal Studies*, 16:2 (2007), 208.

[10] Margit Mayer, 'The "right to the city" in the context of shifting mottos of urban social movements', *City*, 13:2–3 (2009), 367.

[11] On citizenship, see Mark Purcell, 'Citizenship and the right to the global city: reimagining the capitalist world order', *International Journal of Urban and Regional Research*, 27:3 (2003), 564–90. On eviction processes, see Gautam Bhan, '"This is no longer the city I once knew". Evictions, the urban poor and the right to the city in millennial Delhi', *Environment and Urbanization*, 21:1 (2009), 127–42. On urban development and land use policy, see Joceli Macedo, 'Urban land policy and new land tenure paradigms: legitimacy vs. legality in Brazilian cities', *Land Use Policy*, 25:2 (2008), 259–70.

[12] Purcell, 'Citizenship and the right to the global city', 577 (emphasis original).

[13] Ibid., 573.

Social movements are formed and rallied, both in the First World and in the global south, in reaction to struggles against 'privatisation, speculation, eviction and displacement'.[14] While these social movements use the right to the city as a moral claim, they apply it in different ways. For example, NGOs and advocacy groups use the right to the city as the basis to advocate for social equity and justice in urban development. Other social movements build on the right to the city where inhabitants in cities experience dispossession and exclusion. In this manner, the right to the city is sought through 'political and social action' and is 'an opposition demand, which challenges the claims of the rich and powerful'.[15]

In South African cities, and in Durban in particular, the state employed three strategies to eradicate informal urban settlements known as shacks. First, it withdrew services such as water and electricity. Second, it used state violence to prevent the expansion of settlements. Third, it destroyed settlements.[16] The state's action towards inhabitants in shacks in cities such as Durban has stimulated the emergence of important social movements since 2001. These social movements used 'road blocks and vote strikes' as strategies to demand that city residents should 'make their own decisions about where they would like to live'.[17] The demand of such social movements 'has been generalised into a collective demand for the right to the city'.[18] For example, in Durban a 'shack dwellers movement' emerged in 2005 'to pursue a politics of the poor, by and for the poor', owing to their experiences of exclusion.[19]

A more recent example comes from a study by Victoria Stead on Aitarak Laran, an urban settlement located in Dili, the capital city of Timor-Leste. The state issued an eviction order to residents of this settlement in 2010 to move within 30 days so that construction of a new National Library and Culture Centre could proceed.[20] This caused residents of Aitarak Laran to assert their claims to urban land on which they have lived for many years. The strategy they used to demand that they be allowed to continue to live on this land was through a 'language of rights, and appeals based on citizenship and membership of the nation'.[21] This strategy was pursued with the support of several civil society organisations and resonates with the right to the city as a moral framework for political action and resistance.[22]

Although these cases demonstrate that the 'right to the city' is a useful theoretical tool for analysing social movements and struggles over urban land, the framework

---

[14] Mayer, 'The "right to the city" in the context of shifting mottos', 367.

[15] Ibid.

[16] Richard Pithouse, 'Abahlali baseMjondolo and the struggle for the right to the city in Durban, South Africa', in Ana Sugranyes and Charlotte Mathivet (eds), *Cities for All: proposals and experiences towards the right to the city* (Santiago 2010), 135.

[17] Ibid.

[18] Ibid.

[19] Ibid., 136.

[20] Victoria Stead, 'Homeland, territory, property: contesting land, state, and nation in urban Timor-Leste', *Political Geography*, 45 (2014), 1.

[21] Ibid., 5.

[22] Ibid., 10.

has not been explicitly employed in the analysis of similar struggles in Honiara or in other Pacific Islands towns and cities. Taking as my point of departure Stead's recent and productive application of the framework in the case of Dili, I explore how the right to the city framework can help illuminate the strategies people use to access land in Honiara. I suggest that many lower- and middle-class residents of Honiara city have responded to their ongoing experience of exclusion by employing discursive strategies to access urban land that resonate strongly with Lefebvre's concept.

While the Solomon Islands constitution recognises and protects a citizen's right to property,[23] many lower- and middle-class inhabitants of Honiara struggling for inclusion continue to experience exclusion. Inclusion connotes access to services or land that the city has to offer,[24] whereas exclusion means the 'removal of access of people from landscapes'.[25] Exclusion encompasses 'regulation, force, the market, and legitimation'.[26] In a recent and influential book on land in Southeast Asia, Hall et al. described these four 'powers of exclusion' as follows: regulation concerns the law regulating land access and use, the market concerns the commodification of land, legitimation concerns the moral justification for exclusion, and force concerns acts or threats of violence such as forceful eviction.[27] Building on this schema, I consider access 'as the ability to benefit from objects, persons, institutions and symbols'.[28]

The increasing number of informal settlements suggests that many lower- and middle-class inhabitants in Honiara struggle to gain access to urban land through the 'formal' market and regulatory orders. This reveals a tension between inclusion and exclusion that resonates with the experiences of cities in other parts of world as spaces of inequality and exclusion. How people gain access to land in the face of these multiple exclusions depends on 'social practices and values' shaped by 'indigenous morality and non-market relationships'.[29] When framed through identity narratives such as those of 'landowner' and 'citizen', these sorts of relationships determine entitlement and exclusion, which resonates with narratives theorised through a right to the city framework.

Several recent studies from Papua New Guinea, Solomon Islands and Timor-Leste highlight the importance of social relationships for access to land and how this contributes to contestations over land.[30] These studies focus on settler and landowner

---

[23] Constitution of Solomon Islands, secs 8 and 9.

[24] See Mayer, 'The "right to the city" in the context of shifting mottos'.

[25] Siobhan McDonnell, 'Exploring the cultural power of land law in Vanuatu'.

[26] See Derek Hall, Philip Hirsch and Tania Murray Li, *Powers of Exclusion: land dilemmas in Southeast Asia* (Singapore 2011), 4–5.

[27] Ibid. See also Siobhan McDonnell, 'Exploring the cultural power of land law in Vanuatu'.

[28] Jesse C. Ribot and Nancy L. Peluso, 'A theory of access', *Rural Sociology*, 68:2 (2003), 153. See also Pyone M. Thu, 'Access to land and livelihoods in post-conflict Timor-Leste', *Australian Geographer*, 43:2 (2012), 197–214.

[29] George N. Curry, Gina Koczberski and John Connell, 'Introduction: enacting modernity in the Pacific?', *Australian Geographer*, 43:2 (2012), 119. See also Thu, 'Access to land and livelihoods'.

[30] George N. Curry and Gina Koczberski, 'Finding common ground: relational concepts of land tenure and economy in the oil palm frontier of Papua New Guinea', *Geographical Journal*, 175:2 (2009), 98–111; Thu, 'Access to land and livelihoods'; Allen, 'Land, identity and conflict on

narratives expressed through an 'ideology of customary landownership'. This ideology portrays landowners as automatic citizens, and the landowner identity is used to assert claims to customary land.[31] Claims to urban land, in contrast, are 'inextricably tied to the legitimacy of the state. The state underpins the rights of [settlers] to live within the Honiara town boundary'.[32] In this sense, the state plays a critical role in producing and reproducing the categories of landowner and settler. In turn, these categories and identities shape the strategies that people employ to assert their claims to land in Honiara, with lower- and middle-class residents of Honiara using both landowner and settler narratives to advance their case for inclusion.

Honiara as an urban landscape has evolved through a long historical process of land alienation. As Filer has observed, the 'alienation of people from land' can transform over time to become 'alienation of land by people'.[33] This process begins with the categorisation of land as property, and people as landowners. In the next stage, people's ownership becomes translated into legal titles that can be transferred to others. If the original landowners are involved in transferring these legal titles to others, this counts as a case of the 'alienation of land by people', but if it is done without their knowledge or consent, this 'counts as a case of expropriation'.[34] Expropriation is a legal conveyance process that can create dispossession or exclusion if the new owners remove or evict former owners from the land.[35] Following Filer, I discuss Honiara's historical context by examining these processes of alienation and how they have provided the conditions for social exclusion in the expanding urban space.

## HONIARA: HISTORICAL CONTEXT

The Honiara landscape was under customary land tenure during the period of British colonial rule. Under the local rules of custom, the tenure arrangement followed a matrilineal pattern. Individuals and families belonging to the Tandai, Malango and Ghaobata tribal groups owned the Honiara land area and could exercise their rights to this customary land.[36] A person's membership of these tribal groups

---

Guadalcanal'; Gina Koczberski, George N. Curry and Jesse Anjen, 'Changing land tenure and informal land markets in the oil palm frontier regions of Papua New Guinea: the challenge for land reform', *Australian Geographer*, 43:2 (2012), 181–96.

[31] Colin Filer, 'Compensation, rent and power in Papua New Guinea', in Susan Toft (ed.), *Compensation for Resource Development in Papua New Guinea* (Canberra 1997), 156–89; Colin Filer, 'Custom, law and ideology in Papua New Guinea', *Asia Pacific Journal of Anthropology*, 7:1 (2006), 65–84. See also McDonnell, 'Exploring the cultural power of land law in Vanuatu'.

[32] Matthew G. Allen, 'Land, identity and conflict on Guadalcanal', 175.

[33] See Colin Filer, Siobhan McDonnell and Matthew G. Allen, 'Introduction', in Siobhan McDonnell, Matthew G. Allen and Colin Filer (eds), *Kastom, Property and Ideology: land transformations in contemporary Melanesia* (Canberra forthcoming).

[34] Ibid.

[35] Ibid.

[36] See Colin H. Allan, *Customary Land Tenure in the British Solomon Islands Protectorate: report of the special lands commission* (Honiara 1957).

through birth determined their right of access to this customary land. Other special arrangements such as compensation, marriage, warfare or gifts would also make it possible for a person to access and use this land.[37]

The alienation of customary land in the Honiara area commenced through a historical series of land transactions. First, in 1886, European traders Thomas Gervin Kelly, John Williams and Thomas Woodhouse purchased approximately 60 square miles of land on the north coast of Guadalcanal for £60 worth of trade goods. This land area included the core of the present city of Honiara from Point Cruz to Tenaru, including Kukum and Lunga. The vendors were Woothia (Uvothea), chief of Lungga; Allea, chief of Nanago; and his son Manungo.[38] The traders then sold this land on to Karl Oscar Svensen's Marau Company in 1898.[39] In 1907, Svensen and his partners Alex Rabuth and Joe d'Oliverya bought an additional area to the west, bordering on Point Cruz and known as 'Ta-wtu' or Mamara Plantation. William Dumphy, an employee of Svensen, then bought an additional area to the east of Tenaru, named Tenavatu, around 1910.[40] The language of the land deeds for these transactions was based on Western legal constructions, which categorised land as property, and vendors as landowners.

When the British established Solomon Islands as a protectorate in 1893, the colonial government introduced land laws that recognised and protected the property interests of the traders.[41] The laws also allowed for the conveyancing of the core land area comprising Kukum and Lunga to Levers Pacific Plantation Company (later Levers Solomon Ltd).[42] Mamara plantation estate remained Svensen's property, and following his death in 1943, his children sold all his property to R.C. Symes Plantation Company. The original landowners were not consulted or involved in these land conveyances, which could also be regarded as instances of further expropriation under Filer's typology. Levers Pacific Plantation Company, as the new owner of the Kukum and Tenavatu estates, controlled much of this landscape and proceeded to exclude the original landowners.

Guadalcanal landowners have drawn upon customary landownership principles in continuing to reassert their rights to the Honiara landscape. This resonates with Filer's suggestion of a 'double movement' of property rights. He has observed that 'steps taken towards the partial or complete alienation of customary rights are continually compensated or counterbalanced by steps taken in the opposite direction,

---

[37] See Gideon Zoleveke, 'Traditional ownership and land policy', in Peter Lamour (ed.), *Land in Solomon Islands* (Suva 1979), 1–9.

[38] For a copy of the land deed, see Great Britain, High Commission for Western Pacific Islands, land claims registers 1886–1936, Auckland, University of Auckland Special Collections (hereinafter UASC), WPHC 18/I/2, carton 1227358, register B. See also Clive Moore, 'Honiara: arrival city and Pacific hybrid living space', this issue.

[39] Graeme A. Golden, *The Early European Settlers of the Solomon Islands* (Melbourne 1993), 203.

[40] Ibid. See also Moore, 'Honiara: arrival city'.

[41] The early colonial land laws were the Queen's Regulation No. 4 of 1896 and Queen's Regulation No. 3 of 1900, with subsequent amendments.

[42] Moore, 'Honiara: arrival city'.

towards the reassertion of such rights'.[43] This 'double movement' characterisation provides a useful basis for explaining the ongoing reassertion of claims by Guadalcanal customary landowners to the Honiara landscape.

Landowners first complained to the colonial authorities, claiming that the core land area, known as Mataniko Kukum Estate, where Honiara is situated, was unfairly alienated. Gilchrist Gibbs Alexander, the lands commissioner[44] appointed in 1919 to investigate previous land alienations in the protectorate, dealt with the Honiara claim.[45] He recommended a survey at the expense of Levers Company of 'all the land to the east of the Mataniko river' and the titles held by the company. He also recommended that 'the land to the west of the Mataniko river including all coconut trees planted by Levers Pacific Plantation … revert to the native owners and to be excluded from Levers Pacific Plantation title'.[46] Alexander resigned towards the end of 1920 and was replaced by Frederick Beaumont Philips to complete the work of the lands commission, referred to as the Philips Commission. Philips reviewed the land claim and confirmed Alexander's recommendation. The secretary of state formalised this recommendation by publishing it in the *Western Pacific High Commission Gazette* in 1924. An indenture in 1926 between the high commissioner for the Western Pacific and Levers Pacific Plantations Ltd of land situated at Kukum and elsewhere was confirmed by a conveyance registered in the Land Registry Office.[47]

After World War II, the colonial government decided to move its administrative headquarters from the small island of Tulagi in the Central District to Honiara on Guadalcanal on at least two grounds. First, the withdrawal of US forces in 1945 had left substantial infrastructure built on alienated land in Honiara, which the colonial administration wished to utilise.[48] Second, Guadalcanal was identified as having potential land area for agriculture development.[49] During this period, Honiara was also regarded as having an 'underpopulated and largely alienated hinterland'.[50]

In 1947, Levers Pacific Plantation Ltd sold its freehold Kukum estate to the colonial government for £2,174, a substantial amount compared with when the land

---

[43] Colin Filer, 'The double movement of immovable property rights in Papua New Guinea', *Journal of Pacific History*, 49:1 (2014), 78.

[44] Alexander resigned towards the end of 1920 after investigating 29 of 55 land claims.

[45] This is known as Claim 17.

[46] Resident commissioner, British Solomon Islands, Land claim no. 17, Matanikau, Kookoom Estate. – Transmits a report on the claim by Mr. G.G. Alexander lands commissioner, 24 Jan. 1922, UASC, WPHC 4/IV inwards correspondence, MP series, 1875–1941, MP no. 5/1922 – MP no. 3523/1922, WPHC MP no. 450/1922.

[47] Levers Plantation Limited Pty Ltd/Lever Solomon Limited archives, legal papers continued from reel 1, 1932 to 1986, available from Canberra, Pacific Manuscript Bureau, PMB 1121, reel 2.

[48] Morgan Wairiu, 'History of forestry industry in Solomon Islands: the case of Guadalcanal', *Journal of Pacific History*, 42:2 (2007), 236.

[49] Michael E.P. Bellam, 'The colonial city: Honiara, a Pacific Islands "case study"', *Pacific Viewpoint*, 11:1 (1970), 70.

[50] Ibid.

was first sold for £60 of trade goods. The conveyance was done without the consent of original landowners, another instance of expropriation. Later, the crown surveyor undertook yet more surveying work during 1953–54, to create the Honiara township boundaries.[51] The state assumed a monopoly over the Honiara landscape, which was divided from north to south into three sections with separate titles. The commissioner of lands applied to the registrar of titles to register the title of government to these sections in accordance with the Land and Titles Ordinance.[52] This legislation introduced the Torrens title system of land registration, which grants an indefeasibility of title to parties with a registered property interest.

In November 1963, Baranamba Hoai of Mataniko village disputed the commissioner of lands' application to register title to the Honiara landscape. He claimed that the land to the east of the Mataniko River known as Kukum estate belonged to the Habala and Kakau lines of Mataniko, on the grounds that no agreement had been signed between the government and landowners for the sale of this land area, nor had any payment been made.[53] The registrar of titles conducted an inquiry on the claim and requested that Hoai and his witnesses give information regarding the reasons and grounds for the claim. Following this inquiry, the registrar rejected Hoai's claim because no reliable evidence supported it. I suggest that Hoai's claim was an instance of a 'cry' and a 'demand' as discussed above. He was influenced to make such claim based on moral justification, but it was bound to fail because the alienation of the Kukum estate was based on a series of land transactions validated through a legal process.

Later the registrar applied to the Western Pacific High Court to make a ruling on his decision and whether he was authorised to register the title of government to the land area under dispute. The court affirmed the registrar's decision and held that Hoai was resurrecting an old claim that had been settled in 1924 and was binding on parties concerned.[54] It also held that the 'application of government for the registration of the land under dispute should be granted'.[55] The court's decision legitimised the state's property interest to Honiara by allowing its title to be registered. The court acted 'not only as an arbiter of justice but also as a parallel administrative and executive body'[56] responsible for perpetuating the alienation of Honiara land from its original landowners. This experience provided the conditions

---

[51] Lands and Mines Dept B.S.I.P. annual report 1953/54, 1955, UASC, WPHC 16/II/165/3/2. For an outline of the amount of survey work required in and around Honiara, see Duties surveyor B.S.I.P., 1956, UASC, WPHC 16/II/165/3/7.

[52] This land legislation was enacted in 1959, then amended in 1964. Land and Titles (Amendment) Ordinance No. 22 of 1964. It was later revised and consolidated as the Land and Titles Ordinance 1968.

[53] See *In the Matter of the Lands and Titles Ordinance, 1959 and in the Matter of certain questions reserved for consideration by the Court under section 113 (1) thereof*, exhibit A, civil case no. 3 of 1964, High Court of the Western Pacific, Civil Jurisdiction, available from Solomon Islands National Archives.

[54] Ibid. See also Moore, 'Honiara: arrival city'.

[55] *In the Matter of the Lands and Titles Ordinance, 1959*.

[56] Bhan, '"This is no longer the city I once knew"', 134.

for the ongoing struggle by Guadalcanal customary landowners over the Honiara land area and has shaped the kinds of strategies that they have developed to assert their claims.

Honiara became recognised as the capital city of Solomon Islands, established on land purchased by the state through a series of alienations during the 19th and early 20th century. It became the hub for people from various parts of Solomon Islands to claim residency and automatic citizenship. In 1960 the government introduced temporary housing area (THA) schemes on state land within the town boundary to cater for the influx of people to Honiara and to address the issue of squatters and peri-urban growth.[57] The government allowed people to settle on state land through the grant of a temporary occupancy licence (TOL) and the payment of an annual nominal fee of SI$5 or $10.[58] The issuing of TOLs provided people with some form of legal security to access urban land in order to discourage 'large scale illegal settlement on other urban lands'.[59] While the TOL system may be read as an attempt by the state to recognise the claims of settlers over urban land they have occupied, it has done little to address the issue of Guadalcanal landowner grievances associated with the alienation of land for Honiara.

By the mid-1980s, 'THAs accommodated 23 per cent of Honiara's population ... those THAs outside the town's boundaries numbered around 15, with an estimated population of 1,308 persons'.[60] Over the years, however, THAs have become overrun owing to the increase in rural-to-urban migration. The increase in people settling in and around Honiara as a result of the Tension has also contributed to this trend. Many of those migrating to Honiara have an expectation as citizens to share in the benefits that the national capital has to offer. Poor town planning, expensive housing and inefficient administration of urban land have all contributed to the breakdown of the TOL system. In 2006 a household survey funded by AusAID through the Solomon Islands Institutional Strengthening Lands and Administration Project reported that only ten out of 3,000 households had a valid TOL.[61]

Today the number of informal settlements has increased to about 30 within the Honiara town boundary, and at least six others have 'encroached on customary land'.[62] Although on a much smaller scale, the increase in Honiara's informal settlements resonates with Maia's analysis of squatter settlements in Brazil. She has argued that

---

[57] Donovan Storey, 'The peri-urban Pacific: from exclusive to inclusive cities', *Asia Pacific Viewpoint*, 44:3 (2003), 269.

[58] See Milner Tozaka and James Nage, 'Administering squatter settlements in Honiara', in Peter Larmour, Ron Crocombe and Anna Taunga (eds), *Land, People and Government* (Suva 1981), 115–18; Storey, 'The peri-urban Pacific', 269.

[59] Storey, 'The peri-urban Pacific', 269.

[60] Ibid.

[61] Cited in United Nations Human Settlements Programme, 'Solomon Islands: Honiara urban profile', 2012, 15, http://unhabitat.org/books/solomon-islands-honiara-urban-profile/ (accessed 13 Oct. 2015).

[62] Ibid., 8 and 15.

> illegal occupation reflects the incapacity of the state to adequately attend to the demand for housing by the poor. Excluded from the official housing programmes and at the margin of the market, the poor adopt their own informal strategies to gain access to land for their housing needs.[63]

Following Maia's analysis, I suggest that the increase in informal settlements in Honiara is shaped by the ongoing struggle over urban land engaged in by both Guadalcanal landowners and settlers from other islands. These Honiara urban dwellers establish informal settlements as a political reaction justified through a moral lens owing to experiences of alienation and exclusion associated with the processes of urbanisation.

## HONIARA: URBAN CONTEXT AND STRATEGIES

Honiara town is located on 22.73 square kilometres of state land and has a current population of approximately 60,000. The land in Honiara is used predominantly for government and commercial offices, private homes, stores, hotels and small-scale industry. With the rapid increase in rural-to-urban migration and population growth, land in Honiara has become a limited resource. As a result, within and around Honiara, many lower- and middle-income earners coming from other parts of the country as well as Guadalcanal landowners continue to struggle to access and acquire urban land.

Several actors involved in the conveyance of urban land engage in speculative dealings. Certain individuals with money, including politicians and government officers associated with the Ministry of Lands, Housing and Survey, have secured more than one area of land within the Honiara town boundary. Some of these individuals are transferring their property rights to these lands at high market values affordable only to high-income earners and investors. Some officers in the Ministry of Lands, Housing and Survey are also alleged to have been involved in mismanagement and corrupt land dealings.[64] This has caused land prices in Honiara to be highly speculative.

The individual market transactions in land are occurring in Honiara at prices that many lower- and middle-class residents of Honiara cannot afford. For example, in 2010 the premier of Guadalcanal expressed concern over Levers Solomon Limited (LSL) subdividing and selling land in the Lunga area at very expensive prices.[65] He requested that Levers sell land at 'reasonable and affordable prices' to encourage 'individuals and businesses' to invest in Guadalcanal Province.[66] Although the concerns of the premier were reasonable, no mechanism exists to regulate land markets

---

[63] Maria L. Maia, 'Land use regulations and rights to the city: squatter settlements in Recife, Brazil', *Land Use Policy*, 12:2 (1995), 177.

[64] See Mike Puia, 'Woman heads top post in lands', *Island Sun*, 31 Jan. 2012.

[65] Ednal Palmer, 'Land row ... Guadalcanal wants to be part of Lungga land sale', *Solomon Star*, 31 Mar. 2010.

[66] Ibid.

in Honiara. Hence, Levers, as holders of the fixed-term estate over the Lunga land area, continued to sell land to individuals and investors at a high price.

One of the strategies adopted to claim land in and around Honiara by many lower- and middle-income earners who are either Guadalcanal landowners or settlers is through landowner and settler narratives. These narratives demonstrate how people frame entitlement and exclusion claims within the sort of moral discourse that has been theorised under the rubric of the right to the city.[67] For example, in a study of land, conflict and settlement in the rural areas east of Honiara, Allen has demonstrated that Guadalcanal landowners' 'claims to land' are 'framed by claims of indigeneity', whereas Malaitan settlers frame their claims in terms of being the 'the workers and builders of the nation'.[68] These sorts of narratives shaped the strategies and contestations over land in and around Honiara, which in turn contributed to the violent conflict from 1998 to 2000.

Guadalcanal landowners continue to claim through print media and submissions to the government that the alienation of Honiara was unfair and that they were not compensated for being dispossessed of their land. Their claim is part of a list of demands by Indigenous people of Guadalcanal submitted to the central government in 1988 and resubmitted in 1999. These demands included returning alienated land in and around Honiara to landowners, paying rental for Honiara to landowners, and the state enacting legislation to control settler migration to Honiara.[69] The state's failure to address these demands adequately was central to the formation of the militant group first known as the Guadalcanal Revolutionary Army (GRA) but later known as the Isatabu Freedom Fighters (IFF) and then the Isatabu Freedom Movement (IFM). This group was encouraged by the political rhetoric from the Guadalcanal provincial government in relation to the demands for the return of alienated land and compensation. Considerable support occurred throughout Guadalcanal for the movement, and its members were mobilised to evict settlers forcefully.

Guadalcanal landowners use the landowner and indigeneity narrative as a strategy to reassert their claim to the entire Honiara land area. Chief Andrew Kuvu, who represents north Guadalcanal Indigenous tribal groups, reasserts their ownership of the alienated land from Lunga to Tenaru.[70] Andrew S. Orea, one of the landowners, has alleged that Kuvu was illegally harvesting cocoa and coconut from this land. He also alleged that another landowner, Jemuel Gu, was selling plots of land from within this contested land area.[71] George Vari, another landowner and chairman of the Lunga Tenaru Trust Board, argued against the claim of

---

[67] Filer, 'Compensation, rent and power in Papua New Guinea'; Filer, 'Custom, law and ideology in Papua New Guinea'. See also McDonnell, 'Exploring the cultural power of land law in Vanuatu'.

[68] Matthew G. Allen, 'Land, identity and conflict on Guadalcanal', 172.

[69] 'Petition by the Indigenous people of Guadalcanal', 1988, http://www.comofinquiry.gov.sb/claims/Petition%20by%20Indigenous%20People%20of%20Guadalcanal.pdf (accessed 13 Oct. 2015). See also Alfred Sasako, 'The day and forces that changed Solomon Islands', *Fiji Islands Business*, July 2003, 38–41.

[70] See 'Landowners caution', *Solomon Star*, 4 July 2011.

[71] A.S. Orea, 'Who is Kuvu?', *Solomon Star*, 15 Dec. 2009.

Guadalcanal provincial leaders that the Lunga land belongs to the Guadalcanal Province and its people, and asserted that Lunga specifically belongs to the Malango people, its tribe and families.[72]

These claims and counterclaims to the entire Honiara landscape by Guadalcanal landowners are not homogenous. Recourse to the landowner or indigeneity narrative to claim ownership of the Honiara land area would almost certainly fail in law because such claims are best seen as underpinned by moral discourses that cannot be enforced through a judicial process.[73] The commissioner of lands holds the perpetual estate title of alienated land in and around Honiara on behalf of the state. Fixed-term estate titles created from this landscape are held by individuals or business entities. For example, LSL holds the fixed-term estate of the land known as the Tenavatu estate, from Lunga to Tenaru, despite Guadalcanal landowners' ongoing demands for the return of alienated land.

The growth of informal settlements in Honiara has been driven by the migration and settlement of people from other islands on state land.[74] Perceived development and socio-economic opportunities shape the pattern of internal migration, as elsewhere in Melanesia. The concentration of educational, medical and employment opportunities in Honiara and surrounding areas of north Guadalcanal act as 'pull motives' attracting people to Guadalcanal.[75] People move to Guadalcanal and develop strategies to access plots of land in and around Honiara because of all the opportunities and attractions offered by the town. But as Paul Jones has highlighted, 'many hoping for improved life-styles and some form of utopia invariably end up in despair, as reflected in increasing poverty levels' and the rapid growth of squatter and informal settlements.[76] The increase in informal settlements continues to put a lot of stress on Guadalcanal landowner resources such as land.

Given the limited supply of urban land and the cost of housing, many Honiara residents, mostly lower- or middle-class Solomon Islanders, find it extremely challenging to access well-located and affordable urban land for residential purposes. Consequently many of these people end up living in informal settlements or build and settle on land to which they have no legal title. As Robert Neuwith has observed based on his experience of living in squatter communities in various developing countries, people build on land they do not own because they are 'desperate for work and a place to live that they can afford'.[77] This is true for the Honiara urban context,

---

[72] George Vari, 'Lunga land ownership', *Solomon Star*, 16 May 2012.

[73] Mayer, 'The "right to the city" in the context of shifting mottos', 367.

[74] See Bellam, 'The colonial city'; Nicholas K. Gagahe, 'The process of internal movement in Solomon Islands: the case of Malaita', *Asia-Pacific Population Journal*, 15:2 (2000), 53–75; John Connell on behalf of the South Pacific Commission and the International Labour Organisation, 'Migration, employment and development in the South Pacific: country report no. 16: Solomon Islands', 1983, http://staging.ilo.org/public/libdoc/ilo/1983/83B09_735_engl.pdf (accessed 13 Oct. 2015).

[75] Matthew G. Allen, 'Land, identity and conflict on Guadalcanal', 168.

[76] Jones, 'Searching for a little bit of utopia'.

[77] Robert Neuwirth, 'Squatters and the cities of tomorrow', *City*, 11:1 (2007), 71.

where people become informal settlers out of desperation and despair at not being able to access urban land through formal mechanisms.

Some of the settlers who have recently built on urban land that they do not own justify their claims using the narrative of being displaced during the conflict of 1998–2003. To evict them would result in a further displacement. These settlers access and occupy urban land in groups defined by provincial areas or island affiliation, creating a strong sense of group identity, security and protection.[78] Guadalcanal landowners or the holders of a legal title to any land occupied by settlers in and around Honiara are likely to find it difficult to enforce their claim through legal means. While the court will issue an eviction order on the basis of legal title, enforcing such an order and getting people to recognise it is likely to prove extremely challenging in practice. It can create tensions around issues of inclusion and exclusion.

The Solomon Islands National Sports Council's (NSC) plan to build a national sports stadium in the Burns Creek area is a case in point. The NSC received the perpetual estate title to land in this area that was occupied by settlers. The *Solomon Star* reported in 2012 that settlers were 'given some time to leave their homes since the NSC took title over the proposed land',[79] yet settlers continued to reside on the land. With the financial help of their member of parliament (MP), they built a clinic right in the middle of the land that NSC had earmarked for a playing field. This seemingly reassured the settlers, who believed that if an MP funded the building of a clinic on the land, they gained legitimacy in continuing to occupy it. As citizens, the settlers felt they should continue living on this land unless alternative urban land was provided for their relocation. The NSC criticised the MP for failing to contact the Honiara City Council or the minister of lands to find out the status of the land before funding the construction of the clinic building.[80] In October 2013, the NSC announced that the sport stadium groundwork would not continue because the settlers refused 'to leave the land earmarked for the stadium'.[81] The strategy used by the settlers to continue living on this land resonates with the kind of strategy theorised through the right to the city framework.

Finally, people make claims to access land in and around Honiara based on the notion of vacant spaces as 'waste land'. The idea of waste land originates from colonial government land laws enacted in 1896 and 1900. These land laws made land considered as waste land or unoccupied available for purchase by individuals, investors and business entities,[82] opening up large areas of land for alienation. Today the term 'waste land' is no longer recognised in law, although some settlers

---

[78] Connell and Curtain made similar observations for Port Moresby and Lae. See John Connell and Richard Curtain, 'The political economy of urbanization in Melanesia', *Singapore Journal of Tropical Geography*, 3:2 (1982), 127.

[79] 'NSC to put in work plan', *Solomon Star*, 27 June 2012.

[80] Carlos Aruwafu, 'NSC: Ete's excuse lame', *Solomon Star*, 24 Oct. 2012.

[81] 'NSC powerless', *Solomon Star*, 30 Oct. 2013.

[82] The Solomons (Land) Regulation No. 4 of 1896 defined waste land as 'land being vacant by reason of the extinction of the original native owners and their descendants'. Following the enactment of the Waste Land Regulation of 1900, as amended by Queen's Regulation No. 1 of 1901,

still use it to assert their claim to vacant spaces in Honiara. They consider 'waste land' as land that is not useful and that the state will not require for development purposes. But the use of waste land to claim 'swampy places, valleys, riverbanks or steep gullies' in Honiara is a basis for future struggle and contestation over urban land.[83]

## CONCLUSION

The discussion in this paper has focused on strategies that Guadalcanal landowners and settlers deploy to assert their rights to urban land owing to ongoing experiences of exclusion. Guadalcanal landowners who assert customary rights over Honiara land area consider this land area home. Settlers are migrants, and many of them have lived most of their lives in and around Honiara. Many settlers live in informal settlements and 'have limited opportunities beyond the town'.[84] The issue of access to land for residency purposes is shaped by the processes of urbanisation, which creates class struggles. Such class struggles are translated into landowner and settler categories that urban dwellers draw on to assert their rights of access to Honiara urban land.

    The strategies that Guadalcanal landowners and settlers use to assert their claims to urban land in Honiara differ in scale. For Guadalcanal landowners, a collective militant group was formed to advance their land claims, and this resulted in the forceful eviction of settlers. Since then, Guadalcanal landowners have constantly reasserted their claims to the entire Honiara land area through political actions such as petitions to the central government. Settlers' claims concern patches of land in and around Honiara that they have occupied or intend to access, despite not having legal title. This difference in scale determines the kinds of strategies used by Guadalcanal landowners and settlers to assert their rights over Honiara urban land. I have suggested that these strategies can be usefully understood in terms of the right to the city, which I interpret as a moral framework for analysing political action in the context of urban exclusion.

    The application of the right to the city in a Pacific context is useful because it provides a theoretical basis for discussion of the relationship between moral and legal claims over urban land in Honiara. Central to this discussion is the examination of the history of land alienation in the Honiara area and the ways in which this history has provided the conditions for exclusion. Understanding this history and the strategies that Guadalcanal landowners and settlers have deployed to assert their rights to urban land is crucial for urbanisation policy formulation as Honiara town continues to develop. In my mind, further research is needed on the relationship between 'right to the city' and urbanisation in a Pacific context.

repealed and consolidated by Queen's Regulation No. 2 of 1904, the definition of waste land was amended to mean land that was not owned, cultivated or occupied by any Native.
[83] Satish Chand and Charles Yala, 'Informal land systems within urban settlements in Honiara and Port Moresby', *Making Land Work*, 2 vols (Canberra 2008), II, 85–106.
[84] Gina Koczberski, George N. Curry and John Connell, 'Full circle or spiralling out of control? State violence and the control of urbanisation in Papua New Guinea', *Urban Studies*, 38:11 (2001), 2028.

# Index